P9-EJH-895

The DRIVER

MY DANGEROUS PURSUIT OF SPEED
AND TRUTH IN THE OUTLAW RACING WORLD

Alexander Roy

HarperEntertainment
An Imprint of HarperCollins*Publishers*

HarperCollins books may be purchased for educational, business, or sales promotional use. For information please write: Special Markets Department, HarperCollins Publishers, 10 East 53rd Street, New York, NY 10022.

FIRST EDITION

Designed by Daniel Lagin

Library of Congress Cataloging-in-Publication Data

Roy, Alexander.
   The driver : my dangerous pursuit of speed and truth in the outlaw racing world / Alex-ander Roy.—1st ed.
   p. cm.
   ISBN: 978-0-06-122793-6
   ISBN-10: 0-06-122793-5
   1. Roy, Alexander.   2. Automobile racing drivers—United States—Biography.   3. Auto-mobile racing.   I. Title.

GV1032.R68A3 2007
796.72092—dc22   2007019431
[B]

07 08 09 10 11 WBC/RRD 10 9 8 7 6 5 4 3 2 1

THIS BOOK IS DEDICATED TO

Owen and Aidan Weismann

Julian Lai

Amelia Rose Karasinski

Ella Simon Kruntschev

Mia Acutt

Jack Kenny (RCAF)

and my father

We are, all of us,
growing volcanoes that approach the hour of their eruption;
but how near or distant that is,
nobody knows.

—**FRIEDRICH NIETZSCHE**

Contents

Prologue

"Alex Roy from Gumball!?" said Mark, client advisor at Jackie Cooper BMW in Oklahoma City. "Me and the guys couldn't believe it when we Googled you. We knew something was up when we saw all the antennas and gear inside. Totally awesome, man. Definitely the coolest car we've ever had in here. All the customers who come by ask about it. What are you doing in Oklahoma?"

"It's a long story, but listen, I'm just boarding a flight out right now. How quickly can you get that car on a truck back to New York? Money is no object. I need it back in time to ship to Europe for Gumball."

"I'd say . . . within twenty-four hours. Let me make a couple of calls."

I sat back for the surreal two-hour and fifty-four-minute flight to L.A., during which I would survey the 1,342 miles I'd hoped to cross by car in fourteen hours and eight minutes.

My phone rang. I caught the eye of the flight attendant three rows ahead, having just started her pretakeoff survey of bag placement, seat belt tautness, and—

It was Mark from BMW. "Mark, I've got five seconds to takeoff, so whatever it costs, just do it."

"Alex—"

The flight attendant approached. "Mark, whatever it costs—"

"I'm sorry," said the attendant, "but you must turn that off *now.*"

"Mark, just do it."

"Sir! If you don't turn off that phone—"

"Alex, the police are here—"

"—I *will* call security!"

"Hello? Alex, the police want to know where you are and—"

I dry heaved, dropping the phone in my lap.

"Thank you, *sir!*" She walked away. My hands shook as I lifted the phone. Mark was gone. I turned off the ringer. My thumbs vibrated like tuning forks as I laboriously typed my attorney, Seth, a priority e-mail, ending with *they must NOT get inside that car.* I hit send just as the plane began taxiing. If my stomach hadn't been empty, I'd have thrown up.

Part 1 Rendezvous

CHAPTER 1

The Divinity of Purpose

It was a gorgeous morning, heaps of snow having escaped the streets' salting in the wake of the previous night's storm, their knee-high peaks not yet capped with soot from passing cars and trucks.

My cell phone rang as I descended the subway station steps at the corner of Sixth Avenue and Bleecker Street, mere seconds before I would have disappeared into the station and out of range for the next half hour.

"Is this Alexander Roy?"

There was only one reason for such a call.

"This is Dr. Johnson at Beth Israel Hospital."

The world slowed.

"As your father's medical-care proxy, you must give permission for any time-critical procedure during a life-threatening or . . . Mr. Roy? Mr. Roy, can you hear me?"

The bus rumbling mere feet away, the cacophony of voices echoing off the subway station's tiled walls just ahead, the deep hot rushing roar of air out of the station entrance as a train pulled in—all were muted by the gravity of events to which I could only react, and never control.

"Mr. Roy?"

"I'll be there in fifteen minutes."

"There's no time. We need your permission to perform an emergency tracheostomy immediately."

"Or else?"

"Your father will die."

OCTOBER 1999

My father was very secretive about his past. While I was a child, the notion of my climbing up his leg to ask a question—to scale the seemingly indomitable mountain that was my father—was terrifying.

My father had always described himself as a lion, and so had everyone else. He'd lost everything during the Second World War—his brother, his friends, his childhood home—and fled with his surviving family to New York City. He joined the U.S. Army at seventeen, landed at Normandy, was shot and wounded twice, and rode with the lead units into Buchenwald concentration camp. After the war he started life anew, founded the family business in 1954, met my mother in 1970, had two sons he sent to private school, bought a Cadillac, and earned (and saved) enough for us to live comfortably. Even his enemies—and these were restricted to business competitors—respected him, trading insults over the phone every week for decades. He spoke fluent French and Spanish, and conversational German, Russian, and Polish. All agreed he was a gifted painter, photographer, and pianist. My brother and I knew better than to interrupt his weekday postwork relaxation time, during which he plucked at the precious custom-made flamenco guitar he'd bought in Seville. He loved work, and intended to work until the day he died. Surrender was inconceivable.

I never believed it possible that he could be withered by cancer, his deep radio-commercial-grade voice cracking from multiple surgeries and chemotherapy, lying in a hospital bed 15 minutes from where we'd lived for more than twenty years. I'd always assumed he'd live to see me married with children. That was his greatest wish.

My greatest wish was for him to reveal what he'd *really* done between the war and his meeting my mother, a nearly twenty-five-year gap that had been left largely unexplained. My mother's curiosity went further, as the frequent business trips he'd taken when they first met had continued through the late 1970s, ending abruptly in 1980.

Time was now running out.

Radioactive pellets had been placed in his neck to fight a cancerous tumor, and the resultant swelling made breathing painfully difficult. The doctors recommended, and my father consented to, a tracheostomy—whereby a hole was cut in his neck and a breathing tube inserted down his throat. His body, already greatly weakened by months of treatment, reacted badly to the procedure, and I spent long nights beside his hospital bed watching him sleep under heavy sedation.

The swelling persisted for weeks after the pellets were removed, and in heavy-lidded moments of near wakefulness his feet danced slowly under the sheets, both hands raised like claws.

"I wonder what he's dreaming about," said the wife of the patient in the neighboring bed.

"Driving," I said.

Once the tube was finally removed, he began daily, mostly unconscious visits to a hyperbaric oxygen chamber intended to accelerate the closure and healing of his throat.

"He won't be able to speak for some time," one doctor warned as he handed me a pad and paper, "but you can try this."

My father's eyes darted wildly during his first few days of wakefulness, his hands too shaky for anything but scrawling gashes through the paper. Clarity slowly returned to his gestures, and he resumed looking me in the eyes and nodding as I asked him yes/no questions about the business I knew he missed. He struggled to push words up through his ragged, constricted throat. I stared at his mouth and raced like an auctioneer through phrases I wanted to spare him the pain of attempting to utter.

He pointed at the pad and paper, wrote furiously, then turned the pad toward me.

Throat

Dry

Air

Fire

"I'll get you more water," I said, bringing the straw to his mouth.

He swiped it aside angrily and wrote again.

Operation

"The tracheostomy?" He nodded. "What about it?"

Never

Again

Pain

"You don't want to have a tracheostomy again?"

Prefer

Die

"C'mon," I said, false optimism tugging at the corners of my mouth. "That's so unlike you."

Suddenly and with vicious strength he grabbed my wrist, pulled my face to his, and whispered through quivering lips.

"You . . . cannot . . . allow . . . it."

"But—" I mouthed in disbelief.

He glowered at me, eyes wide with volcanic anger, and pushed the pad against my chest.

Prefer

Die

DECEMBER 1999

"Mr. Roy!" Dr. Johnson blurted through the phone. "If you can hear me, I need your permission right now if we are to save your father's life."

"What," I said, my eyes welling with tears even as I spoke with literally deadly clarity, "are the odds of his survival without the procedure?"

"*Very* low. Every passing minute increases the likelihood of oxygen deprivation and brain damage, if he survives."

"Do it now," I said, in tears.

MARCH 2000

My father revealed many fascinating things on his deathbed. One was that he'd faked a heart attack in 1995 in order to trick me into moving home to New York from Paris, where I'd been busy finding myself through bartending, wearing a scarf, and attempting to write a novel set in Japan—a country I'd never been to. Another was that he didn't appear to remember the second tracheostomy, or the ensuing weeks, which was a great relief. Yet another was that he kept a storage room outside the city that had remained unknown to anyone—me, my mother, even Genia, the company bookkeeper of twenty-two years in whom he'd placed sole responsibility for paying the bills he so frequently lost between our mailbox and his office desk.

"What's so important about the storage room?" I said, interrupting his slow, measured monologue. He'd regained the tone but not the pace of his natural speech.

"A box," he intoned.

"What's in it?"

"Pictures."

"From the war?"

"No."

"What," I said, trying to conceal my excitement, "do you want me to do with it?"

He paused far longer than I expected, as if he hadn't until that very moment decided what to do with this incalculable treasure. He'd already rewritten his will and trust documents innumerable times, having recited from memory every painting, book, and piece of wartime memorabilia he'd amassed, recalling the origin and value of each with scientific precision. His face hardened, and I later came to believe it was then that he'd accepted his impending death, because it was the first time he'd expressed determination not merely to postpone death, but to accomplish one last task before it was too late.

I immediately set off, as per his halting instructions, to retrieve the albums and bring them to my apartment.

"Do *not*," he'd said in his James Earl Jones voice as I walked out of his hospital room, "open the box until I tell you. And don't tell your mother. Don't tell anyone."

My father still owned the 1977 Cadillac Fleetwood Brougham he'd bought upon moving to New York from California. It had been driven a mere thousand miles a year for twenty-three years, and he took great pride in being able to park it unlocked anywhere in Manhattan without fear of theft. He admired the soft (I called it hallucinatory) ride and passenger space for seven. I was embarrassed by the broken window controls, the cracked seat leather, the black felt roof lining that sagged on passengers' heads whenever driving over a bump, and the fact that no self-respecting car thief would steal it even when parked overnight, unlocked, in lower Manhattan. He refused any suggestion that it be replaced, insisting that new cars were too small and uncomfortable at any price. The list of unworthy cars included any new Mercedes, BMW, Cadillac, or Lexus manufactured after 1989. He liked demonstrating the Cadillac's merits by tricking friends into "going for a ride" during which, five blocks from the garage, he'd claim to have forgotten something at home and the "ride" was cut short. His dream car was a Citroën CX, a teardrop-shaped French car considered quite futuristic when first unveiled in 1974. Rarely ever seen in the United States and out of production for years, the CX's alleged onetime primacy guaranteed he would never buy another car.

"You have the box?" he said.

"At home."

"How's the Cadillac?"

"Terrible," I said, deadpan.

"I don't want to hear it. Did you open it?"

"No."

"If you had, you'd already be asking me."

"About what happened after the war?"

"Be quiet and listen."

I braced myself. I had dozens of theories—prior marriage, bad divorce, bigamy, jail, the OSS or CIA. None seemed far-fetched.

"Cannonball Run," he said, "with Burt Reynolds."

This was when I suspected he'd not fully recovered from the second tracheostomy. The doctors had warned he might never fully recover, and even if he did, there was the possibility of brain damage. It had always been common for him to drop one conversational thread and pick up another (often parallel but occasionally tangential) topic. Although some considered this the mark of genius, he'd recently begun repeating stories, and *this* tangent was—

"All true," he continued, "there really *was* a Cannonball Run. The nonsense in the movie . . . most of that happened—" He lurched, *almost* coughing, which I feared might rupture his IV, ending our conversation as it had several times before.

My eyes darted to the door and the nurses' desk just beyond.

"I'm . . . okay," he groaned.

We shared a silent moment as he gathered his strength, fighting the drug-induced fatigue with anger and resentment.

"Did you know," he said with a surge of energy, as if he'd just won a temporary, albeit false, victory over his body's sickly shell, "I had sports cars my whole life?"

"Yes, Dad," I said. "I knew that."

"Before you and your brother. A new one every year after I got out of the service. I had everything—Porsches, Ferraris, MGs, Austin-Healeys. Even when the company was doing badly and I slept on your grandparents' couch. Back then you could drive as fast as you wanted, in Europe, in the States. Those were great days. Then I met your mother. I had a blue Porsche 911 Targa. What a terrific car. She hated it. The noise . . . the clutch. Then we had you. Then there was the first Cannonball. I knew I had to do it."

"What?"

"Listen!" he rasped.

"But how come—"

"I didn't tell you? Because of your mother. She was so upset when she found out. She caught me talking about it with Sascha Orbach. My poor friend Sascha. I think he died. I lost touch with him. I lost touch with him . . ."

His eyes lost focus. My mind reeled. I wanted—*needed*—him to proceed.

"Sascha," he said, "he . . . tried to get a Citroën CX. Or maybe it was an SM. I can't remember. Wait . . . do you know . . . what the Cannonball record is?"

I shook my head.

"Thirty-two hours, fifty-one minutes," he said. "Nonstop. New York to L.A."

"Impossible."

"It's true. In 1979."

"Wait," I said. "You did the Cannonball?"

"Sascha and I began planning. But your mother... heard me on the phone. She would have left. You were so little." He shook his head slightly. "So I told her I was going on a business trip."

"Hold on—"

"Listen to me! We thought we could win. We had fuel tables, a fuzz-buster. Everything. But the car broke down. Sascha thought it was sabotage. Then your mother found out from Sascha's wife."

"But... why didn't you tell me before?"

"Think! Your mother would have died if you tried anything like that. You remember when you wanted me to take you to the car show to see the Porsches and Ferraris? We did everything we could to stop you from having a car."

That *was* true, all through high school and college.

"But," he said, "there's something else you need to know."

I shook my head in amazement.

"Listen!" he said sternly, his tone hardening. "Do you know why Brock Yates canceled the Cannonball? It grew too big. Parties and bullshit. There were leaks. The police knew the drivers' names before the start. Tagalongs. Copycats. Everyone thought someone would be killed. But there were serious drivers who wanted to continue. Secret races."

"C'mon."

"It's true. People talked about how to keep going after Yates shut it down. How to keep it secret. Safe. No press. You have to vet drivers. The organizers must be anonymous. The cars have to leave at different times, from different places."

His eyes lost focus. "No one has ever beaten thirty-two hours."

This was the first thing he said that *wasn't* a surprise.

"Rumors," he said, "more races... thought they could beat 32:51. Even thirty-two. Some said even thirty. Sascha said thirty-two was the wall. He told everyone we could beat it."

"Did you?"

"No."

I was strangely relieved. If he had—and never told me—I would have felt terribly betrayed, unaware of what had driven him, ignorant of what I might have inherited—

"But," he said, "I heard someone came close."

"Impossible. That's 3,000 miles."

"It's less." He smiled faintly. "Thirty-two fifty-one. In a Jaguar. A terrible car."

"Terrible." I smirked. "But still, they had to have averaged at least—" I was as terrible at math as Jaguar was at building cars, at least in 1979. I tried to guess the size of a Jaguar's fuel tank. "If it's just under 3,000 miles, with fuel stops and tickets, they had to have averaged at least 100 mph, right?"

"That's the secret. What Sascha knew."

"What is?"

"Stealth. Math. If you don't get a ticket, 32:51 . . . is only in the mid-eighties."

"Are you sure? Eight-five doesn't seem that fast."

"Everyone says that. Everyone who's never done it. Or tried."

This I would have to check when I got home.

"I don't feel well," he said. He was lying. There was too much strength in his voice. It was completely unlike him to reveal so much at any one time without a motive. Like a good teacher, he wanted me to infer the meaning of his stories, but clearly I'd yet to make the great leap. He reached for the pain-killer button. I scrambled back through our conversation, looking for what I'd failed to grasp.

"One more question," I lied.

"What do you want?"

"What," I said, "does all this have to do with the box?"

"Just pictures. Sascha. Me. My pictures." He leaned back and closed his eyes. "He . . . called me."

Sascha was dead, or at least I thought he was. "Who called?"

"He called . . ." his voice trailed off. "He called."

I was losing him. Maybe he was lying *and* unwell. There was a fair chance—given his medication and treatments—he wouldn't resume this conversation tomorrow. I had to push.

"*Who* called?"

"The Driver."

"The driver? What driver?"

"I don't know." Maybe I'd already lost him.

"After Cannonball," he whispered.

"Brock Yates . . . called *you*?"

My father slowly turned his head toward me. "No. The . . . *Driver.*"

The painkillers *had* to be kicking in. "Wait," I said, "who's this . . . driver?"

"Sascha . . . I thought it was Sascha. Calling me."

"So who called you?"

"I'm tired. I don't know. He won't stop calling me. Strange. Did you know I have the best memory? I never forget." I nodded in sympathetic agreement, silently mouthing *I know.* "Because," he said, "he never stopped attacking the wall."

"This . . ." I hesitated. "This . . . driver?"

"The Driver," he groaned, "against the wall."

"On one of these secret races."

"Yes."

"And why did he call you now?"

"He can't . . . he can't attack the wall alone. Trust . . . who to trust?"

"Trust who?"

"To go . . . against the wall. He called Sascha. My God, was it twenty years ago? My memory . . . my memory. Sascha knows. Sascha knows. But no one has done it."

"Hold on," I said, "when did he—"

"Sascha wanted to go, but his wife. Your mother. Sascha told everyone we could beat it. If we'd finished. In '79. But the sabotage. Sabotage, he said. Sabotage."

"So . . . you were sabotaged? In '79?"

"I don't know," he rasped, "but he can't find Sascha, so he found me."

"Didn't Sascha pass away some time ago?"

"I can't remember . . . I mean yes. Do *you* know how to reach him?"

"No." I could have cried.

"Yesterday," he said, "he said . . . it was sabotage."

"*Who* said *what* yesterday? The Driver?"

"He knows . . . he knows."

We sat in silence as I struggled to filter truth from medically induced hallucination. I knew nothing of dementia or memory disorders, but there *was* one sure way to test his lucidity.

"Dad," I said gently, "do you remember your Social Security and bank account numbers?"

"Don't insult me." He recited the numbers perfectly.

"But why this whole story—"

"Find him. Race."

"Me?"

"Beat thirty-two. It's possible. Sascha knows how. Sabotage," he rasped. "He knows. It doesn't matter. Thirty-two. Just go."

"Dad . . . I don't know anything about racing."

"Think you can't, but you can. Only now. You're so young. No children. If you ever do it." He leaned back again, seemingly ready to pass out.

"But . . . but how will I find this . . . Driver?"

His eyes briefly lit up. *"Un rendezvous."*

"A meeting? How?"

"Enough. Come back tomorrow."

CHAPTER 2

Rendezvous

I was blessed with two sweet, kind, loving eccentric parents. My father's parents were German Jews who moved to Brussels in 1934 and then escaped the Nazis and emigrated to the United States in 1942. My father helped liberate the concentration camps, returned with a Purple Heart, and founded Europe By Car, the family business. My mother escaped Communist East Germany at twenty and moved to New York in 1965 hoping to meet Elvis. They met on an American Airlines flight from New York to Paris in 1970. Henry Roy was a single, forty-three-year-old war veteran and businessman who dressed like Austin Powers. Ingeborg Schneider was a petite blond twenty-seven-year-old ex-schoolteacher, ex–au pair, ex-model-turned-stewardess who liked to wear go-go outfits and go dancing with her five stewardess roommates. They made a maturity pact before getting married and having me—he quit smoking, shaved his mustache, and stopped wearing vertically striped pants. She stopped dressing like she was sixteen and partying with the pot-smoking gay Japanese fashion designer who'd adopted her as his muse.

I was born nine months later.

I had a normal childhood, lived in Manhattan, and went to good schools. I studied piano and took art classes. I graduated from New York University with a 3.5 GPA. I double-majored in politics and journalism, with a minor in urban studies, a euphemism for criminology. I volunteered for various charities and gave money when I had it. My father wanted me to take over the family business. My mother wanted me to become an architect.

I'd always wanted to be a judge, or, if I could have made a living at it and my father had stopped telling me it was a surefire way of remaining poor, an artist.

I was quite sure I'd be married with children by the eve of the millennium, the year I turned twenty-nine.

Things didn't go as planned.

SPRING 1995

My father had a very strong work ethic, and I had to work from the age of fourteen on. I've been (in very rough order) a beachboy in Saint-Tropez, a masseur to leathery French women of substantial age and girth, a hi-fi salesman on lower Broadway in Manhattan, an Urban Outfitters pant folder (later promoted to store greeter), an executive assistant at a failing record company, a protocol assistant for an unpopular New York City mayor, and a criminal investigator for the New York Legal Aid Society. I've also waited tables, parked cars, driven a Parisian taxi, and bartended at an Australian pub in Paris frequented by foreign criminals who'd left home and joined the French Foreign Legion to escape prosecution.

I'd taken these jobs as a way of buying time until forced to choose a career path, all the while struggling to write the Great American Novel, when, one night in Paris, a Tasmanian legionnaire lifted me off the sawdust-littered pub floor and announced that I had a "good 'ead" and should shave it immediately.

A few days later I was standing in the petite bathroom of my Paris sublet inspecting my hairline when the answering machine beeped in the next room. I watched the machine vibrate and move across the desk as my father's deep voice emerged from the speaker—I had to place my hand on the device to keep it from falling to the floor.

"My son," he announced with biblical intensity, "I've been thinking about your situation for some time. I've decided that it's best for you to come home and be by my side. I've been ill for several days and your brother is very young. The stress of raising your brother alone is causing me terrible heart problems. Only you can help me. Only you can help save the business. You must stop this nonsense about writing a novel and come home now. I can only imagine your terrible living conditions and urge you to consider your future. Of course, I would help you with a place to live and a car."

This might be a good deal.

I'd wanted a car ever since my catastrophic accident on Christmas Eve 1991. A cab had broadsided my trusty Nissan and we smashed into the front doors of a synagogue on Fifth Avenue. I'd been glad my parents weren't pious.

I called him immediately. "A car?" I asked.

"You want to know what kind of car I'll get you?"

"Yes."

"Aren't you worried about my heart condition?"

"You've been saying that since I was ten."

"I had a heart attack last week."

"Why didn't you call me?"

"I didn't want to worry you." This was very suspicious. "Come home," he said, "and we can discuss your car."

"Are you going to be okay?"

"I don't know."

I suspected my father was exaggerating because he thought (correctly) that my still-unfinished nine-hundred-page Great American Novel might never be completed while I spent my days smoking in local cafes and picking up long-legged French girls too easily impressed by a young American with a laptop.

He'd had three heart attacks in ten years.

I bought a ticket home the next day.

SUMMER 1999

There are moments in each of our lives when something so dramatic happens that one can barely remember what life was like before. These moments reshape the prism through which we see everything that follows. These moments define the chapters in our lives, and how we react to them defines who we are.

This is why we must now discuss the first time I saw *Rendezvous*, the greatest car-racing movie of all time.

I was standing in a sparsely populated club in New York called Void. A twenty-foot-wide screen hung on Void's rear wall. A projector flickered. The following appeared on-screen, in French:

No special effects of any kind were used in the filming of this movie.

The speakers thumped with a beating heart, and a decades-old blurry image appeared. A camera had been mounted on the front bumper of a car speeding up a ramp—its engine howled and its tires squealed as the driver turned onto a wide boulevard lined with trees. It was dawn in some foreign city. As the driver accelerated, the lane stripes bled into a single line and out of the mist appeared the Arc de Triomphe, centerpiece to the world's most dangerous intersection—the Etoile. With ten major boulevards and six mi-nor streets intersecting in a single twelve-lane traffic circle without traffic lights, it was . . .

Impossible. This had to be staged. It couldn't be done.

There had to have been spotters, side streets closed off, assistants with police tape and funny little megaphones waving one arm overhead to hold back the onlookers.

I was sure to spot them if I looked. And I looked.

I felt like those people who, on May 7, 1824, heard the first strings of the first movement of Beethoven's Ninth, or maybe the first college kids in 1969 to lower the record needle through a haze of pot smoke onto Led Zeppelin I.

These examples are really too obvious, because, as the driver drove into the Arc de Triomphe–Etoile intersection at 100 mph without slowing, nearly hitting three other cars before turning onto the Champs-Elysées, I knew that I was seeing something seemingly impossible yet very real, something very *very* far beyond what had previously seemed feasible—something abso-lutely, utterly unrepeatable.

The car barreled down the Champs-Elysées at over 120 mph and ran a red light.

This was Russian roulette with five out of six chambers loaded.

There was no music. No special effects. No editing. There were only two characters—the driver, whose every feeling was expressed through the en-gine's howls, tires' squeals, and the split-second decisions he made as the car cut left and right through the wide boulevard and narrow streets, and Paris itself, revealing new dangers as the sun rose through the mist, the city allow-ing the first inhabitants to emerge as the driver defied the red lights, nearly killing those few who dared cross the street.

This was a snuff film on wheels.

For nine minutes I stood paralyzed, utterly speechless, until the driver stopped the car in front of the Montmartre cathedral overlooking the city. Out of the haze a lone beautiful blonde climbed the cathedral steps toward the camera. The driver entered the frame, face unseen, kissed her, and the screen went black.

Before I saw *Rendezvous,* plans for my final hours totally precluded any form of dangerous sports like car racing. After seeing *Rendezvous,* it led to a single question.

Could I make my own Rendezvous?

This more than captured my imagination—like a ghost it hovered be-side me as I tried to sleep. It interrupted my conversations such that my attention wandered even from the Czech model I'd once thought it so important to take on a date. We might be married today if only she'd understood the *why*. I must have sounded like an idiot to her, but it wasn't the language barrier. Her confusion made it easy to delete her number from my phone.

As to why, well, the first half of the answer would be comprehensible only to those who've seen *Rendezvous*. The second half of the answer, the part that has earned me friends I'd otherwise never have met, *that* was the part best understood by the types of people I'd made fun of as a kid.

Why was I going to make my own *Rendezvous*?

Because of what my father said. Because of *Rendezvous*. Because of The Driver.

Little did I know this would be only the first of many dumb questions I'd ask myself, and attempt to answer in a car. Until I'd seen *Rendezvous* I'd always assumed a car was something one bought and drove within a given set of limits—first, basic traffic law; second, one's skill. *Rendezvous* showed a car to be something else, and way more than, as many people joke, an expression of the owner's manhood.

A car isn't just an expression of our taste and finances.

How many times have I walked past Cipriani on West Broadway, home of innumerable husband-hunting, fake-breasted girls who work in public relations, only to see a handsome young banker pull up in a brand-new red Ferrari F360? The model/actresses swoon. The driver sits with his friends and explains the options he chose this time—*carbon brakes, racing exhaust*—and how he couldn't get it exactly the way he wanted. He talks about how fast he drove downtown from the Upper East Side, four miles away. His friends are impressed until one remarks that *he's* soon taking delivery of the even newer F430. "A lot more power," the friend brags, flashing his Panerai diving watch and smiling at the girls at the next table. "You should order one." The 360 driver smirks with jealousy, knowing he will when his lease runs out.

Not one of these people will ever hunt, cave-dive or race, or attempt anything that would endanger their purebred dog, Italian navy diving watch, or custom-ordered car, let alone their own safety, unless well paid, forced, or shamed into it.

This is the message of *Rendezvous*—it's not what you have, it's what you *do* with it.

Rendezvous demonstrated what one can do, *must* do, if one owns a car like a Ferrari. There is no dignity in bragging about one's car when it has never surpassed 50 percent of its maximum speed, or in comparing diving watches that have never seen the ocean, let alone a shower, or in driving to a restaurant where the girls see not a car but the promise of the rest of their lives pulling up in front of expensive restaurants in bright red sheet metal and tan leather. There is only the absurd cash outlay for the best engineering on four wheels, the question of what equally outrageous challenge it must be put to, and whether that test will be sufficient to please the god of decadence from whose domain the car has been borrowed. To do any less is far worse than wearing $200 sneakers for a pleasant stroll, or domesticating an animal meant to roam free—it's eating McDonald's in Paris, it's watching porn instead of having sex with one's girlfriend, it's returning from war with one's gun unfired. Such second-rate decadence is worse than bad taste. It is not a victimless crime. It's an insult to everyone who can't afford the option.

SUMMER 2000

"*Rendezvous* in New York?" said my best friend, Paul Weismann. "Are you insane?" I hadn't expected this response. "You're absolutely out of your mind." He shook his head. "And in New York? Are you nuts?"

Paul was a former semiprofessional race-car driver who, in high school, had taught me to drive stick on his 1987 Ford Mustang GT. He never forgave me for running over a squirrel the first time I shifted into second gear. I trusted his judgment more than anyone else alive, and not just when it came to cars.

My father once said that one was lucky to have one real friend in life, and although I'm blessed to have several, Paul had been the sturdiest and wisest accomplice when it came to my most ambitious (i.e., dangerous) ideas. He rightly occupied a near-paternal place among our mutual longtime friends, and for reasons lost even to us, those closest to him called him the ceremonial patronymic "The Weis."

"So you won't help me?" I pleaded. "We could make film history."

"*I* might be able to do it," The Weis said as he shook his head, "but I think *you'd* need a lot more driving experience, and a specially prepped car."

"So you'll do it with me?"

"No way. Too dangerous. Besides, you don't need a copilot. That French guy didn't have one. The whole thing is worse than dangerous. It's pointless."

I paused—slightly hurt.

"It's *not* pointless."

"Well"—The Weis smirked—"your dad was almost certainly referring to Paris—"

"—which is a little impractical at this point."

"But why are you doing *this*?"

There was no point trying to explain the *why*. The Weis was a rational person who did a cost/benefit analysis on everything. Whenever I knew I'd lose a debate with him, it was time to invent a seemingly good *new* reason that might get him to go along, which, even after twenty years of friendship, seldom worked.

"First of all," I said, "it's good practice for Paris, and secondly ... the whole point of redoing *Rendezvous* in Paris is to get The Driver's attention so he'll contact me. But buying the appropriate car, shipping it to Paris, shooting it, publicizing it ... it seems like an expensive long shot. Doing this in New York will be a lot cheaper, and if I post the video on the Internet, it'll get to him eventually."

The Weis shook his head. "I'm afraid I think you just made that all up, but I'll give you credit—it'll be a lot cheaper. But a bad idea at a lower price is still a bad idea. Let's think about this. Your dad said the only way to find The Driver is by having a 'Rendezvous,' which you think means a *Rendezvous* in Paris, which means a Paris run is some kind of road test for entry into this ridiculous club he's running."

"But *Rendezvous* in New York will be a lot more dramatic."

"*If* The Driver is watching street racing videos on the Internet."

"Wouldn't he?"

"Somehow, a secretive guy who's been organizing illegal cross-country races for the last twenty years doesn't seem like the kind of guy who's sifting through crappy street-racing Websites hoping to find you."

"But it'll make good practice."

"For something you may have to do anyway, if you're going to be stubborn about this bullshit."

"But I *want* to do this in New York. It's my city."

"Now you're getting into other issues." The Weis shook his head. "Promise me one thing. You've got your brother and mother to look after. Just write up a will before you try."

"Done, but will you help?"

"Who loves *this* guy?" The Weis smiled.

"*That* guy."

"Let's be practical ... you really think you can lap Manhattan in twenty minutes or less?"

"Actually, The Weis, I was thinking of a Ford Crown Victoria, painted like a taxi, or a police car."

"Those might work if you ditched the paint job idea, but there's really only one choice."

"What's left?"

"A Subaru WRX."

Rendezvous remained shrouded in mythology greater than the Gumball 3000, Cannonball Run, and all the illegal underground races ever, combined.

The facts were these: In 1976, the highly respected French director Claude Lelouch mounted a 16mm color camera to the front bumper of a Mercedes 450 SEL 6.9. Departing the west side of Paris just after dawn, Lelouch drove across the city in less than nine minutes, finishing in front of the Sacré-Coeur cathedral in Montmartre, where the stunning Gunilla Friden (his then girlfriend, who had been Miss Sweden, 1968) ran up the cathedral steps to embrace the black-turtle-necked driver.

Lelouch allegedly screened the film in Paris in 1978, was arrested, the film permanently banned in France and Lelouch forbidden ever to speak of it. This seemed to explain why the film was almost impossible to obtain for nearly twenty-five years, restricted to $50 VHS copies traded over the Internet and shown among car fanatics.

Rendezvous in New York wouldn't be easy. The Paris *Rendezvous* route was just over seven miles. Manhattan Island was 13.4 miles long, a circumferential route twice that, and the island wasn't ringed by a single road, which would force me to run multiple red lights on city streets. The most obvious problems were that even the world's best driver probably couldn't cover a 26-mile course in under twenty minutes, I wasn't nearly *that* good, and even the world's biggest car fan would have to be strapped down to sit through anything that long.

I had to shorten the route, skipping Manhattan's northernmost quarter around Inwood and Washington Heights. Given the reputation of those neighborhoods' police precincts, this would have obvious additional benefits.

The start line was obvious—the World Trade Center. The WTC was the most dramatic location in lower Manhattan, and it was only two blocks from Manhattan's southern tip and the beginning of the FDR Drive.

The final time target was twenty minutes or less.

On the final run there'd be no stopping for anything, except a jaywalker.

Maybe.

"A Subaru," said The Weis.

"I hadn't thought of that."

"It's on every reviewer's top-ten list."

"I know, I know—"

"There's really no other car," The Weis explained. "Think about it. If you were on a track, a Porsche or Ferrari would be the obvious choice, but New York streets suck. The closest thing would be dirt roads, like on Paris-Dakar or the Baja 1000. You need a car with big fat tires, lots of suspension travel, four-wheel drive, and tons of acceleration."

"If I ditch the four-wheel drive," I said, "it sounds like a cab *would* work, like a Ford Crown Vic."

"That's why cabbies use them, but they still won't have the handling you want."

I owned an Audi S4, a fantastic four-wheel-drive turbocharged sedan that fit 90 percent of the bill. The primary problem was that it sat low to the ground.

"You can't use the Audi," said The Weis, reading my mind. "That was the last car you and your dad ever sat in together. Show some respect."

Lelouch had a single spotter at the north end of the Louvre tunnel—I'd need a lot more help than that, and a lot more redundancy.

With a stack of nondisclosure agreements and a crate of two-way radios, I intended to ask at least a dozen trusted friends/accomplices to stand guard at the traffic lights and block westbound traffic. This would be yet another problem, as there was absolutely no upside for my blockers other than bragging rights, something that would put me in jail for multiple crimes long before the statute of limitations ran out.

And there was yet *another* problem, which was that my girlfriend at the time refused to cooperate in the final touch which might elevate my effort into distant orbit around Lelouch's achievement.

She refused to meet me at the finish line.

My heart fractured hourly over this refusal. Her reasons made perfect sense, but I'd hoped that beyond her accusations of irresponsibility she might grasp the leap I was attempting to make between this admittedly absurd plan and the kernel of purpose my father had bestowed upon me. I'd long believed that for every thousand acts of pointlessness, there was one that justified the vain hopes of those who'd failed, that I, in this instance, would not become a statistic, and that she might surprise me.

Famous last words.

Other than The Weis, there was really only one other friend I trusted in this endeavor. Jon Goodrich, who shall hereafter be referred to as Nine, had been the coolest nonsnob at my high school's rival school.

Nine was one of the only private school kids I knew who dropped out of college, but, to his credit, he did it out of loyalty, choosing to go into the family business, which, like mine, involved cars. In the summer of 1990, Nine was rumored to have set the fastest-ever time from Manhattan's Upper East Side to Riverdale in the Bronx, the suburb where our schools lay. This seemed a good opening upon which to build a friendship, and it was around that time Nine became close friends with The Weis. Given the latter's lack of patience for bullshit, social climbers, liars, and trust-fund kids, I knew Nine was one of us.

This was the other thing that bound us. Pater Goodrich had passed away not long before my own, and my father had immediately given Nine a job at Europe By Car. When my father passed away, I quickly learned not only who my real friends were, but how grateful and loyal Nine was, and would prove to be.

One more thing.

Nine's first answer was always yes.

"This is one of the worst ideas you've ever had," said Nine. "What does The Weis think?"

"He's already agreed to help."

"Don't lie to *this* guy." Nine shook his head.

"Seriously."

"That's bullshit." He leaned back on my sofa. "So what's the plan?"

My plan was to have Nine organize the traffic-intersection blocking teams, one at the Harlem entrance of the West Side Highway, and one each at every westbound traffic intersection on the West Side Highway between Fifty-ninth Street and the World Trade Center. Radio interference prevented use of the RadioShack walkie-talkies I'd already tested, so we'd default to a sequential cell-phone tree that would alert the blockers to don their reflective-orange traffic officer vests, step out into each intersection, and hold up a bright red police baton. Each would prevent westbound traffic from turning south onto the West Side Highway, hopefully just long enough for me to run every red light between Fifty-ninth Street and the finish line. I hoped that would be fifteen seconds or less per blocker, or whatever it took to avoid my having an accident, and them getting arrested for police impersonation.

"Dude," said Nine, "I knew this was a bad idea, but that's the worst fucking plan ever."

"You have a better plan?"

"You have a better idea?"

"No."

Nine scratched his stubble. "And The Weis signed off on this?"

"Yup."

"Do I have to call him to see if you're lying?"

"C'mon," I said.

"Then I'm in."

"Who loves *this* guy?"

"This guy!"

"Nine, you know I'm putting you in charge of recruiting the traffic blockers."

"I figured. Who do you trust?"

"You."

"Does anyone owe you money?"

"Not that I know of." I squinted. "Why do you ask?"

"Because they would be the first people to ask."

"Hadn't thought of that." I nodded. "Any other suggestions?"

"No ex-girlfriends."

I loved Nine.

"We're almost ready," I told Nine.

It had taken a year to complete dozens of reconnaissance runs. I knew every pothole, every bump, every radar trap, and the general location of every NYPD patrol car on Manhattan's perimeter. I'd waited for winter's end so as to remap the route, knowing that however well the Department of Transportation refilled the potholes, new ones would emerge through spring and summer. I knew that Monday morning between 3:30 and 4:00 would be safest, since most nightclubs and bars closed early Sundays and there would be fewer drunk drivers, let alone innocent bystanders, than any other night of the week. I knew that late summer was best, as temperatures were dropping (reducing pedestrian traffic) and rain would be infrequent. I knew the garage guy near my Wall Street office would stash the car undercover for at least a week, long enough for any potential police investigation to die down so I could move the car to The Weis's Long Island country house for a few months.

Each morning I awoke with my sheets churned and twisted, the elasticized corners of the mattress cover pulled loose. My pillow was often so damp that the first time I noticed it I ran to the bathroom to find a thermometer. It read 98.6 degrees.

My greatest fear had begun to manifest itself.

I could never live with the thought that anyone else had been harmed by my actions.

Despite the confidence I projected to my accomplices, I knew I'd rather fail than risk another's life.

"When's the first practice?" said Nine.

"I'll tell you once I've talked to The Weis."

That night in bed, I watched the headlights of passing cars break upon the window blinds, splitting into dozens of parallel beams cast upon the ceiling. They moved from one end of my bedroom, slowly at first, then faster and faster as the car approached, to the other before disappearing as instantly as if the car had fallen off a cliff.

CHAPTER 3

God Is Speed

The first practice run was scheduled for the following Sunday. I wouldn't use the traffic-intersection blockers this time—I'd save them for the final run, just in case one of them leaked to the authorities.

I'd taken girls I wanted to impress on my reconnaissance runs, but for moral reasons I'd have to practice alone—it was far too dangerous. I'd never driven alone in any competitive or semiprofessional manner, and I was unexpectedly terrified at not having a rational voice in the seat beside me.

Although it would provide damning evidence in the event of an accident, I Velcro-mounted a camcorder to the dashtop. In the event of my death I wanted to at least *prove* there'd been a reason, however impenetrable.

I'd already driven the S4 down to a quarter tank of fuel so as to mitigate the chance of fire, and I removed all loose items from the car's interior—an accident would turn pens, lighters, and loose change into shrapnel.

I napped in my clothes from 8 P.M. Sunday until jolted awake by my alarm at 1:30 the next morning. I scanned the notes I'd made during my reconnaissance drives, but left them behind so as to deprive the police of critical evidence.

The practice lap time target was 30 minutes.

My first and last pencil-written remarks were identical.

Breathe

My second (and second-to-last) remarks were also identical.

Do no harm

I laughed out loud at my citation of the Hippocratic Oath.

If I broke it, *I'd* be the one needing a doctor.

It was a short drive down Broadway, west across Canal Street, then south on the West Side Highway. I might have stopped myself at any moment if only a companion had suggested it, but the fear caused by the empty passenger seat was replaced by the rush I felt in knowing I *was* going to do it.

I tried to clear my thoughts as I approached the red light at the WTC start line—the southbound intersection just a few hundred feet north of the entrance to the tunnel looping counterclockwise underneath the Staten Island Ferry Terminal toward the FDR Drive.

I lowered the driver's side window. It was a clear, humid night.

I exhaled upon the suction cups of my Valentine 1 radar/laser detector, attaching it just below and to the left of the rearview mirror. The V1 had saved me many times. It would have been inconceivable to attempt this without it.

I placed the camcorder on the dash at the last possible moment. Its presence would immediately tip off any police officer who might pull up right before the start of the worst car-related crime ever committed in New York City.

I pressed record.

My finger slid off the button with the first hint of sweat. The red recording light below the lens began flashing, reflecting off the windshield glass to warn any car ahead of my arrival. I'd forgotten to put a piece of tape over the light, but it was too late.

I craned my head, scanning for police. All clear. The dash clock read 2:26.

The traffic light turned green.

I gently let out the clutch, depressed the gas, and headed into the tunnel.

The tunnel lights turned night to day, the Audi's interior flashing yellow and black as I passed under the sodium vapor bulbs. The exhaust roared off the white-tiled walls and ceiling, then the twin turbos spooled up, whining like an aircraft engine at takeoff.

I hope no one's on the emergency pedestrian walkway

67

I crossed the double white line, veering left from the outside lane toward the inside. Fourth crime of the run.

The black square night of the tunnel exit was in sight. I floored it and burst from the tunnel, the ancient rusting-brown old Staten Island Ferry Terminal to my right, Wall Street's high towers looming to my left, the night's hot air buffeting my shaved head—

81

I recalled my reconnaissance notes—the right-side concrete lane divider ended just before the Brooklyn-Battery Tunnel ventilation building and Heliport Pier, allowing traffic to merge from the right.

I coasted right, around the gentle turn underneath the bridge, the deep roar of dozens of cars overhead—the bridge, Manhattan itself, speaking to me with anger at my passing. The third ambush point was clear.

If clear, stay left and accelerate on Straightaway 2

The hot wind blasted against my ear.

86

It would be impossible to hear the V1. I'd have to—

92

—take my eyes off the road but—

102

—that would be too dangerous.

111

One hundred and eleven miles per hour.

In New York City.

114

On Manhattan Island.

116

I never thought it possible—

118

—to hold it this long.

119

The Manhattan Bridge lay approximately 1,000 feet away.

120

A siren wailed to my left, echoing somewhere within the residential projects. I wished the anonymous victim luck.

121

I raced under the Manhattan Bridge. At this speed even the roar of the cars running perpendicular overhead was a mere sideshow.

129

I love New York.

Breathe

90

I approached the complex Thirty-fourth Street exit—an idiotically designed simultaneous on/off merge running from Twenty-fifth to Twenty-eighth Street—an intersection so dangerous (even at legal speeds) I couldn't believe litigious Manhattanites hadn't forced the Department of Transportation to close it.

Thuthump

Yes.

The road grew even worse on the leftward ramp up and over Thirty-second Street—the surface resembling the wreckage left by Vietnam-era cluster bombs meant to impede the passage of critical supplies along the Ho Chi Minh Trail.

The first of the NYS DMV's terrific rules was that, for anyone who was a New York State driver's license holder, moving violations occurring *outside* New York State did not appear on one's driver history, and such points do not accrue against one's driver's license. Since virtually every rally and illegal race I'd enter in the future would occur outside New York, this was a great relief.

The countervailing bad rule was that violations within New York State *did* generate points on one's license, and an automatic suspension occured if one earned eleven points within a rolling eighteen-month period. Preparation demanded careful study of the DMV point system.

I knew before my first practice that my potential violation point total would be in the hundreds, but I was comforted by the second-best NYS DMV rule:

Points accrued for any given violation are subtracted from the running total every eighteen months.

This meant that no matter how many points I accrued, I'd have my license back eighteen months after the final run—unless a perceptive traffic court judge figured out exactly what I'd been trying to do, in which case I might never be able to drive again.

Once in court, *if* a judge converted one or more reckless driving violations into criminal felony charges, I'd be sentenced to between thirty days and six months in jail. A judge would have every right to call my actions reckless, just as I'd know in my heart that I'd taken every precaution, through reconnaissance and practice, to mitigate the possibility of endangering bystanders. If I hadn't thought it was safe (or even possible) to attempt the lap, I wouldn't have tried.

Since I *was* guilty, and since I couldn't possibly explain *why* without the court making an example of and/or institutionalizing me, I'd plead guilty, accept my civic responsibility, and do the time without complaint.

Six months in jail and the permanent loss of my license in New York State?

This would never deter people like me.

The likely punishment—an eighteen-month license suspension—might have seemed like a long time, but New York City had an excellent mass transit system, and most Americans, myself included, needed more exercise.

The Most Dangerous Turn in New York City occurred at the intersection of the Harlem River Drive North and the George Washington Bridge access road—a high-speed left exit ramp ascending several stories before banking ninety degrees left. A right-hand merge lay at the end of the turn—at the precise point at which one had to bear right for the Second Most Dangerous Turn in New York City—the upcoming right exit toward the Henry Hudson Parkway South.

If a cop merged right behind me . . . Police officers waited their whole careers for traffic stops like this.

144

I passed the 167th Street on-ramp, braked—*no cop.*

136

Brake more.

—bore left toward—

Harder.

114

Harder!

81

—made the turn—

Yes

—and safely navigated the Most Dangerous Turn in New York City.

YES!

I accelerated West over 179th Street and bore right toward the Henry Hudson Parkway South exit. And made it. I passed the halfway mark.

I moved past fear, past philosophy, past the recognition of landmarks and their meaning, past internal debate, past rationalizations, and defaulted to something I'd never been very good at except when it mattered, and this was the first time it really mattered.

In theory, I had so far committed the following:

51 Moving Violations, including

24 Speeding Violations

14 Reckless Driving Violations

13 Improper Lane Changes

This brought my theoretical total moving violation projection to:

354 points

Enough to have my license suspended thirty-two times.

The final stretch ran four and a half miles from Fifty-ninth Street—where a series of red lights had to be run on the next and final attempt—to the finish line. I reasoned that stopping at the reds on the practice runs might in fact be a fantastic psychological exercise—on the final run my desperate urge to accelerate *through* the reds would probably be unstoppable.

I rolled past the World Trade Center at 2:54 A.M. I'd left at 2:26. I lapped Manhattan in twenty-seven minutes. I beat my target by three minutes. I'd committed 109 moving violations. I'd spotted two police cars. I'd earned a theoretical 731 points against my license, sufficient for sixty-six license suspensions.

And I'd never felt better. Ever.

I felt something I hadn't felt since losing my virginity—a surreptitious, revelatory sense of awakening born of accomplishment—but this, unlike that, had been completed alone, and with skill.

I thought I might have grasped a piece of Lelouch's *why*.

I'd made vicious, violent, terrible, irresponsible love to this city—*my* city. And I'd done it alone.

And I was going to do it again.

Faster.

"So," said Nine, "where's the car now?"

"Parked near my office, ready for one last practice run."

"When?" said Nine.

"Sunday," I said, "or the week after. Weather depending."

"Sounds good."

"The final run," I said, "will be one week after that."

Everything was a go—Jon, the car, the fake construction workers, everything.

It was Monday afternoon.

And tomorrow, well, tomorrow was Tuesday. Primary Day. September 11, 2001.

CHAPTER 4

Crossing the Rubicon

SEPTEMBER 11, 2001

I suspected something was wrong when I tuned in Howard Stern—even through soap-clogged ears I heard his typical cadence replaced by intermittent remarks and dead air. I grabbed a towel, ran out onto the fire escape, and saw the black shape of the second plane across the North Tower's face.

It was just after nine o'clock in the morning.

The South Tower exploded northward. I, who'd long considered myself an intelligent person capable of logical jumps, didn't even guess what had happened.

My father was extraordinarily protective of his sons, but I couldn't remember him speaking more then a few words to me until I turned ten. "Stop complaining," he'd say before I did, or "Come sit," a euphemism for keeping him company while I did homework. His wisdom was revealed on fragmentary tablets, and only at twelve did I first realize the difference in having a father one generation older than those of my friends. Sometimes he inexplicably stopped midstory, then continued another from weeks or months earlier, and the stories would converge in an uncomfortable moment whose meaning remained unclear to me for years. Only in my twenties did I grasp that their conclusions were withheld until I'd reached the age at which he'd lived them.

"You're such a complainer," was his answer to my request for a new G.I. Joe action figure. "You've no idea how lucky you are. The Luftwaffe bombed our house when *I* was your age, in Brussels. Everyone panicked. My best friend Jojo's parents said everyone should go to the station to get a train to

Paris, but Tata said that was suicide. You remember your grandfather Tata, don't you? Jojo wanted to stay with us and he cried when they dragged him away. We didn't own a car and Tata couldn't drive, but my brother Jack—he'd just turned seventeen—suggested we break into the Citroën dealer and steal a car. Jack read all the car magazines. Jack said the newer ones had easier clutches and he could figure it out. When we got there all the windows were smashed. All the new models had been stolen. We heard the explosions getting closer. The Junkers were flying over the city. In the back we found an older-model Citroën with a hand crank, and your Tata and I got on our knees and cranked and cranked until it started. We sat in the front and your aunt Janette and Mama got in the back, and we picked up an older couple Tata knew and—"

My father told me this story more than once, always pausing in the same place.

"—and . . . Jack . . . he struggled to keep the car going. There were people everywhere, and the engine stalled every time he stopped to avoid hitting someone. And people were trying to climb into the car. And they were on top. And Jack—"

At this point he always stopped, eyes slightly out of focus, and just barely stopped himself from crying before continuing.

"My poor brother, my poor Jack. He fought with the transmission and got the engine started again. He always got it started."

Jack was killed five years later. He joined the Royal Canadian Air Force, rapidly completed navigator and flight engineer training, and was shot down over Munich in the closing days of the war.

"What," I asked the first time my father told this story, "happened to Jojo?"

"What do you think? The Nazis strafed the train and killed them all."

"What about your house?"

"It's still there. So is the building where Tata had his matchbook factory."

I didn't know what to make of this.

"Tata had to start over again, in Paris. But he never complained. Then the Nazis took Paris, and we fled to Toulouse and he started over again. And Tata never complained. Then they came to Toulouse and we fled to Spain. He had many friends in shipping. He wanted to take us to New York, but some of the boats full of refugees to America were turned back, so Tata found a boat to Canada. And he started over again. And still he never complained."

All this precipitated because of the new swivel-arm G.I. Joe available for

$11.99 at the Lamston's across the street, or $8.99 with the coupon I was poised to show him before he began.

"You listen to me with this toy you want. Don't be a complainer. Do your best with what you have. Never give up. And don't panic."

"But all I wanted was—"

"Enough."

Don't panic.

And I didn't, standing in the shower that Tuesday morning. My staff would just be arriving at the Europe By Car office on William Street, three blocks east of the World Trade Center. Europe By Car was the last family-owned independent European car rental agency in the United States. We were the last fish in a sea of larger sharks. I was responsible not only for my brother and mother, but for this legacy my father left me, and that meant looking after our employees, a second family that had been part of my life ever since I'd been a secretary there during high school summers.

I had to turn the staff around, send them home, get them out of the black smoke and away from whatever was happening. The rest of the staff would still be on the subway, heading south toward the disaster. They would emerge on Broadway, one block east of the Trade Center, the worst possible place to be in case the buildings fell. My knowledge of structural engineering failures was based on a boyhood visit to Pisa, and a domino-style toppling toward the east would crush the seven-story building in which we worked.

I'd still have to go down there myself and wait for them. It was my responsibility.

I called Alfred, but all cell circuits were busy.

I ran south on West Broadway, the streets strangely devoid of rush-hour traffic, people clustered around stationary cars with their windows down, radios blaring local news. I ran down the center of the road as far as Canal Street, almost halfway to my office, stopped to catch my breath, and was nearly run over by a convoy of fire trucks and unmarked police cars heading in the same direction. I chased after them until, just a few blocks north of the Trade Center, a police officer stopped me from going any farther.

I called the office. All circuits were still busy.

I ran east and south, passing a group of gawkers silently surrounding an aircraft engine smoldering in the middle of the street. I made it as far as Broadway and Liberty, one block east of the Trade Center, and looked up.

The South Tower loomed above, paper and debris drifting down and collecting at the feet of the crowd around me. Tiny specks fell from the top. People were jumping.

I didn't quite believe or understand how or why, but the building's top began to shake, the tower's grand vertical lines blurring in what had to be some entirely explicable optical effect of the heat and thickening smoke, when suddenly the tower's length began to compress, enormous pieces cascading onto the fire trucks and police cars visible below. The crowd began screaming above the rumble of the great structure's fall.

Then I remembered more paternal advice born of the war—advice so obvious that I didn't need to recall the story ending with it.

Don't stick around burning buildings—

But it was too late. The crowd began to turn and flee toward me. I hesitated to help a woman who'd fallen over her own high heels. I tried to hand her one of her shoes, but she grabbed my wrist and pulled me east toward Nassau Street. I took one last look over my shoulder, but the tower was gone, engulfed in a cloud half the building's former height. A ten-story-tall tidal wave of gray smoke and debris headed straight toward us.

I ran after her, passing Nassau Street, hopping over abandoned briefcases and shoes and glasses. I couldn't know how much time I had before I was overwhelmed by this seemingly fatal wall. William Street was less than a block away. If I could just make it there, I might find safety in the lobby of the Chase Bank—certainly the sturdiest building within range.

The bank's entrance was filled with people trying to get inside.

Seconds remained.

I spied a dump truck, but the space beneath it was full of people.

That left only the Mobile Fried Chicken van, the one place I'd sought to avoid since moving the office downtown a year and a half earlier. I sprinted, crouching behind whatever safety the large yellow van might offer, hoping its inventory of frozen chicken would offer some protection. It didn't occur to me that I might get boiled in a rain of cooking oil, grease, and crispy wings.

"Do you believe in God?" I once asked my father.

I'd never been a religious person. My mother, who grew up in East Germany and never met her handsome, literary father, a *Panzergrenadier* officer killed in the siege of Sebastopol in 1944, had, despite everything, remained an innocent soul with faith in the ultimate goodness of people. My father was an atheist who'd renounced even the secular Judaism of his parents, the only unit of his extended family to escape the concentration camps. He believed in basic tenets of goodness common to all religions, and, he hoped, other atheists— honesty, hard work, and loyalty. What he saw when his U.S. Army unit liberated Buchenwald turned out the light upon whatever faith he had remaining.

"Please," he said, pursing his lips.

The rumble grew closer. I fell into a fetal position and pulled my messenger bag over my head.

It was time to pull out whatever prayers I knew, except that I didn't know any.

"Here it comes!" someone yelled.

I prayed that whatever God was listening would grant me this one reprieve and forgive my minor sins. I couldn't remember any major ones, and I wondered how many minor ones equaled . . . but by then it was too late to equivocate or lie to the creator(s).

If I make it, I'll be good, or at least better, and live, really LIVE—

The cloud washed over me.

It was empty, a cloud of dust so thick that I inhaled what tasted like bits of wet paper. I could possibly hold my breath for sixty seconds, then I would be in trouble. I opened my eyes. I could barely see my own hands. It was as dark as an undersea cave where mutated fish navigate by their own luminescence.

Silence. Then sirens. Screams. Finished.

With both hands I reached down and pulled up a damp clump of debris. I squeezed, confused, and dropped something with the size and weight of a baseball. Whatever was accumulating was thick enough to suffocate me if I didn't get inside and find air.

I crawled along the edge of the van, feeling my way to its rear bumper. Heat rises, firemen say. Stay low. But there was no fire, and staying low meant kicking up more of the debris and dust that passed through the shirt I'd pulled over my nose and mouth.

A nearby woman called out for help, but I couldn't see, let alone find, her.

I stood in a half crouch, as if this would protect me from whatever else might fall from above. My office lobby had to be no more than fifty feet away. I walked slowly in what seemed the right direction, both hands thrust out like a blind man who's lost his cane, and stumbled on a curb as my limited air gave out.

I wasn't going to make it. I crawled over the curb, reached out, and felt steps.

"So you don't believe in anything?" I asked my father a month before he died.

His voice was scarred from the twin tracheostomies he'd endured, making him, despite his weakness, even more imposing.

"Only once . . . did anything ever happen to make me believe in something . . . else. I was in the U.S. Army hospital near Saumur, in France. There's a tank museum there now. I can't remember the year. You should go see it."

We'd been there together. More than once. He'd long feared losing his memory, and his stories were increasingly underscored with items he didn't want to forget, and wanted me to know he remembered. "I was sitting outside in the woods, laughing at how pathetic my injury was when so many others there had lost arms, legs. Then my heart seized. I thought it was subconscious guilt at my good fortune. I thought I was paralyzed. I couldn't speak. I couldn't call for help. When I came to I knew something bad had happened." His eyes welled up. "A few days later they gave me a letter. My brother Jack . . . my poor brother Jack . . . was dead. Shot down. Jack was dead."

He paused. "I don't know. How could I have known? Maybe there's something. There has to be something . . . to explain how . . ."

A door opened against my shoulder. Two sets of hands grabbed me, raised me up, and pulled me inside. It was Jerry and Stavros, the Greek father and son who'd opened a deli in our lobby just a few weeks earlier. Several people screamed when they saw me, and as I was helped past the mirror behind the counter I understood why. I was white from head to toe, as if spray-painted, and from a single point on my right temple a line of blood splayed out across my neck and shoulder.

"What do you want me to do with the business?" I asked my father a week before he died, just a few days before his revelation about The Driver.

"You want to write, you want to paint. You think you want to do something else. But never forget, Europe By Car must survive. It's the one thing that has made everything possible. Since the war. Since I came here with Tata. Everything you have comes from that. From the business."

Someone doused my head with water, revealing only a superficial cut, and then my right hand, VP, and surrogate brother Alfred Celentano, and the rest of the Europe By Car staff emerged from a side door leading to the emergency stairs. I saw the momentary fear on his face replaced by relief, and then I realized not only how lucky I'd been, but also how irresponsible.

That was the first time I truly understood my father's inner conflict, and the choice he'd made. I had inherited not only his desire to find The Driver, but also his responsibilities. Just as he had backed out of the Cannonball for his family, I'd have to give up my quest for as long as it took to look after the business.

How could I ever have risked my life on a quest to find The Driver without considering what might happen to my mother, my brother, Alfred and the staff that had been family to me my whole life?

My father had left me the company's reins, and yet there was no line of succession, no life insurance, no single person to step into my place. Alfred, however trustworthy and capable, couldn't run it alone, and although in the year and a half since his death I'd assumed his quest to find The Driver, I had not yet safeguarded the legacy left me.

I'd find The Driver, but first I'd save the business.

And nothing would stop me.

Then I'd find The Driver.

And nothing would stop me.

SEPTEMBER 17, 2001

I drove to Alfred's house in Westchester for the Discussion. Despite being the proudest of successful immigrant capitalists, my father had retained a near-Japanese sense of socialist loyalty and honor to those who'd helped him. In the forty-six years my father ran the company, only a handful of people had ever been fired (and then only for theft), and there had never been a mass layoff.

Alfred's poker face was nowhere near as good as The Weis's. "So what are you going to do?" he asked.

I already knew. I had not only a moral imperative to do the right thing, but also a selfish one—I needed not only Alfred's respect and trust, but the staff's as well.

"We're going to do exactly what my dad would do. No layoffs. I have no idea what's going to happen, so we're going to hedge our bets for a month or two. Everyone keeps their jobs and takes a 20 percent pay cut and one day off a week. We'll cut my salary to zero. You take a cut which we'll figure out when we get back to the office next week. We sit tight for a month and see what happens. If we go under, I give you my word that we'll start over and I'll take you with me."

The blood rushed back into Alfred's cheeks. "I think that's what your father would have wanted."

"I'm just glad he didn't live to see this."

"Me, too."

Thirteen months later, Alfred and I were proven right.

It was time to rewrite my will. I didn't tell them what I intended to do.

There was only one way to find The Driver.

I had to find the events where he might recruit drivers of sufficient experience and preparation for an utterly illegal, secret, nonstop race crosscountry. Twenty-two years after the end of Cannonball, the pool of interested, *qualified* entrants had to be minuscule. These few, eager for more than weekend track days, would gravitate toward the next closest thing.

There was only one logical place to look, an event named after a fictitious race depicted only in film, its true origins having long swirled and disappeared into the fog of Cannonball mythology.

The Gumball 3000.

Officially, the Gumball was a rally without time, speed, or distance-related trophies, but if it was *merely* a rally, then why was hard information so scarce? Why did virtually every fan and aspiring entrant refer to it as a race? Why was it so hard to identify past winners of the cryptically named Gumball Spirit Trophy? Why didn't Gumball stop entrants from claiming "victory" on their personal websites? Why did fans worship oddly named legends such as Lonman and Kimble? Why—even among car aficionados—was Gumball discussed in hushed, reverential tones as if it were the Cannonball incarnate?

It was obvious. Gumball was either a surreptitious race *disguised* as a rally, or tacitly allowing entrants to race under its legal umbrella.

The next Gumball would leave New York for L.A.—a virtual tribute to the real Cannonball—in late April 2002, a mere six months away. I needed a year to research and prepare. Rumors suggested Gumball would return stateside in 2003.

I'd be ready.

NOVEMBER 2002

"Gumball. That's where I'm gonna find him. I *know* it."

"So," said The Weis, "we're back to this Driver business."

We sat in the library of his family's country house in Long Island. We had to discuss this out of earshot of his parents—my surrogate family since my parents divorced when I was nineteen. The Weis was the only Weismann who would entertain my most reckless ideas without reaching for the TV remote, often waiting weeks for the opportunity to deliver a memorized backlog of insults to his best friend.

"I thought you gave this up."

I frowned with false indignation. "That's how you talk to me?"

"Idiot. What makes you think he'll be there?"

"This Gumball thing is as underground as you can get. It's expensive, it's impossible to get in . . . if he's not there, then I'm sure he's watching. Maybe someone there will know him."

"And how do you intend to find him, or them?"

"If he's there he'll find me. If not, there's only one way to get his attention."

"Be serious."

"I have to win the Gumball." The Weis shook his head. "Okay, maybe not *win*," I said, "but I can come close . . . maybe."

"And this is a real race?"

"Not officially, but a lot of people treat it like one."

"Where was the last one?"

"New York to L.A."

"And the one before that?"

"London to Russia and back, via Sweden."

"And this one?"

"San Fran to Miami."

"But what are the rules?"

"The entry form says it's not a race, but I think that's so it doesn't get shut down by the police."

"Has there ever been an accident? Anyone killed?"

"I searched online for 'Gumball death.' Didn't find anything."

"Why's the route always different?"

"Maybe no one will have them back."

"Aliray, there *have* to be rules."

"Maybe it's like the real Cannonball back in the day. The only rule is—"

"—there are no rules." We both paused.

"So"—I leaned forward—"will you come with me?"

"This sounds pretty dangerous."

"But—"

"No."

"No . . . but you'll think about it?"

"Dude . . . no."

I couldn't believe my closest friend—the only person I knew with actual racing experience, the person who'd taught me to drive, the one person I'd let drive my car although he terrified me every time he took the wheel—would let me risk my life without him there to mitigate my paying the final price.

"Aliray," said The Weis, using the nickname given to me by his mother and now used by all my closest friends, "this sounds really, *really* dangerous."

I smiled faintly. "I'm pretty sure *I've* got eight lives left."

The Weis frowned quizzically. I tapped my chest in reference to the two lung tests I'd taken since 9/11. He nodded.

"Actually, The Weis, it might be seven."

"Seven?"

"The Manhattan lap leaves me seven, which means one dumb mistake for each of the five days of the rally, and two left over . . . just in case."

"I love you, Aliray, but you can't guilt me into this—"

"Don't worry, I'll find someone else."

"—but I'll help you prep the car . . . whatever it takes."

CHAPTER 5

The World's Best Bad Idea of All Time

DECEMBER 2002

We are all subject to nature's forces, as are our creations. Thin air affects a mountain climber's lungs, depriving him of oxygen and slowing his reactions—just as Colorado's high altitude necessitates cars' fuel systems to run different mixtures. Marathoners train and run differently in extreme heat and cold—just as the air temperature through an engine's intake changes its performance. Beachgoers wear sandals, hikers boots, and were they to trade, passersby would laugh and point. Summer tires skid in snow, and winter tires are unsafe on hot days. People require food and water, cars fuel, water, lubricant, and brake fluid.

All things must adapt to their conditions in order to thrive, function, and survive, and strict adherence to regimen is the difference between modesty and excellence. Only athletes trained from youth through physical maturity will be ready to perform best—and win—during their prime years. Only a car properly broken in, maintained, and driven will reach its optimal performance and remain reliable over the long term.

My father's 1987 Porsche 911, which in late 2000 I'd bought back virtually undriven from the film producer to whom he'd sold it in 1988, was such a car. Even with 92,000 miles it had inexplicably improved every year with nothing more than annual oil changes and inspections. I knew I'd give the 911 to my as-yet-unborn son.

My Audi S4, alas, was not such a car. Despite all we had shared, it was plagued with recurring turbo-hose ruptures. I needed to replace it.

But, before acquiring the right car for Gumball, before I could approach potential copilots who already owned more suitable cars, I needed an edge, a strategy, a lock on entry.

"You are absolutely out of your mind," said my attorney, Seth Friedland. I knew he'd say that. "It's a felony," he continued, "and I don't need to—"

"Seth, I don't have a suitable car or copilot. I'm running out of time to fill out this Gumball application. I need to tell them something outrageous if I'm gonna get into this thing."

Seth was straight out of a *Law & Order* casting call. Fiftyish, short, handsome, and impeccably dressed in a pin-striped suit with suspenders, he spoke with the confidence and authority of the attorney every TV criminal wished he could afford. Seth and I had met right after the 9/11 attacks nearly destroyed the office building we shared. I was fighting our landlord over compensation for the professional cleaning necessary to make the EBC office habitable, and Seth was the only other tenant willing to join the fight. Seth reminded me of my own father, and this was the first test of his willingness to aid in my quest.

"Maybe," said Seth, bringing his hands together as if in prayer, "you should do some research. You're a creative guy. Surely you can come up with a better idea."

It was too late for that.

The Gumball Rally, Cannonball Run 1 and *2, Cannonball!,* and *Death Race 2000.*

Most of the characters in the films had allegedly been based on real people, so I made a list of all The Drivers and cars from all the films and the few articles I could find about the real races from the 1970s, then divided them into two distinct schools of thought.

The *brute force* camp drove Ferraris, Lamborghinis, or Porsches in the belief that maximum power and speed would make up for time lost to frequent refueling and traffic stops.

The *stealth* camp brought vehicles and disguises meant to confuse and (hopefully) pacify the authorities—the most ambitious being *The Gumball Rally*'s fake police car, and *Cannonball Run*'s fake ambulance (Burt Reynolds's Transcon Medevac) and fake priests (Sammy Davis Jr. and a drunk-on-set Dean Martin in a Ferrari 308).

Although Yates himself had Cannonballed in the actual Transcon Medevac, with his wife as the fake patient, there was no evidence anyone else had ever used such disguises in real life.

I knew exactly which camp I fell into.

"I've done the research," I said, "and I'm completely serious."

"As your attorney—"

"Seth, have you seen *The Gumball Rally*?"

"No, but I don't need to, to know that impersonating the police is a really, really, really bad idea. What about if—" Then, in a moment of joint Thomas Edison–level revelatory insight that would forever bind us, change me, and greatly increase Seth's billable hours in an area of law in which there is virtually no precedent, he said, "—you drove . . . a *foreign* police car?"

"Now *that*," I exclaimed, "is worth $385 an hour!"

"I was joking," said Seth.

"But it might work!" I shot back, slapping my shaved head with both hands.

"It's a long shot."

"It's certainly better than driving cross-country in an NYPD cruiser."

"I suppose"—Seth rubbed his chin—"it *might* buy you time, if you *and* the car looked sufficiently different from local law enforcement."

There was a limited selection of foreign police uniforms available on eBay, none of which were suitable. They were mostly wool, came in limited sizes (I had no idea who my copilot would be), and looked too much like American police uniforms. The most aesthetic uniforms—the French Cycle Gendarmes and English Riot Police—had the word *police* spelled P-O-L-I-C-E across both sleeves.

I might as well race *myself* to jail.

I looked at the 2003 Gumball route: San Francisco to Las Vegas, Tucson, San Antonio, New Orleans, and Miami. Much as I felt bad even thinking it, most of the police departments along this route would likely employ officers lacking in, shall we say, a cultured sense of humor. Such gentlemen would have *no* sympathy for a bald New Yorker in a black turtleneck speeding in a foreign car, but something told me they were just going to *love* (if not, at worst, be utterly confused by) a serious-looking man in a strange uniform and foreign police car.

It made no sense.

It made perfect sense.

There was really only one country whose police force would garner the appropriate respect. The country that invented the highway, the only country in the world without speed limits, a country whose cars were respected (and bought) even by their most fearsome enemies.

I'd create a fake German Police Car. I'd become one of the Polizei.

At worst I might offend my Jewish cousins in Los Angeles, but there was little chance they'd find out—they didn't follow car racing, let alone Gumball. There was the slight chance I might run across the South's lone Jewish police officer in what would be the most hilariously tragic traffic stop of all time. I decided to bring a pocket Torah just in case. I guessed this would hardly be the strangest item I'd end up bringing.

There was one other thing about the Polizei—something that added an extra dose of irony which would come to protect me over many traffic stops.

Germany has no highway patrol, at least not a dedicated force as we do in the United States, but I'd seen pictures online of a Polizei Porsche 911, and I recalled seeing pictures of various Mercedes and VWs—

I'd call myself Team Polizei. It was in bad taste. *Illegal.* Insane. *Perfect.*

I sprinted home and filled out the online Gumball application.

"This is Julie Brangstrup," came the voice over the crackling overseas connection.

A young, female, English voice. I was momentarily optimistic that some friend had given my number to *his* good friend, or cousin, or neighbor visiting New York, and my weekend plans were about to improve dramatically.

"Who?" I said.

"I'm calling from Gumball 3000."

"Hold on a second, I'm driving. Let me just pull over. Okay, what did you say?" I didn't want to appear the overexcited amateur, but it was too late.

"You've been accepted for the 2003 Rally."

"That *is* good news," I said calmly.

"We really enjoyed your application. Are you absolutely serious about this Poliz . . . how do you pronounce it?"

"Polizei."

"Ah, German," she said. "Of course. And you're absolutely serious about this . . . Team Polizei?"

"Absolutely serious."

"That's a new one."

"Thank you," I said with genuine pride.

"And yet you haven't decided on a car?"

Dammit. I hadn't expected this call so soon. Had it been two . . . three weeks? "I'm afraid"—I paused—"that's a secret."

"And I'm afraid that won't do. We like to have a unique mix of cars, you see. We can't have a hundred fifty Porsches show up at the start."

"I see."

"And your copilot will be?"

I was in trouble. "That's"—I lamely pretended to cough—"also a secret."

"That just won't do. I hope you don't think us unreasonable, but for insurance purposes we simply must know these things in advance."

"Of course. I promise you this. We shall bring an actual German Police Car."

"And we"—she chuckled with her first hint of levity—"look forward to seeing it."

JANUARY 2000

"I hate BMWs," said my father.

His Cadillac had broken down again; repairs would take weeks. My 1996 Audi A4 had just been struck, for the second time in three years, by a New York City taxi. I'd traded it in and bought the vaunted Audi S4, the twin-turbocharged version of their small sedan. My father hated it, but it was the only way—barring taxis—to get him to the hospital for his treatments.

Car shopping was the only time we spent together outside the office and hospital. We had a ritual—I suggested cars, he rejected them. I took him to dealerships, he asked to leave. I took him home, he lectured on long-discontinued cars superior to everything we'd seen.

"What about a nice 740?" I asked. "Paul's parents have had one for six years. They love it."

"Too small. I can fit four people in the back of the Cadillac."

"Then get the iL model," I said, "You know, the long-wheelbase version."

"But it's rear-wheel drive. It's got that big hump in the center of the backseat."

"I don't think it has the hump anymore."

"They're overpriced," said my father. "And," he said, "the ride is terrible."

"*Car and Driver* said it was very comfortable."

"They wouldn't say that if they'd compared it to my Cadillac."

I didn't even bother suggesting a *new* Cadillac. Everyone knew they were truly terrible at that time.

"I guess," I said, "you wouldn't consider a big Audi."

"Overpriced. And the ride is terrible, like your S4."

"That's ridiculous."

I had to prop him up against the lobby wall as we waited for a taxi. The doormen who'd known us for two decades looked on quietly. They knew better than to offer him help.

We rode in silence to the Mercedes dealer on Fifth Avenue, where, despite my support, he nearly fell onto the sidewalk.

Together we inched through the revolving doors, then shuffled toward a gorgeous black S-class. I helped him into the driver's seat.

"Awesome," I said.

"Terrible. Look at this interior," he said. "I remember my 450 SEL 6.9. I think it was a '79. You should have seen the interior. You could take a flame-thrower to the dash, like we used in the war. Not a scratch. If Mercedes had been in charge of building those pillboxes—"

"I remember," I said, "you told me."

"Look!" he said, fingering the plastic buttons. "Terrible."

"Let's head over to Audi. It's only a block from Lexus, just off the West Side Highway."

"I hate the West Side Highway."

"Too hard to get a cab?" I said.

"No, I just hate it."

A salesman helped us through the front door, and I hoped this would warm my father to the BMW 7-series on display right inside the entrance. I could see in the salesman's eyes the struggle to overlook my father's disheveled appearance. My father was way past caring about fashion. Today he wore his favorite pants, just as he had yesterday, still paint-splattered from the last remaining hobby he had patience or energy for.

He sat in the driver's seat. "It feels like a Messerschmitt." Messerschmitt was one of the primary manufacturers of Luftwaffe fighters during the Second World War. "It's too German."

"But built like a tank," I said, regretting it immediately.

"But not as good as my 6.9."

"C'mon," I said. "That was thirty years ago."

"My Cadillac is a '77. It'll be fixed soon."

There was one car *I* wanted to see—an extraordinarily rare car I'd never seen in person—and I'd read on the BMW forum that one of them was actually here.

"Do you have the M5?" I asked.

"Right over here," said the salesman, who led us toward a jet-black M5 in the far corner.

The best of any given BMW wears the M badge. Except for the badges, such models are to the untrained eye almost indistinguishable from their lesser and far cheaper brethren.

"I know you like this," said my father.

"I do."

"How much is it?"

"Around $80,000," said the salesmen with disdain, as if that might deter us from asking more questions.

"C'est cher," my father said in French. *It's expensive.*

"Je sais," I said. *I know.*

The salesman looked out the window. He'd seen this before.

"When you've earned it," my father said in English, "buy yourself a used one."

"Really?"

"All young men need such a car once in their lives. Once you've outgrown the need for it, you'll be a man."

"But," I said, "you had that '79 911, and the '87."

"But I didn't need them. And I sold them. This"—he placed one hand on the M5's roof—"is such a car. When you're ready, find a used one."

"I'm afraid," the salesman chimed in, "they're very rare."

"The German police use them," said my father.

"That *was* true," said the salesman, "but now they use M3s."

"There was a secret unit," said my father. "Always the best cars. Porsche, Mercedes. A few years ago they had M5s—" He paused, lost in thought. "Don't speed in Germany," he said quietly. "They will catch you, the Germans."

"There aren't any speed limits in Germany," said the salesman. "That's why BMWs are engineered the way they are."

"But," said my father without looking at him, "they will still come for you. If they want you. Let's go."

DECEMBER 2002

In a bizarre confluence of bad luck, timing, and opportunity, my beloved S4 disappeared from a West Village parking spot. I couldn't believe a thief overcame both the Audi *and* aftermarket antitheft systems, *and* the impressive looking Club I'd placed on the steering wheel. I didn't care about the car being stolen. All I cared about was that the S4 was the last car my father had ridden in beside me.

I had to find it. I had to see it. In any condition.

I spent that night in bed feeling my first-ever empathy with those who taped "Lost Pet" flyers to the neighborhood lampposts.

My phone rang the next morning at 9:01. "I've got good news and bad news," said the police officer.

"Bad news first," I said, my father's son.

"The car's been stripped."

"Where is it?"

"Somebody drove the crap out of it. Dumped it in the Jersey swamps. It's in a lot in Newark."

This was like a Kentucky Derby–winning Thoroughbred being kidnapped, forced into pulling tourists around Central Park for one day, then shot and dumped in the East River. I'd have felt better if the thieves had shipped the car to Mexico and sold it to some car-loving mobster who won drag races against men he'd then tie to the bumper and drag through town.

"Is it drivable?"

"Unlikely."

"Call Paul at Par Cars," I said, writing down the number. "He'll pick it up." And sell it for me, as soon as possible, to someone who'd nurse it toward better days in a second life. I was willing to take a loss to see this happen.

I wanted an M5.

I scoured the Internet for used M5s in BMW's green or blue—traditional Polizei colors. What the salesman had said in 2000 remained true—M5s *were* rare. Buying a new one at $90,000+ was inconceivable. I called dozens of BMW dealers, placed myself on their used M5 mailing lists, and prayed.

FEBRUARY 2003

"Who the—" sputtered Paul Reznick of Par Porsche, at whose dealership I'd arranged inspection of my new purchase, "—who...who the hell owned this? Who sold you *this* M5?"

"Why do you ask?" I said.

"It's all wrong."

"What's wrong?"

"Probably gray market. We'll have to check the VIN numbers. Look at the air dam and mirrors—not U.S. spec. And look at the paint on the front right. All resprayed. Some kind of accident. And it looks like a European model that was only partially converted. The dash is wrong, too, and the radio is set to German."

"Should I give it back?"

"And look at this," Paul said, sitting in the driver's seat. "Only 5,700 miles after three years. Barely driven. Strange."

"You think this thing's gonna make it?"

"The 5-series *is* built like brick shithouse," Paul said.

"How long for the modifications?"

"Don't ask," said The Weis. "I'm still not coming."

"Guess what I'm calling my team."

"Try me."

"Team Polizei . . . awesome, right?"

"Aliray, I've known you a long time . . . but this . . . this!"

"I've got the uniforms and everything."

There was silence between us, the first such silence in as long as I could remember. Neither of us was ever at a loss, ever.

"You," he said, "really *are* crazy. I wish you the best of luck. Really."

"Is there any chance," I said, "any chance at all, that you'll reconsider?"

"I told you . . . if you want help prepping the car, fine. But I'm not coming with you. Not for this. Not on Gumball."

I needed a copilot. Badly. The criteria were harsh, but if *I* could meet them, someone else had to be able to. I needed someone with:

1. Experience driving stick, with club and/or actual racing experience.
2. Ten days free. Two days' preparation time and time zone adjustment, six days of Gumballing, and two days of drinking, bragging, and recovery. This one is a notorious job and marriage buster for many Gumballers. You'd be surprised how many wealthy people *don't* have ten days to spare, at least not for something like this. Those with enough money to do Gumball are usually too busy with work (in banking, law, etc.), or married to spouses who'd prefer to be taken on a nice safe vacation during their limited joint free time.
3. The willingness to drive aggressively, but not recklessly.
4. A clean driving record.
5. A clean criminal record.
6. A full head of hair. Two bald men in German police uniforms? Too Teutonic.
7. The ability to pass a drug test.
8. $8,000, for half the entry fee.
9. At least $10,000 more in disposable income.
10. Shamelessness sufficient to wear a fake police uniform for a week.
11. Fearlessness sufficient to wear a fake police uniform for a week.
12. A really good sense of humor.
13. Knowledge of foreign accents, preferably German.
14. A serious girlfriend, wife, if not children. Any of these, especially

children, would mitigate the likelihood of a gloriously suicidal pass killing us both.

The Weis was theoretically perfect; he was getting married that August. I would have suggested he ask his fiancée Astrid's approval, except that she was my ex-girlfriend.

Nine was next, but I couldn't possibly ask him to sacrifice the money he was saving for his engagement to Becky, his adorably fit twenty-six-year-old blond girlfriend. All his male friends strongly supported this union, but they'd probably also (if only out of jealousy) tell him he was crazy *not* to accompany me. I didn't want Gumball to become a point of contention so early in their relationship.

I'd have to go outside my immediate circle. Money would be key—I had tons of friends who met almost all the criteria, save the money. I couldn't possibly afford to pay my copilot's way, let alone front the $8,000 deposit without an ironclad commitment. I'd read posts on the Gumball forums about copilots who'd backed out at the last minute, forcing The Drivers to attempt to sell their slots. Gumball's contract forbade this, and I couldn't risk it. If someone had the money, I was reluctant but ready to compromise on the other criteria, as a last resort.

The most obvious demographic were the very people I'd often mocked for their hubris and empty materialism—bankers between the ages of twenty-seven and thirty-five. They were the most likely to have $18,000 to blow, yet the least likely to approach Gumball as anything other than a series of parties punctuated by daily road trips. I couldn't imagine spending a week in a car (and a hotel room) with someone I had nothing in common with, but I had no alternative.

MARCH 2003

"I've got the perfect person," said my dear friend Alex Chantecaille.

"Let's hear it."

"My boyfriend, Dave."

This sounded bad. When it came to cars, there were only three kinds of women: the rare few who actually knew how to drive, those who were terrified of their boyfriends' driving, and those who thought their boyfriends were the best drivers ever, even if they sucked.

"Why Dave?" I asked.

"He's the *best* driver. You have to meet him." Oh boy. "Call him," she said. "You'll see."

"What's his last name?"

"Maher."

I was desperate. With only four weeks to departure, I'd sat through dozens of interviews, almost all of them beginning and ending with, as expected, a late-twentysomething banker explaining how he was going to "kick ass," "kick *some* ass," "kick ass *and* take names," and/or "kick *all* their asses."

At least the latter was ambitious.

I awaited Dave Maher at La Goulue, a highly rated French restaurant on Madison Avenue that I would never have gone to unless I was meeting my mother for lunch, or interviewing a Gumball driver who'd suggested it because he lived in the neighborhood.

Although I liked Chantecaille—she was one of the few New York socialites who, like Melanie, was genuinely intelligent and lacking in pretension— I was ready to dislike Maher as soon as I saw him.

A tall, classically handsome all-American banker type with tousled short black hair, he looked like a young Shakespearean actor who'd rejected the role of Superman because the film was beneath him.

"You must be Alex," he said stiffly.

"Drink?"

"I'll take a beer."

Finally, someone without airs. "Chantecaille," I said, "tells me you're a *great* driver."

"Well, I like going to the track. Club events. You?"

And finally, someone with real driving experience—professional track experience superior to mine.

"Not really," I said. "Did some Audi Club events. Whaddya drive?"

"A Porsche 930."

The lightweight, turbocharged, and exceedingly rare (in uncrashed condition) Porsche 930 was one of the most dangerous 911 variants ever made. Nine once said 930 owners who hadn't met the nearest tree were damn good drivers, or liars.

"Four-speed?" I asked, just to make sure he wasn't lying.

"Yup."

He owned one. "Maher, how old *are* you?"

"Twenty-seven," he said, followed by an instantly resentful, "Why?"

"Because," I said, "anyone who owns that car is lucky to be alive. Anyone who owns that car under forty must be fucking good."

He pursed his lips. "I'm pretty good. Getting better."

Proud, but modest. I didn't think I'd *ever* heard a Porsche or Ferrari driver under forty admit to being anything less than "fucking great" behind the wheel.

"Do you drink?" I asked.

"As much as anyone else, I guess, but not on school nights."

I knew Chantecaille. He was telling the truth. "Drugs?" I asked.

"C'mon."

I knew where he worked. Morgan Stanley tested regularly.

"So Gumball," he said, "what do you know about the rules. How does it work?"

"No idea."

"I know it's a rally . . . but it looks like some of these guys take it pretty seriously."

"So do I."

"What kind of car are you going to bring?"

"A 2000 M5."

Our time together on this earth, and my premature assumption of a grossly inflated bill for two drinks, depended on the correct answer—followed by *precisely* the right question.

"Good Gumball car," he said with knowing sincerity. "Big V8. How's the fuel economy?"

In that instant Maher became the first interviewee in banking to demonstrate *any* knowledge of math, fuel economy, and/or Gumball car selection. Given how many I'd interviewed, I felt bad for their clients.

"Twenty-two on the highway," I said.

"Bet that's a lot worse at Gumball speeds."

"Maher," I said, deadpan, "do you think you have a sense of humor?"

"None."

Sarcasm cloaked in nonchalance, a clean criminal and driving record, ten days free—he'd be perfect, especially if we were pulled over by actual police. I didn't need to ask him if he could afford it—he wasn't the type of person who'd have shown up and wasted a stranger's time if he couldn't.

"Maher," I said, leaning back with my undrunk glass of red wine in hand, as if asking Watson why he'd accompany Holmes on yet another outing he thought futile, "why exactly do you want to do this?"

"I've wanted to go since the moment I watched the cars leave New York last year."

"But," I said, "why are you *here*?"

"Everybody talks about Gumball, but no one really wants to go and put it on the line."

He'd just given me the single most critical piece of information I required. There was more to the proud, distant, yet surprisingly modest Maher, but I could wait to learn the rest during the 200-odd hours we'd spend planning, preparing, and driving over the next six weeks.

"Why are *you* doing it?" he said forcefully. Clearly there *was* more to Maher—he was ready to take Gumball as professionally as I was, and wasn't going to put his life in the hands of a stranger with unknown motivations.

"Maher, have you seen *Cannonball Run* or *Gumball Rally*?"

"Of course."

"If they still ran the Cannonball, I'd do that, but they don't, so it's this."

Maher couldn't quite stop the hint of a smile, his first visible expression of emotion.

"So are we on?" he asked, his eyes locked to mine.

"Here's the schedule," I said, pulling out a pen with which to write on my cloth napkin. "I need you at my place on the following dates for race prep and help with shipping."

"Done."

"Good." I smiled surreptitiously. "Now let's talk about what I've got planned."

Maher listened to me without interruption for over an hour.

CHAPTER 6

I, Spy

I had arrived at the Fairmont Hotel five days earlier to await FedEx delivery of my heavily insured secret Polizei gear, and to identify, observe, learn from, befriend, and—if the latter wasn't possible—spy on arriving Gumballers.

For no reason other than force of will, I retained a distant hope that The Driver, if he was here, would, despite his best efforts to remain anonymous, inadvertently and telepathically reveal himself to me.

If he's here—even if he's only watching—there's only one way to find him.
I had to get his attention.

I had to determine whether Gumball actually was—despite official statements to the contrary—a race, and if not, whether there was a tacit race within Gumball, and if so, who was participating; then, if possible, identify the organizer (if one existed), join, or get invited to join.

I parked my as-yet-unmarked M5 in the back of the hotel garage's lowest floor as far as possible from Gumball's reserved spots—its lone rear-facing New York State license plate almost flush with the wall. I scoured the interior, leaving no sign of the car's owner, origin, or purpose.

After lunch I strolled around the hotel's perimeter, introduced myself to the entire hotel staff, tipped as many as I could afford to, then asked those I'd tipped if they would be kind enough to subtly notify me if any Gumballers arrived. I then studied maps of San Francisco and its environs, and asked the concierge about traffic congestion the night of Gumball's departure.

That night at ten, my cell phone rang.

"What the f—" The Weis demanded. "*What* are you doing?"

This meant he missed me. "Why are we talking?" I fired back.

"Why are you answering the phone?"

"I'm resting."

"Shouldn't you be busy getting ready or something?"

"I *am* busy," I said. "Busy resting."

"Why don't you do something constructive, like study San Fran's exit points?"

"You're an idiot. I already bought the maps."

"Then why don't you get in your car and check the exit points in person?"

"If you're so smart"—I pondered a comeback that wouldn't require me to do as he suggested—"then I *will*!"

"You're too lazy."

"I hate you."

"Enjoy!"

It was a great idea. I hung up, called the concierge, and demanded the cheapest rental car deliverable within the hour. I didn't want to drive the M5 unless absolutely necessary.

SUNDAY, APRIL 13, 2003
GUMBALL-4

"Now why are we talking?" The Weis actually sounded angry.

"To talk strategy," I said.

"I mean why are we talking *now*? Did you forget the time difference? It's six o'clock in the morning!!" he yelled.

"You need to be up for work soon anyway."

"It's Sunday!"

"Oh yeah."

"*You* better pray you didn't wake my fiancée!!!"

"I know her. She's a heavy sleeper."

"I hate you."

"Ready for strategy?"

"Fine."

"The Golden Gate Bridge is out."

"You actually went there last night?"

"You inspired me, so now you get a wake-up call every morning until I've checked all the exit points, and I wanna talk about them."

"I really do hate you."

"I'll be quick. Let's talk about why the Golden Gate Bridge is out."

"Tell me what you saw. Cops, cameras, everything."

TUESDAY, APRIL 15, 2003
GUMBALL-2

I stopped by the garage again to check on the M5. She was safe.

In the lobby I approached the concierge, a well-coiffed gray-haired gentleman.

"Ah, Mr. Roy, your Federal Express boxes are here. Would you like them brought to your room?"

Thank God. "Have them brought to the garage, but *not* the Gumball area. Lower level, in the back."

"Right away."

It was time to unpack and install my secret equipment, then sticker the car, but I had one more question only The Weis could answer at this hour.

"My God," he groaned, his fiancée snoring in the background, "what time is it?"

"Six-thirty New York time. Aren't I a nice guy? One quick question. How do you say 'enemy drivers' in German?"

"*Die Fiend-Piloten.*" Then he hung up.

CHAPTER 7

Die Fiend-Piloten

WEDNESDAY, APRIL 16, 2003
GUMBALL-1
MORNING

I periodically strolled outside for a cigarette and to play a game indulged in by car lovers—the identification, by sound alone, of approaching cars. The Fairmont sat atop Nob Hill, one of San Francisco's tallest, and with every distant roar of large engines in the city below, my heart raced at what my foes might bring to battle.

I strolled back inside as a large group of rowdy high-schoolers on a class trip was checking in.

Suddenly, through a gap in the mass of writhing teenagers, I caught a glimpse of a girl so exquisitely gorgeous that I was stunned at my failure to spot her entering the hotel.

"That chick is soooo hot," one teenager said to another.

I hated the thought of hitting on someone's girlfriend, more so if he enjoyed working out, especially if he had a bad temper, and certainly if he had a criminal history.

But no single red-blooded American male could pass up a chance like this. I walked over to her.

"It's getting messy in here," I said. "Do you have a light?"

I buried my lighter behind the keys in my pants pocket so that she couldn't see the Bic's distinctive outline.

"Of course," she said in the Queen's English, bemused smile spreading across her face. A Gumball driver, I hoped, and not merely a rally girlfriend.

"Alex Roy." I smiled back. "Join me?"

"Kira," she said, "and yes, thank you."

Even in sneakers she was nearly six feet tall, and with unexpected and temporary strength, I pushed and held open the heavy glass door, watched with delight how her loose black track pants tightened with each long stride, and followed her outside.

"By the way," she said, turning toward me with lighter in hand, "my boyfriend will be here any minute." But of course he would. "Perhaps"—her smile widened as I searched for a response of appropriately tactical nonchalance—"you know him?"

Since I didn't know who *she* was, I couldn't possibly guess. "I think so," I lied.

"Charles Morgan?"

I *knew* this name, but couldn't place it.

"Kira, darling!" came a grown Englishman's voice over my shoulder. "Who's your new friend?"

Once I turned, I knew that the English gentleman before me—a slender fiftyish man with short hair having just begun to gray, as understated, handsome, and charismatic as Sean Connery's Bond in his prime—was in fact *the* Charles Morgan, grandson of the venerated H.F.S. Morgan, founder of Morgan Motor Cars, manufacturers of the delightfully bizarre three-wheeled Morgan driven by Peter Sellers in the 1968 movie *The Party*. Founded in 1910, the pace of Morgan's design evolution was charmingly glacial—wing-fendered roadsters of enormous power mated to ultra-light chassis of wood, steel, and now, aluminum.

"This is Alex," she said without hesitation.

"Well, jolly good!" He smiled warmly, pumping my hand. "But I'm afraid Kira and I must be off! Shall we see you later? But of course we will!"

This would be the last time I spotted a woman on a rally and assumed she was available, unmarried, unpaid and/or not spoken for in some way— legally or financially.

I love cars. I love sports cars. I love racing. I've even come to love watching car racing on TV—sometimes, and only for up to the ten-minute limit tolerated by any of my girlfriends. But Gumball wasn't taking place on a track—a short, specialized loop with fuel, mechanics, spare parts, and medical support one lap and minutes away—which meant that virtually everything race cars were designed for was irrelevant.

Success on the Gumball *had* to be based on endurance, reliability, fuel economy, police evasion, and, despite the highly conspicuous stickers required by Gumball, stealth.

By this measure, there was only one possible car more appropriate than mine: a dirty-brown 1980s Mercedes turbo diesel station wagon.

Any other cars, whether psychological crutches, rolling jewelry, or priceless works of automotive art, couldn't be as well suited to the task.

I was utterly confident in my technical preparedness.

But my heart still sank when the rumbles and wails of Gumball cars began echoing in the surrounding streets.

"Holy shit!" said one of the high-schoolers surreptitiously smoking out of sight of his teachers inside. "Guys! You gotta come see this!"

A lemon-yellow Ferrari 360 with custom body-color-matched Sparco racing seats, five-point race harnesses, and nineteen-inch chrome aftermarket wheels pulled into the Fairmont's driveway. Immediately an all-male teenage crowd gathered to snap pictures, point, lecture, and debate the car's every facet. They were soon joined by a small group of passersby, bellhops, and a passing cabdriver who each recited loud, overlapping, sometimes contradictory, and often obscure details of the 360's performance. It was as if all but their involuntary organs had been overwhelmed by a hypnotic invisible gas secretly developed in Italy—99.9 percent effective within ten feet of any Ferrari's prancing horse badge.

I knew from reading *Car and Driver* that the 360 was a highly rated track car costing approximately $200,000, but I also knew from the Ferrari chat boards that two hours on rough roads would give The Driver hemorrhoids. More importantly, I *also* knew that it drank 16 mpg on the highway—in tests far below Gumball speeds. Totally inappropriate.

I watched the gawkers. I admired the car. Of course it was art. Of course it was amazing. Of course the driver could beat me on a track.

But it's not the car with which to win a cross-country race.

Nor were the similarly and outrageously expensive supercars forming a line behind the yellow 360. The supercars were vastly outnumbered by a slow parade of $50,000 to $100,000 cars possessing at least 85 percent of their performance—numerous BMW M3s, Mercedes SLs, and Porsche 911 variants. Cars that may have hidden extraordinary modifications—the lone blue Ford Mustang, white Toyota Supra, and green Mini Cooper—were laughed at or completely overlooked—but not by me.

Few of the cars had the telltale sign of a Valentine 1 radar detector—two small circles on the windshield, indicating that one had been suction-mounted, pulled down, and stashed away. What little evidence I spotted was of other detector models (which I considered no better than bricks) mounted low and/or off center—proof of ignorance at how radar detectors work.

The drivers and copilots emerged from their cars, smiled, laughed, and shook hands with one another, dampening my hopes for public displays of competitive animosity.

These were not the hard-core illegal underground racers I was looking for.

All eyes fell upon a very low car as it gingerly entered the Fairmont driveway.

I'd read every issue of *Car and Driver*, *Road & Track*, and *Automobile* magazine published in the United States since 1983, and I'd never even seen a picture of the steel-gray car that rolled up in front of me.

It whirred like a taxiing airplane's turbine, its smooth-sloped semicircular wraparound windshield and cockpit as far forward as a fighter plane's, five clawed spokes forming each of its matte silver wheels, the engine beneath its long rear deck emitting secondary hisses and barks as the rpms fell to idle.

Even parked, it looked like a mythological beast exiled from its herd that had returned for vengeance, muscles coiled as it lay low, leaning forward on its rear haunches, poised to strike like a meteor—first at the pack leader, then its mate, then the weaker and younger, then the cubs, to feast lazily before trotting back to its lair, beheading any passing unicorns on its way.

"Koenigsegg," said a young black-haired Englishman wearing a pair of colorful Piloti driving shoes. "Very nice."

"How much is it, Nicholas?" said a brunette next to him.

"I believe it's seven hundred," said Nicholas. "*Thousand dollars.*"

The long right-side door clicked, moved outward from the car. Then it silently rotated on its forward hinge to ninety degrees and clicked in place.

A skinny Middle Eastern college kid with a baseball cap worn askew and expensive colorful sweats climbed out. A goateed friend in similar sweats emerged from the lobby, the two embraced, and a rapid exchange began in impenetrable London slang.

A third man arrived and entered the conversation, now in hushed tones. Although he was a serious-looking thirtyish blond Englishman in a dress shirt and slacks corporate enough to have afforded the car, his body language within the trio suggested a more subservient role.

"Have you seen the police car?" said the brunette.

"Now that's funny," said Nicholas, surveying the girls in the crowd around the Koenigsegg. "What kind of car?"

"Some blue BMW."

"Now that *is* funny. An M car, I hope."

"What's an M car?"

"A BMW with a lot more power. Not for you, darling. Who's driving?"

"I didn't see who, but it has New York plates!"

"At least someone has a sense of humor. I'm bored here. Let's go to the bar, my dear."

I waited for them to enter the revolving doors before following, but before I could, I was stopped by the sound of something coming. *Something big.*

The Koenigsegg—like almost all Porsches—was a gentleman's car designed with ironic subtlety. Despite its purpose, it *was* possible to drive it without scattering pigeons, stopping pacemakers, and painting the streets with rubber. But whatever was coming was not such a car.

The terrible noise approached—a single note played within every octave of the audible spectrum's lower half—an enormous engine mated to an aftermarket exhaust intended to wake up, annoy, anger, intimidate, and command the attention of anyone in earshot.

Its arrival was not intended as a surprise. Its presence was meant to offend.

Then I saw it—a jet-black plastic-clad Texas-plated Chevrolet Avalanche 4×4 truck—a hideous showcase of American automotive shamelessness—as it clawed its way over the curb and stopped on the Fairmont sidewalk.

Onlookers turned and pointed with white-faced mortification as the driver revved the engine and a flock of birds took flight from the stone perches on the Fairmont's facade. The truck's huge chrome rims gleamed in the sun, which also highlighted bright red jerry cans chained to either side of the enormous spare bolted to the rear deck, and the pairs of floodlights affixed to the roof, hood, and front bumpers. A Confederate flag filled the rear window, a second small Confederate flag graced the hood, and twin seven-foot radio aerials danced against the blue sky.

The Avalanche driver, a shaggy, black-haired, goateed cowboy, killed the engine, opened his high door, stepped down onto the pavement, and yelled, *"Awwwww yeeeeaaaaahhhh!"*

"Hey," a bellhop called out as he pointed at the Avalanche's plates. "What does that mean?"

"D-V-L B-L-R," I read out loud. "Devil something or other?"

"That's right!" the cowboy yelled at us as he approached. "Devil Baller!"

"Alex Roy," I said, offering my hand.

"Richard Rawlings! How the hell ya doin'?" He suddenly turned toward the crowd surrounding his Avalanche. "It ain't gonna hurt ya!" he yelled, and headed back to the truck. "At least not yet!"

Rawlings opened his driver's door, stood on the high running board, and regaled the crowd. "That's right! Beefed up with a three-quarter-ton chassis and a 502 big block!"

The Avalanche's fuel economy and handling would be terrible.

But with those jerry cans... I walked over to peek inside at the Avalanche's interior.

Holy shit.

Rawlings had installed virtually everything I had in the M5—radar detector, CB radio, two (!) police radio scanners—along with a stack of backup paper maps I'd reasoned I wouldn't need because of my GPS.

Rawlings was now Polizei Enemy number one.

I began scoping out the cars in the hotel garage.

A yellow Porsche 996 Turbo X50's left rear sat on its red-rimmed spare.

I remembered one thing I'd forgotten.

The M5 rode on wheels and tires too large to fit a donut—let alone a full-size spare—in the trunk. I was stuck with a temporary inflation kit, which was basically a small pump with a foam canister. It was now four years old and it had never been tested.

If I got a flat, I'd lose a fortune and have to drop out not only of Gumball, but of the *race*.

I'd have to wait another year to find The Driver.

My fear of a flat was but a pebble in the shadow of what I felt upon seeing the four-foot CB aerial two cars down. It was only the second big aerial after Rawlings's. I walked up to a black Ferrari 550 Maranello.

The exterior was stock. A Valentine 1 was suction-mounted top center of the windshield. A police radio scanner was professionally mounted between the seats. A CB radio hung under the glove box.

The car had Texas plates. He *had* to know Rawlings, and if two or more technically prepared drivers knew one another ... *we had the beginnings of a race.*

I'd found the first, tenuous, possible sign. I was one small step closer to finding The Driver.

CHAPTER 8

Dorsia

WEDNESDAY, APRIL 16, 2003
FAIRMONT HOTEL GARAGE
GUMBALL-1

I'd lost track of how many times I'd been asked where and how to get into the Gumball kickoff party. I'd heard there was one party on the roof, a second one at nearby club, then a secret after-hours party at yet another club. "Your badge is your only access," the Gumball staffers warned, "so *do not* lose it."

"Where's the party?" I asked each and every one I saw, often multiple times.

"As we said, seven P.M., on the rooftop."

"What about the *other* party, the *big* party?"

"We'll let you know."

I was reminded of Bret Easton Ellis's *American Psycho*. The protagonist, Patrick Bateman—serial killer/banker plagued with insecurity over his social standing—is obsessed with getting into, eating at, saying he ate at, and/or *being seen in* New York's most exclusive fictional restaurant, Dorsia.

Whenever its name is uttered, a delightfully loaded ritual begins.

"Lunch at Dorsia?"

"Dorsia? Impossible to get a reservation."

Or—

"Have you been to Dorsia?"

"Dorsia? Impossible to get in."

Or—

"Can I bring one more person?"

"To Dorsia? Are you insane?"

Dorsia entered my vernacular, becoming the Holy Grail of my social life. Once I turned twenty-one and could get into bars legally, Dorsia became any one of the new clubs. Even once I passed through the velvet ropes of one Dorsia, another Dorsia beckoned. Dorsia became a basement restaurant with an unlisted reservations number, then an after-hours club with a secret door and open bar after dawn, then a Bulgarian prince's loft packed with models. Yet no matter how many Dorsias I somehow talked my way into, the same people— or type of people—were there, and I wondered if *this* was it, if *this* was all there was, and if there might not be some other Dorsia I'd not yet heard of.

I eventually abandoned that self-perpetuating quest and became grateful for a night of sushi, war movies, and Gran Turismo with The Weis or Nine, and whichever girlfriend had the patience to wait up until their departure.

But now there was a new Dorsia. *And The Driver might be there.*

My CB-radio antenna base mount wasn't locking to the M5's trunk lid. I was trying to install a four-foot antenna—effective up to five critical miles— which would make mine the third tallest after Rawlings and the one on the Texas-plated Ferrari.

It was time for the emergency backup RadioShack 12-inch antenna and magnetic mount. I slapped it on the roof with a satisfying *thunk*. I wondered at what speed it might fly off and smash another Gumballer's windshield.

I wanted to ask Maher what he was wearing, but he'd already gone upstairs to bask in the attention already given him—at six three he was the tallest Gumballer of 2003—by most of the unattached (and some of the attached) women on the rally. It *had* to be dressy, even if the invite didn't say so. A tuxedo would therefore be perfect. But I hadn't packed one.

My parents agreed on almost everything except party protocol. My mother said to *dress* as if one owned the place, and my father said to *act* like one owned the place.

I'd go with Mom on this one. I put on my black pin-striped suit, white dress shirt, bloodred tie, and black shoes, inserted a crisply folded white pocket square in my jacket pocket, clipped a silver tie bar to my tie, and inserted my favorite cuff links—one a tiny barometer, the other an inclinometer— in my cuffs.

"Roy!" Maher called out from between two girls with their backs to me. "What took you so long?"

"Forgive me, ladies, but I've got to borrow Maher for a few minutes."

"Thank goodness!" said Jessica, a gorgeous young photographer from Stockholm. "We're done with him anyway!"

"Great party girls," said Maher as I led him into a corner so I could survey the room. "I love Gumball already. You need to learn how to relax. Those two girls I was talking to are with two more blondes smoking on the balcony. All four of them are with this guy Eyhab from London, and he brought two cars *and* a support truck!"

"Who is this guy? What's he driving? I want to see him."

"There." Maher nodded across the room.

A well-tanned, handsome, athletic man of medium height with short, curly black hair—somewhere between thirty-two and forty, and probably of Middle Eastern descent—stood in the far corner. He wore a black T-shirt that read *China White*—the Dorsia of 2003 London. A tall brunette had just walked up to him, and Eyhab flashed a broad white smile of sincere joy contrasting with the serious demeanor of the two enormous men beside him.

The two wore large black bug-eye sunglasses, Gumball's signature black baseball caps with reflective stripes, black shoes, jeans, and T-shirts.

One of them was a guy I'd met in the lobby named Rob. "I know that guy!" I said.

"You know Eyhab?"

"No, the guy on the left. Rob. One of the big guys. Nice guy."

"Looks like a good friend to have."

"Great guy," I said. "Let's go introduce ourselves to this Eyhab."

Rob and his partner moved in and out of Eyhab's orbit based on the proximity of other people, the second one even putting an enormous arm around Eyhab's shoulders in an unsubtle gesture of *I-may-have-to-shield-your-body-with-mine-while-Rob-returns-fire.* The second man moved in front of Eyhab as we approached. When Rob spotted me, he leaned over to Eyhab and whispered in his ear.

"These guys are okay," Eyhab said to the man blocking our path, who immediately stood aside.

"Alex," said Rob, "this is Eyhab."

"Good to meet you, Mr. Police Car Man!"

At any other time and place Eyhab and his entourage would have been the most bizarre people in the room, yet among all the Gumballers I'd seen or met in the last few days, they were by far—from the instant we'd met—the warmest, most unintentionally hilarious, and human.

"And," Rob said, "this is Mike."

"A pleasure," said Mike.

"And this," I said, "is Maher. My copilot."

"I heard," Maher said to Eyhab, "you brought a couple of cars."

"I'm driving the Murcielago, my girlfriend's taking the 360 with Jess."

"Nice," Maher and I said in unplanned unison.

"Rob and Mike," said Eyhab, "are in charge of logistics and support."

"High-speed support," said Rob.

"Lincoln Navigator," said Mike.

"I heard *you* two," Eyhab said as his grin further widened, "are in that Polizei M5."

"You," I said "are the first person who actually pronounced it correctly."

"We're the good guys," said Eyhab, "so please don't pull us over."

Oh. My. God.

The whole point of Team Polizei was to confuse and/or amuse *real* cops so as to avoid tickets or jail time. But if Eyhab actually thought we might use our police lights on him—*we could actually use the lights as an offensive weapon on other Gumballers.* It might not work in daylight, but at night . . . they'd never know if the flashing lights behind them were real or my *StuttgartAutobahnVerfolgungAchtungPolizei M5.*

They'd have to slow down every time, just in case. We might even be able to pull one over if we used the PA system.

But we'd lose valuable time. Better just to pass anyone who fell for it.

"Don't worry," I said, "you guys are safe."

"I'd like a water. Care to join us at the bar?" Eyhab may have *looked* exactly like the poster boy for Gumballer playboy, but he wanted a water. *Maybe he's just not drinking tonight . . . because he's here to race.* He was clearly someone to keep an eye on. He'd be hard to miss.

"We'll catch up with you later," I said, jabbing Maher with my elbow. "Tell me what else you learned."

"Rawlings, the cowboy guy in the tricked-out Avalanche, is not as crazy as he looks. I think he's an ex-cop or fireman who made a bunch of money."

"Has he seen our car?"

"Yeah, but he doesn't know we're the guys driving it."

"Good. Let's go find him."

Maher led me out onto a terrace packed with at least fifty Gumballers. Even in my suit I shivered against the brisk evening air. Near the ledge a bare arm raised a beer bottle over a cowboy hat. "I see him," I said, and began slowly and politely inching toward our quarry.

"That blonde"—Maher leaned closer to me and nodded at a tall woman in her late thirties, in tight jeans and a low-cut T-shirt—"is his wife. I heard them talking about their kids. She's also his copilot."

That *might* mean—even if he was as serious about racing as his preparations suggested—he might back off in the critical moment of commitment that was the difference between first place and second.

"Interesting. Who are the guys with him?"

"The one on the right"—a boyish thirtysomething with professionally cut yet shaggy dirty-blond hair and expensive-looking tinted glasses—"is Dennis Collins."

"Collins have kids?"

"I'm not a mind reader," said Maher.

I watched Rawlings jab Dennis in the arm. "They seem to know each other."

"Old friends."

"What car is Collins in?"

"Black 550 Maranello."

"Maher, *that's* the Ferrari with the huge aerial and the scanner! They have almost all the same stuff *we* do! Did they tell you anything else?"

"Dude, I just met them, I wasn't gonna interrogate them. Relax."

I stared at the jovial contingent from Texas—the four of *them* laughing as they ordered another round—while *I'd* come to stalk the crowd in cold sobriety.

The Collins brothers were now Polizei Enemy number two.

I snapped out of it upon spotting a beautiful blond girl's face hovering a full head above everyone else on the terrace.

"Yeah." Maher sighed. "I saw her before. She's gotta be six three . . . *my* height. Jodie Kidd, famous English model. I heard she races professionally."

"Finally, a model who does something."

"Yeah." Maher nodded approvingly. "Next to her . . . see that shorter guy?"

"Everyone's shorter than her."

"That's Joe Macari—"

"The guy who looks like a lovable bulldog? Good work, Maher. I guess you *haven't* been talking to girls all night. So who is he?"

"Check out his hand," said Maher, "for a burn scar. I think he's a retired pro driver. He's in a Mercedes SL55 AMG."

Good car, but shit gas mileage, and no dash space to install equipment.

"What about the frat-brother-looking guy next to Macari?"

"Jamie McCloud. I think he's a banker. He's got an F50."

"Wait, a *Ferrari* F50?"

"The real deal."

The F50 was the Koenigsegg of the late 1990s—a low-slung $500,000 race-prepped barely street-legal Ferrari resembling the cartoon cars ten-year-old boys draw in their notebooks instead of paying attention in class. The few collectors who could even find one never dared to take it out of the garage.

Anyone who brought an F50 this far with friends like Macari wasn't on vacation.

"Is Jodie Kidd riding with one of them?"

"Hmm," said Maher as we both watched her speak down—literally, but only physically—to McLoud and Macari.

"From the looks of her . . ." Maher started.

". . . no one tells her what to do," I finished.

"How old do you think she is?'

"Nineteen," I said, "going on forty. Girls like that never age. Out of your league, Maher. Anyone else?"

"That's it so far."

"Okay, let's reconvene in thirty."

"If we get split up, I'll meet you at the club."

"Club?" I exclaimed. "What club? *You* know where the club is?"

"I'll call you as soon as I know. Dude, you've got your Gumball ID. You'll get in."

People like Maher always got *in,* even without ID.

Fucking Dorsia.

"You're late!" said the Gumball staffer just inside the club entrance. "Just head right upstairs!"

"Dude!" said Maher. "I've been looking for a bald guy in a black suit, and you show up in a white suit? How the hell was I supposed to find you in here?"

We headed to the downstairs bar. "*That* guy," I said, surreptitiously pointing at the slender, knowledgeable Englishman I'd seen outside the hotel that afternoon, "is hard-core veterans. Nicholas Frankl. He does every event, he knows *everybody*. He won the Gumball Spirit Trophy last year in a Porsche 911. He was arrested with a guy named Nick Connor, but they got out and flew to the finish in their jail stripes."

"Holy shit," said Maher. "I spoke to Frankl. A ton of track experience."

"Did he say what he's driving?"

"Mitsubishi EVO."

Of course. The *highly-rated-but-underappreciated-by-car-snobs* EVO was equivalent to the Subaru WRX The Weis had recommended for my

Manhattan run. With a fuel cell it'd be an excellent endurance racer, and at $35,000 it had 95 percent the performance and handling of the Porsches, Ferraris, and Lamborghinis on Gumball.

Only someone with a limited budget—*or Frankl's experience*—drove an EVO.

"What color?" I said.

"Yellow." Maher shook his head.

A veteran? In a yellow car? "Are you sure?" I said.

"I saw it in the garage."

"Frankl better pray the cops are color-blind."

Maybe Frankl wasn't so smart after all. But wait—Frankl was English. He didn't care. Anything short of arrest would have no effect on his license. Frankl was now Polizei Enemy number three.

The Koenigsegg duo walked past.

"I heard that one of the Koenigsegg guys," I whispered, "said to someone he was gonna kick ass, and *that* someone said, 'Even those crazy guys in the police car?' and you know what the Koenigsegg guy said?"

"Just tell me."

"He said, 'Oh, that piece of shit?'"

Maher nodded. "Let's just see how far that Koenigsegg makes it."

There. You see that fortyish redhead in the black leather jacket? That's Alison Cornea. Big Microsoft exec. Rumor is she just got divorced, bought a brand-new M5, and signed up for Gumball. "Gray M5, license plate M-TROUBLE. But we still have to find the *big* drivers. Keep a look out for Kenworthy. I want to know what he's in. And Kim Schmitz."

"I heard Schmitz isn't coming," said Maher. "I heard he was in jail."

"I think a lot of these guys are gonna be in jail before the week's up." We had $3,500 ready for fines, court fees, lawyer fees, bail, bribery, and as-yet-unknown miscellaneous emergency Gumball expenses. "But not us, Maher, not us."

"Did you hear about the after-party?" said a French-accented girl behind me.

Maher nodded and silently mouthed *Let's go.*

This was going to be a long night.

CHAPTER 9

The Eleventh Hour

THURSDAY, APRIL 17, 2003
GUMBALL START DAY

"Good morning, Mr. Roy! This is your eight A.M. wake-up call."

BEEP BEEP BEEP went the alarm I'd set—just in case.

"I hate you, Roy," Maher groaned, then turned and pulled the pillow over his head.

In the middle of the night, half asleep, I overheard him on the phone describing how good the party had been. On his behalf I reset the alarm for 11 A.M.—enough time for him to complete our research.

Quietly I slipped on—for the first time since purchase—my dark blue Polizei pants with the yellow highway patrol stripes, then a white Polizei officer's shirt with "144" and "GB3K" collar dogs, then a dark blue wool Polizei sweater with German flags on each sleeve. If I was ever going to be beaten up, shot, or arrested, today was the day.

It was time for the M5's final refuel before that night's Gumball flag drop. I presumed *everyone* would sneak out for one last refuel, if only to avoid traffic jams at what few gas stations lay between the Fairmont and any one of the city's exit points I'd scouted.

The slow, lazy, or hungover might spend the first hour of Gumball—one of the world's last true adventures—waiting at a gas station.

I stopped before a mirror halfway down the hall to the elevator. I stared at my cleanly shaven head, light pink blotches and streaks where I'd pressed the razor and pulled in long impatient strokes. I wondered why I alone, bleary-eyed and starving, up at 8 A.M. while the others slept off a historic night of festivities, was rushing out to mitigate a theoretical.

Because I was not one of those people. I *might* lose my license or insurance. I *might* lose my car. I *might* be jailed, crippled or killed, or kill someone else. I *might* never do this again. *I* wasn't going to waste time sitting at a gas station.

I sprinted to the elevator, ignored the hotel guests whose eyes pleaded with me to hold the door open for them, stabbed the "Close Door" and "Level G" buttons, ran through the cold, silent garage to my *AutobahnPolizeiInterzsceptor M5,* sped out into the street, and ran the first red light before catching myself.

The speed limit was 35. I cruised at 34.

Suddenly, just as I pulled into the gas station—

DING-DING-DING

—the M5's driver information display lit up below the speedometer: *radiator coolant low.*

I cursed loudly. The attendant inside stared at the uniformed bald man slamming both hands against the steering wheel of the blue police car. He quickly ran toward me, his helpful expression turning to bewilderment once he saw the car's foreign markings.

"Everything okay?" asked the attendant.

"Look under the car!"

"You got a coolant leak! You need—"

"How far is the nearest BMW dealer?"

"Four miles? I'll get you the address!"

Then, with deadly seriousness nearly smothering the utter madness of the idea—an idea that only hours later would become completely logical—my eyes fell upon the police siren and lighting controls. I could *easily* get to BMW in half the time, if only I didn't have to limp there to preserve what little coolant remained before the engine seized completely.

For the first time since 9/11, I prayed, and once again I prayed a desperate secular man's extemporaneous prayer: *Please God or Gods, bless this fake Polizei Interceptor and grant me safe passage clear of police cars on patrol, police on horseback, visiting German dignitaries and tourists, Orthodox Jews over seventy, the police chief's wife walking her dog, off-duty cops going to work, traffic police at intersections—*

Sweat poured down my neck as I pulled into BMW San Francisco—20 glacial minutes later.

"Do you have an appointment?" said the girl at the BMW customer service entrance.

I slowly removed my sunglasses. I glared directly into her eyes.

She froze, looked at my badge, then at the stack of gear on my dash, then at the *AutobahnPolizeiVerfolgungInterzsceptor M5*.

The traffic barrier began to rise.

"Sabotage?!" I yelled at the mechanic.

The other mechanics' heads snapped toward me like weather vanes struck from an unexpected direction.

Sabotage obviously wasn't in the BMW factory service manual.

"It *is* weird," said the mechanic.

I grasped my head in both hands. The mechanics and now several managers murmured and gestured toward me—an angry bald man who wore a foreign dark blue police uniform and motorcycle boots, who on his gun belt carried handcuffs and a squawking radio, who wore a silver badge on his chest and foreign flags on both sleeves. A man whose BMW M5 said *AUTOBAHNPOLIZEISTUTTGARTACHTUNG!* on both sides. A man who spoke perfect English.

"How," I said in a low voice, "could this happen?"

"Well, your radiator has two caps, one fill and one drain. You rolled in here with no radiator fluid 'cause the drain cap was missing." He paused. "You in this Gumball race?" I nodded. "Well then," he said, "that would be a *prit-eeeee* strange coincidence."

That sealed it. Sabotage. Six hours remained until the 2003 Gumball Flag Drop.

Then, in the most sheepish tone ever used by anyone committing the crime of police impersonation, I said, "Can you help me? I'll do—"

"When does this Gumball thing start?"

"Tonight."

"Okay . . . I'll give the cap free, but if you've got some time I got an idea." This sounded bad. He nodded at the car. "You remove the 155 mph speed limiter yet?"

My calculations suggested I wouldn't need to go that fast—or faster—if Gumball was a serious endurance competition. The M5's fuel economy above 100 mph dropped faster than rock groupies' jeans. Gumball's 500-plus mile stages required an endurance racer's fuel strategy—the fewest possible gas stops, each limited to the 3 minutes and 15 seconds necessary for the M5's top-off. Theoretically, 1,000 miles at 90 mph would take less time than at 120 mph, once one subtracted time for extra fuel stops. Or so I hoped.

"No," I said.

"I'll sell you the Dinan Stage 1 engine chip cheap. Removes the limiter. You should get it, just in case."

"Okay. Just in case."

Just in case I tossed my meticulously researched drive plan. I'd just surrendered to mankind's worst, most primitive instinct—subjugating reason and creativity to brute force.

"Just curious," he said, "was this really a German police car?"

I wanted to believe it was an accident. I didn't want to believe any of the Gumballers I'd met—most of whom I liked—would actually sabotage my car. The last thing I wanted to believe was that any of those I'd identified as serious *racers* would do such a thing.

Sabotage.

A little piece of my heart had just been chipped away.

The entire BMW San Francisco staff clapped as I rolled out two hours later in my fully washed, waxed, detailed, fluid-flushed, stickered, striped, police-light and siren-equipped and operational *AutobahnPolizeiVerfolgungInterzsceptorM5*, now theoretically capable of speeds over 175 mph.

I wondered if I'd find out. I wondered if I'd *have* to find out.

I'd let Maher take that leg.

GUMBALL 3000 DRIVER BRIEFING
FAIRMONT HOTEL CONFERENCE HALL

I still didn't have a shred of proof. I knew only the official line. The Gumball 3000 wasn't a race. It was a rally.

I'd called their London office numerous times, and read every page on their website. What little information existed about long-distance, point-to-point endurance racing—all of it, every print article, every online post—mentioned the Gumball 3000. I'd studied the MTV *Jackass* episode about the 2001 London–St. Petersburg Gumball, and although Johnny Knoxville's crew clearly *weren't* racing, they repeatedly referred to "winning" and "the race," as did numerous other drivers. Knoxville even said, "If you know the Cannonball Run . . . it's kind of like that."

Online fan forums referred to "winners"—Kim "Kimble" Schmitz and Rob "Lonman" Kenworthy—but the Gumball Website only mentioned trophies for "Spirit," "Style," and other seemingly arbitrary categories.

And yet—

The 2002 Gumball ran from New York to Los Angeles—a virtual duplicate of the original Cannonball Run route. The Gumball 3000 had clearly inherited both the spirit and mythology of the original Cannonball Run, which was why, despite the official denials, I'd come.

I watched the Gumballers boisterously file into the Fairmont's Louis XIV–style ballroom, their voices echoing off the high ornate ceiling. I counted at least two hundred people—drivers, copilots, serious girlfriends, rally girlfriends, ex-girlfriends, wives, Gumball crew, videographers, reporters, and fans who'd snuck in but whose fresh-faced awe gave them away. Almost all wore sneakers, jeans, and a mix of polo shirts and red Gumball T-shirts. Some donned Gumball's black-and-reflective-silver baseball caps. Some sported Gumball's bright yellow driver bracelets, and most wore Gumball photo ID card driver necklaces, a good number now messy-haired women wearing ill-fitting Gumball Ts, and last night's skirts—and pumps.

There seemed three possibilities: (1) Gumball surreptitiously ran an illegal race under the guise of a rally, (2) Gumball tacitly allowed entrants to race one another, or (3) Gumball *was*—despite rumor, myth, and gossip—merely a rally, albeit the most infamous of such perfectly legal, organized, public road events.

If The Driver wasn't here, surely he'd have sent someone. Surely.

I was certain about Rawlings, Collins, and the as-yet-unseen Lonman. There had to be more.

An Englishman behind me tapped on my shoulder. "You," he said, "the bloke in the police car?"

"That's me."

"Now 'ere's a man"—he turned to his friends—"who's really fookin' crazy!"

"Thanks," I said quietly, suddenly feeling sheepish.

"Pay attention," Maher said to me. "Max is coming out."

I snapped forward to get my first good look at the infamous Maximillion Cooper, Gumball 3000's founder, about whom I knew little beyond rumors he'd raced cars and been a fashion designer. I'd spotted him at the prior night's party, but penetrating his entourage of Gumball staff girls had seemed impossible.

Max entered from a side door and stepped up onto the podium as even *this* crowd fell silent. It was as if Burt Reynolds and David Niven had been kidnapped, then in the next room forced into the DNA-merging teleporter from the sci-fi movie *The Fly,* then their lone offspring handed a potion granting eternal youth, a vertically striped red, white, and blue leather racing jacket, and a pair of light-blue-tinted sunglasses he was forbidden *ever* to remove.

Max took a microphone from a square-jawed young Gregory Peck. "Who's *that* guy?" I said to Maher.

"Handsome Dave. Gumball's Number Two. Don't talk to any girls within twenty feet of him. It's hopeless."

"Welcome," said Max, "to this year's Gumball 3000!"

The room erupted in clapping and cheers of joyful release. My heart quickened as I joined in, whistling and clapping until my palms turned red. The start was now less than four hours away.

"Thank you." The noise subsided. "Thank you very much. I've already heard you've all had your own little Gumballs again getting here..."

Max paused before even louder cheers and laughter, hollers suggesting those who *really* had Gumballed here. I quickly turned to identify them.

"Pay attention," Maher prodded me.

The noise subsided as Max raised the microphone to his mouth once again.

"Cars and people come from pretty much the whole of the world. Obviously we cater to everyone. It doesn't matter who comes in first. So the trophy we give out in Miami at the end is pretty much the Spirit of the Gumball determined throughout the week. It's always a kind of a natural given who that goes to because they've done it in the craziest way. That's the kind of thing we're into, more than who comes in first. Every morning each car will receive a route card indicating the next checkpoint. So that's it. The only rule is to get to the checkpoints safely. So have a safe drive and I hope to see all of you in Miami."

CHAPTER 10

Two Minutes to Midnight

What about the police?

Although I'd taken criminology and urban planning in college, and although I'd tried to apply these to studies of traffic congestion in scholarly journals such as *Transportation, Econometrica,* and the *American Economic Review,* no researcher had ever investigated their convergence with gross flouting of the law by large groups of high-speed cars.

Short of planning a bank heist on a mafioso's secret account, my task was the world's coolest, most gratuitous, and illegal homework assignment of all time.

I intuited two schools of Gumball Driving Theory.

Lone Wolves drove alone, set their own pace, and ignored the primary route suggested by Gumball and taken by the majority of entrants.

Convoyers drove in groups of similar cars and/or like-minded drivers, and followed the recommended route.

Lone Wolves, if far enough ahead of other wolves or convoys—whether on the same or a parallel route—*might* avoid police who had not yet been alerted to Gumball's impending passage or the location of the next checkpoint. *Lone Wolves,* however, risked being caught alone to bear the full brunt of one or more potentially *very* unhappy police officers.

Convoyers, like pack prey trying to avoid predators, *might* avoid police if the convoy was sufficiently numerous relative to pursuing police, especially if the convoyer's vehicle was less conspicuous than other convoyers'. *Convoyers,* however, risked capture by larger numbers of police cars alerted in advance to their passage by the very strategy behind which they hoped to pass unharmed—the convoy's size.

Team Polizei had to control its own destiny. Team Polizei would be a

Lone Wolf. The key was getting out ahead, preferably on an alternate route as far away as possible from other Gumballers.

This was how—other than investigating San Francisco's exit routes—I spent my waking hours in the four days before the other Gumballers arrived. This was why, upon returning from BMW right before the Gumball Driver Briefing, I was possessed by a single thought: parking strategy.

Had I parked in the garage, the M5 would have been trapped among dozens of cars and hundreds of fans blocking any effort to move the car to a more advantageous position on the starting grid in front of the Fairmont.

Screw the garage.

I hit the M5's police lights (in European yellow/green rather than U.S. blue/red), turned onto Mason Street, and headed toward the hotel. The SFPD officers instantly gave my *Polizei M5* the thumbs-up and lifted the barricade. "Love the green lights!" one of the cops yelled as I rolled past at 5 mph.

The street was clear all the way to the start line. I might even be able to park *at* the start line. In my peripheral vision I glimpsed—with sudden optimism—a girl with long dark hair running toward my car.

"I'm sorry!" said the gorgeous cat-eyed Gumball staffer, "but you can't park here just yet. You must return to the garage."

"Max told me to park here," I lied. Then, suddenly remembering an honest, legitimate reason, said, "I'm carrying one of Gumball movie-camera guys."

She looked at me skeptically, then at the *AutobahnPolizeiVerfolgungAchtungM5,* then ordered me to park among what someone higher up felt were lesser entrants—a burgundy Lotus Elise, a stock-grey Porsche 996 convertible, a heavily modified blue Subaru WRX, a silver Nothelle-modified Jaguar S-Type, and a gigantic bright blue Kenworth biodiesel-powered semi.

This could turn out to have serious consequences.

I'd parked at the north end of the block—Mason Street ran southbound—which meant the start line was at the other end, which meant, counting only the cars on the east side of the street, we'd leave in approximately tenth position. *If* Gumballers staged on the street's west side, we'd be twentieth. *If* the cars still in the garage formed a grid in the street's two open lanes, we'd be fortieth off the line.

Or worse.

I pushed through the revolving doors to find hundreds of fans gawking at the now two dozen Gumball cars lined up on *both* sides of the street, with still more lining up to pass through the police tape.

Like a cloud of moths descending upon a row of lanterns, the crowds surrounded the cars as each beeped one by one with alarms being deactivated. Before the drivers could open their doors, they were mobbed by camera-toting fans begging for *just* one shot, then another, and another, until they'd shot every permutation of Gumballers, rally girlfriends, Gumball cars, SFPD, smiling sons, bored wives, sighing daughters, slow-moving grandparents, and crying babies.

Whereas my first thought was annoyance at being unable to move the car, most of the Gumballers were overwhelmingly delighted at their new-found celebrity. They delayed what I considered critical last-minute preparations.

I suddenly realized I'd so far missed the point of this singularly fantastic spectacle—perhaps even of Gumball itself. Casting aside my notions of a secret race within Gumball, the Gumball *event* was clearly both different from and more than what I expected. The cars *were* amazing, and to have so many travel from the farthest garages and seaports and runways, now *here* in one place, at one time, *was* utterly surreal.

In the bright sun they shone—Lamborghinis the yellow of fresh sunflowers, Ferraris in apple red, a Prowler as purple as ripe plums, Mercedes and Bentleys black as night's water, Porsches silver as a ring gifted on one knee, a Lotus the burgundy of Loire grapes, and a sea of blues—one Morgan the impenetrable blue of the deepest Pacific, another the translucent blue of Caribbean shallows, my BMW the blue of Atlantic dawns.

Their owners glowed, too, cheeks flushed with pride and enthusiasm and bluster.

Children ran laughing as the SFPD took chase to prevent their climbing upon the lower-profile Lamborghinis and Ferraris—their raked hoods especially inviting to tiny sneaker-clad feet.

I was suddenly filled with those very children's wonder and excitement, and even at a distance I saw the same joy in so many Gumballers' faces—Collins, Rawlings, Eyhab, Morgan, and others I didn't yet know—beside their cars, mingling with fans.

The gravitational center of the Gumball universe, his shock of light brown hair waving in the late afternoon breeze, our strangely calm P. T. Barnum—Maximillion Cooper—moved slowly through the crowd, answered questions, shook hands with fans, and wished the drivers good luck.

A line of bellhops, hotel staff, and SFPD began politely pushing the crowd back from the driveway entrance.

Maher spotted me, waved his arms, and pointed aggressively toward the M5.

"There goes that crazy guy with the police car," said one of the Englishmen as I walked away.

"Straight to jail," said the other.

"Everything okay?" I said to Maher as we converged at the M5.

"Totally." He beamed. "You?"

"Still waiting on my blow-up doll."

"What," he said, moving only his head slightly toward me like a curious bird, "are you talking about?"

"In-car conference," I said to Maher as I got into the driver's seat.

"You may not think so," Maher said after he closed the door, "but I've been hard at work while you've been shopping. I got a bunch more drivers' names and phone numbers—"

"Kenworthy?"

"No," said Maher, "but I heard he's in a silver GT2!"

"A 911 GT2?"

"With stripes on the hood and a British flag on top!"

The GT2 was the ultimate road-legal race-prepped Porsche 911/996—an ultralightweight 911 turbo with a more powerful engine and roll cage, and stripped of four-wheel drive, air-conditioning, and soundproofing. Any 911 would be conspicuous, but a silver 911 much less so among dozens of red and yellow sports cars.

"I guess," I said, "if you're gonna go all out . . ."

"Now *that*"—Maher shook his head—"is a great car."

"Yeah," I said as he handed me his drivers' list. "Wow . . . All right . . . well, any word on an eighteen-wheeler with two Porsches? The guy with the spotter chopper?"

"That was last year's rumor."

"I *knew* it!" I said, and slapped the steering wheel with satisfaction.

My inflatable doll arrived. "Finally," I said, shoving a wad of cash into my old friend Gloria's pocket.

"Talk about short notice!" She giggled as she handed me the bright pink box whose clear front displayed a red-lipped abomination of Edvard Munch's *The Scream*. I ripped it open and laid the pink latex form over the Polizei M5's windshield.

"Sorry," I said, "but I lost my old one, and the one I bought got a hole in it, but not the way you think."

"If you say so."

"Now, *you* hold her down while I blow her up. And gimme your scarf. It might look weird when I blow—"

"You *sure* have a lot of respect for women."

Fans gathered closer in gasps and hushed disbelief as I struggled not to laugh, my lips locked to the rubber inflation spout on the back of my Chasey Lain Inflatable Fantasy Playmate Love Sex Doll.

Chasey's legs splayed across the hood, then her arms—one under mine and the other over my head. As she filled up, I laid her gloriously pink sunlit form on the hood, plastic nipples turning under Gloria's scarf into small circus tents.

One father shielded his young daughter's eyes and carried her away.

"If you have the police outfits," said Gloria, "why do you need cute little Chasey?"

"Chasey Lain"—my chest heaved—"dragged me through a late puberty."

"That soooooooooo can't be true!!!"

"It's my insurance," I whispered, "in case the cops have a sense of humor."

Five embarrassing minutes later—during which I neither laughed nor doubted my wisdom—I placed a nurse's hat on Chasey and gingerly belted her into the Polizei M5's rear left seat. The crowd stood in silence. One man took his wife's hand and muttered under his breath.

"Perfect," said Gloria. We hugged.

"This guy rocks!" said a teenage boy.

"This guy's such an asshole," said one bystander.

"He might be the smartest one here," said another man. The two men turned to see who'd disagreed. A red-cheeked SFPD officer stepped out of the crowd and with a huge smile his eyes slowly moved over the Polizei M5, then Chasey, then to me, then back to the naysayers. "If you were me," said the officer, "would *you* arrest *this* guy?" He turned and placed a hand on my shoulder. "I've got bad news," he said, my heart dropping. "I'm outta PBA cards, *and* we got a betting pool at the station."

"On . . . ?"

"If you get hit for impersonating a police officer." I froze. "Roy, right? All us guys love this Pol-eeez-eye shit you're doing. Hilarious."

"But . . . what," I gasped, "are my odds?"

"I'm not gonna lie. Bottom-of-a-well bad. Highway patrol ain't like city cops. The good news is I've got fifty bucks says you make it."

"Well . . . I guess . . ."

"You should smile more," he said, "so they'll get the joke. I'll give you a coupla my cards with my number. Not as good as a PBA, but ya never know.

Now get your chin up and do your thing." He took my right hand in both of his, shook it vigorously, gave me the steely look of a man I'd go to war with, and walked away.

I started up the engine, a muted thrum drowning the noise beyond what would be my world for the next five days. Curious faces peered in through the windows, handprints large and small smearing visibility to both sides, muted voices in deep discussion over my next move. I powered up the dash-top-mounted Polizei gear—in full, public view—for the first time, setting off a medley of electronic beeps, alarms, and chimes.

A high school football player knocked on my half-open window. Although I could little afford distraction from my work, I remembered my childhood excitement when my father took me to see the jets streaking skyward at the Paris Air Show, or during New York's Fleet Week aboard the steel-gray monolith that was the flight deck of the U.S.S. *Carl Vinson*. I remembered that—until 24 hours earlier—I was merely a fan, and that I wouldn't even be a *real* Gumballer until the flag dropped in less than 2 hours.

"Yo, dude!" said the teen. "What *is* all that stuff?"

"Get in the passenger seat and I'll show you."

"Can I bring my girl?"

"In the back," I said, "but watch out for the sex doll."

It took them a full minute to get through the jealous crowd surrounding the car, open both right side doors without bumping anyone, and get in.

"This," I began, pointing to the small box suction-mounted to the windshield just left of my rearview mirror, "is a Valentine 1 radar/laser detector, the best one made. If you see a car here with anything else, it's amateur night."

"Some of your buddies"—he shook his head—"were *just* asking where to buy a detector."

"They're screwed," I said. "Valentines are mail-order only. This," I said, pointing to the small controls left of my steering wheel, "is for a Lidatek LE 20/20 laser jammer system, effective against 97 percent of police laser guns in the U.S."

"Is that legal?"

"If I'm caught that's the least of my problems. Now *that*"—I pointed below the glove box—"is a Uniden BC520XL CB radio, for talking to trucks. Magnetic mount antenna goes on the roof."

"Won't that fly off if you're really kicking it at a hundred?"

"We're gonna find out. Now *this*," I said, pointing at the metal half-shoebox unit on the center dashtop, "is a Uniden BC795 digital radio scanner. This picks up police communications—"

"Yeah," he said knowingly, "I saw a coupla these in other cars."

"Which ones?"

"The big black Avalanche." He paused. "Oh yeah . . . and one of the black Ferraris."

"Did you talk to those guys?"

"Yeah, they just got 'em. I guess this scanner's a new one that just came out?"

"That's right," I said, "but the trick is that you can't just buy one and expect it to work. The built-in frequencies aren't enough, and they're all analog. A lot of cops use digital frequencies, so unless you spend a month programming them manually, this thing's almost useless." At least that was my theory. "And then here"—I pulled out a plastic bag from the floor between his girlfriend's legs—"are my magnetic-mount police lights in red, yellow, green, and blue."

"Is *that* legal?"

"We're gonna find out."

"What's that thing you put on top of your back license plate?"

"Laser-diffusing plate cover," I said, "in case the Lidateks don't do it."

"That is soooo awesome." He grinned. "Man, you gotta be the best-prepared guy here. You can't have more stuff than this . . . ?"

"The rest is secret. Here's my card. I'm Alex."

"Jimmy," he said. "Man, if there's anything I can do—"

"Actually," I said, "there is. What are you doing for the next five days?"

"Following you guys online!"

"I could really use your help, you know, for weather and traffic updates."

"You mean"—his eyes lit up—". . . spy, officially, for you guys?"

"You got it."

"Omigod, I'll do anything I can. You rock, dude!"

"Just don't tell anyone."

"I promise."

I turned to his girlfriend in the backseat. "Nice to meet you," I said.

She stared, mesmerized, and mouthed: *Be careful.*

"Hey!" An annoyed-looking bellhop rapped on the window. I lowered it halfway.

"I know you're a guest," he said, "but you've been idling for half an hour. We're choking and suffocating back here."

"Sorry," I said, and killed the engine.

It was time to test the lights. I pulled one blue and one yellow police tear-drop light out of the bag, strung the coiled power cables through both sides' sun visors and overhead handrests, placed—with a satisfyingly loud metal-on-metal *CLI-THUNK*—the lights on the roof just behind the A-pillar, then plugged them into the 12V Y-splitter I'd bought at RadioShack the day before. They clicked and whirred, but there was no way to tell if they worked by looking through the dark-tinted sunroof.

Whoas! and *Yeeeaaahhs!* erupted. *And clapping. People were clapping.*

I felt—despite having done no more than ordering some police lights on eBay for $19.99 each and plugging them in—pride.

"Ent-shool-dee-gung," said a maternal-looking tourist. *"Bitte."*

Uh-oh. A real, live, actual German tourist.

I was pretty sure, given my limited online study of German phrases commonly used by actual Polizei, she'd said, with the greatest possible deference, "Excuse me, please"—perhaps, just in case, I *actually* was a Polizei officer.

"I'm sorry"—I smiled—"but . . . I don't speak any German."

"A-ya!" She burst out laughing. "You are not really Polizei!?!"

"I'm afraid not. I hope I didn't—"

"Not to worry at all . . . *mein Gott!* You must have a picture with my husband and son! Is it okay if I will get them?"

Fans—cameras, pens, and paper in hand—closed in behind me.

"I'd be honored."

I turned to see Maher leaning in through the driver's window.

The roof-mounted police teardrop lights suddenly went dark. "Alex," he said sternly as he emerged to face me, "how long have you been running those lights?"

"Ten or fifteen minutes?"

"Without the engine? Gimme the car keys."

With anticipatory shame I dropped into the passenger seat. Maher turned the key.

Clickclickclickclick

"Battery's dead," he said.

"I'm sorry—"

"Forget it," he said with professional calm, his eyes rapidly scanning the nearest cars and drivers.

"Booster cables," I said with unexpected calm. "I'm on it."

"Yo!" someone called out from the bright blue Subaru two spaces away. I jumped out and ran toward them. "I heard you trying to turn over," said the young black-haired American in Car no. 15, "but our cables won't reach."

"Alex Roy," I said, offering my hand and reading the driver names off the Subaru's rear window. "Fly or Mermel?"

"Dan Mermelstein. Don't worry about it. We'll pull the car around."

"I owe you more than you can ever know."

"Maher!" I yelled over the fans watching and pointing in amusement. "Pop the hood! They're bringing the Subaru around!"

1. Galls StreetThunder Handheld Megaphone   **$79.99**
2. Duracell Type-C Batteries (x8)   **$14.30**
3. Tasting Menu and two Bottles of Sake at Nobu Miami Beach for crew of Gumball no. 15 (Dan Mermelstein and Fly)   **$500**
4. Eight Fully Charged Duracell Type-C Batteries in a Galls Street Thunder Handheld Megaphone While Attempting to Disperse Bystanders Blocking Inter-Gumballer Car-to-Car Emergency Booster Cable Hookup, 16 Minutes Before Parade Lap Departure   **_PRICELESS_**

"ATTENTION ALL BYSTANDERS, PLEASE CLEAR THE AREA IN FRONT OF THE BLUE SUBARU AND BLUE BMW, ATTENTION ALL BYSTANDERS—"

It was too late. The SFPD lifted the police barricade. From out of the garage a row of Gumballers turned the corner onto Mason—filling the previously empty street right in front of us.

"I'm an asshole," I said under my breath. "I'm really—"

"Forget it," Maher replied.

One hour and three minutes remained to the flag drop.

Three interminable minutes until the goddamn parade lap.

Then, in the tradition of other, vastly different, professional motor-sport events, Handsome Dave raised a megaphone to his mouth, and with even his amplified voice barely audible in between a hundred engines' mocking roars and honking horns, he spoke the four long-awaited words: "GENTLEMEN, START YOUR ENGINES!"

McCloud's F40 then led the one hundred-odd cars that hadn't broken down at the start into the world's most expensive traffic jam. Gumball's traditional predeparture parade lap was obviously for the virgins. After the crawl down the switchbacks of Lombard Street, we miraculously found our way back to the Fairmont over an hour later. The veterans who had stayed behind were already slowly rolling up to Handsome Dave for their route cards.

And leaving.

So this was it. No new instructions. No time clock. No punch card.

No one would know where we were, where we stood, how we ranked, what our elapsed point-to-point time was. If anyone was racing, Gumball definitely had nothing to do with it, all the enemies I'd identified were gone.

We had to make ourselves known. I had one goal. Find Rawlings, find the others, and get to the checkpoint. First.

Handsome Dave signaled for us to advance and stop. I pulled the M5 up to the start line and Handsome Dave smiled and handed us two route cards. "Next stop, Reno. Have a good one."

CHAPTER 11

How Old Those Girls Were

GUMBALL FLAG DROP

"Reno," Maher said, looking at the card. I turned right to follow the other Gumballers down California. "Wait, Alex, we gotta wait for our cameraman."

Except for when I'd used him as an excuse for my parking strategy, I'd completely forgotten about Cassius—the thirtysomething English cameraman.

He had balls—I liked him. But now he was costing us. Bringing Cassius was an acceptable risk. There were rumors of a Gumball documentary. If The Driver wasn't here, he might see it.

"Cassius!!!" Maher yelled out the window.

"Use the megaphone!"

Reno was northeast. One could take the Golden Gate *or* Bay Bridge. The Bay Bridge is only two miles through city traffic, and the Golden Gate's five, with police patrols guaranteed. The SFPD would, in the interest of increasing tourism, escort the Gumballers to and over the city's greatest attraction— the Golden Gate Bridge. Every cop stationed or living within 10 miles north of the Golden Gate would be alerted and waiting.

I turned the screen menu's rubber knob to *GPS* and clicked.

"Here comes Cassius!" Maher yelled, dropping back into his seat.

The GPS address-entry screen appeared. I turned the knob to select the letter *R*. Nothing happened.

"What's up?" said Maher, incredulous.

"It's always slow," I said truthfully, my faith in free fall. A never-before-seen message appeared on the map display: *Disc Error.*

Suddenly I understood why my M5 had come so cheap. It was a 2000—the M5's first model year, after which BMW made minor changes for 2001 that were largely conveniences for most. But for Team Polizei, were utterly catastrophic.

My 2003 BMW Navigation United States Mapset DVD didn't work *because my 2000 BMW M5 GPS only read CD-ROMs.*

"Maher, get your maps out!"

"All right!" Cassius pulled his door shut. "We're off!"

I put the car in first gear and gently accelerated. West. Minor problem—the Bay Bridge was east. I couldn't make a U-turn since SFPD motorcycle units sat at every other intersection.

"Gotta make a right ASAP," I said, "for the Bay Bridge."

"Are you sure?" said Maher. "The other guys are headed to the Golden Gate."

"Trust me. Listen!" I turned the scanner volume to maximum and pressed the backlit button labeled *1,* activating the first of the BC796D's ten channel banks, each containing one hundred of the one thousand police frequencies I'd researched online for three months, assumed relevant to a section of one of several potential cross country routes, then uploaded, adding my best guess as to police unit types and acronyms.

SKREWWWW-EEEEECH-SHCHAWWWW

I turned the squelch knob to adjust the scanner's sensitivity. The display lit up: *Sausalito MOB3.*

". . . Ten-twenty-seven on a foreign DL . . ."

"What's he saying?"

"Um . . . MOB3 means 'mobile,' and 'Ten-twenty-seven,' I think that's a request for info . . . on a foreign driver's license! They've got someone already! Where the hell's Sausalito?"

"I think"—Maher frowned—"it's north?"

"North of San Fran!" I laughed, wiping tears of joy from my eyes. "Right across the Golden Gate Bridge!"

"This thing works like this right out of the box?"

"Maher, what did you think I was doing for the last three months?"

The scanner cycled too rapidly for us to follow the chatter. The display lit up: *SFPD Local, CHP A, CHP B, Sausalito PD, Waldo MOB, CHP Air . . .*

"Damn," I said, "I wish we knew exactly where are all these cops were."

"Ten-fourteen northbound—"

CHP B: *". . . copy Ten-twenty-seven—"*

"Code Nine on . . ."

Maher shook his head. *"I* wish we knew what the codes meant."

"...numerous vehicles...high rate of speed...One-oh-one..."

"Now you're talking!" I giggled.

Sausalito PD: *"...APB...multiple vehicles...northbound..."*

An APB was an All Points Bulletin—just like in the movies.

"Bad news for those guys!" I said. "The good news is we haven't picked up anything from Oakland or Berkeley, which is the other side of the Bay Bridge."

"Roy," Maher said with the greatest respect, warmth, love, and gratitude possible between two straight men who'd only recently met and were risking their lives together, when one realized the other was as smart as he'd hoped, "turn that thing to max and pick up the pace! Bay Bridge, baby!"

"Look!" I pointed at a silver convertible cresting a distant hill. "Gumballer?"

"It's those watermelon helmet guys in the Z8! They must be headed the same way."

The entrance to the Bay Bridge was only a few blocks away.

We chased the Z8 over the bridge through dusk rush-hour traffic, weaving across the solid white lines two or three lanes at a time.

"This is incredible," I said, "not a cop in sight."

87

"Yeah," said Maher, "I can't believe we're getting away with this."

91

"Maher, what's the speed limit?"

"Who knows?" he said, uninterested in checking the list I'd earlier told him was in the right-side door pocket. Maher now glanced at the maps. "Follow the signs, *there,* at the end, to 580 West, then 80 East. And pick it up!"

I bore left off the bridge onto I-80/580, its six lanes sprinkled with light commuter traffic cruising at 75 mph.

"I'll take it to 95."

"There's the Z8," said Maher, "they've slowed down."

"Their top's down. If I'm cold they've gotta be freezing."

"They'll have to stop to put it up. Pass 'em."

The Z8's distinctive blue-tinged Xenon headlights disappeared in my rearview mirror.

101

"Maher, the Golden Gate guys, if they're on the west side of the bay... how long until their route intersects ours? Because they're gonna be bringing the whole damn CHP with them, and we need to get past that intersect point before they do."

"Looks like"—Maher ran his finger across the map page—"we hit the I-80/37 interchange in . . . maybe 25 miles. Fifteen minutes at this speed."

"Keep your eyes open as we approach."

"Passing through . . ." Maher said. "Town of Vallejo, California, interchange coming up."

My phone rang. *"Roy . . . Roy! Can y . . . ear me?"* His English voice was smothered by wind and engine noise.

"Who is it?"

". . . all o . . . them nicked . . . the bridge . . . we—"

"Maher, what does *nicked* mean?"

"Maybe 'caught' or 'stopped,' I guess?"

". . . was . . . massacre . . . wh . . . are you?"

"I can't hear you!" I lost the signal.

"Who was it?" said Maher.

"I don't know, but he did say 'massacre.'"

"Interchange," said Maher, "any second now." Maher peered at the interchange's entry ramp. "I don't see anything."

"Cops?"

"That's what I was looking for."

"Gumballers?"

"Nothing."

"The scanner's been quiet," I said, checking that its volume was at maximum. It was.

"Let's hope we passed the main pack," said Maher.

"If not, we're dead."

110

The scanner lit up.

Vacaville PD: *"Ten-twenty-three on those rally vehicles . . ."*

I let off the gas.

"Maher! We *just* passed signs for Vacaville! And we've got Xenons coming up behind us at high speed!"

"I see him," said Maher, "it's the Z8!"

"I'll let him pass . . . wait, hang on!" I yelled. "Yellow Ferrari! Passing on the left shoulder! And the scanner's going crazy!"

DEEDEET!

It was the Valentine 1. My hearing, keenly attuned after ten childhood years of classical piano training, recognized the single *DEEDEET* as a K-band signal, almost always evidence of a police radar gun within (assuming a straight road with no obstructions) four miles in either direction. This instantly set off a series of responses so frequently practiced they were as involuntary as breathing.

I hit mute and kicked the brake, sending every loose object in the car—the map book in Maher's lap, Cassius's spare DV tapes, and all our cell phones—flying forward, my seat punched by the mountain of bags behind me in the sex doll's lap.

I released the brake when the speedometer read 70—moved to the right lane in an effort to hide my *AutobahnPolizei M5* among a cluster of local commuters, and set the cruise control.

"Alex, can we get a warning next time?"

"Just being cautious."

"Hang on, wait, we've got flashing lights coming up fast. Left lane!"

A black-and-white police car flew past us at least 90 mph.

"Whoooaaa!!!" we yelled in unison.

A CHP motorcycle flew past doing at least a hundred.

"WHOOOAAAAAA!" we yelled together.

My body tingled with excitement at our escape. "Good eyes, Maher! You saved us!"

"Looks like we've got a Z8 about to get pulled over. And a yellow Ferrari!"

Five minutes later we spotted a single, stationary set of flashing lights on the right shoulder.

"Slow down more," said Maher as he lowered his window, "so I can get a good shot."

Cold air blasted into the car.

"Looks like," Maher yelled in the wind, "the Z8!"

"Those poor watermelon-helmet guys." I thought I saw both of them on their knees being handcuffed.

Over the next hour we spotted four more sets of flashing lights on the right shoulder—each behind a stopped Gumballer.

"Any cell reception yet, Maher?"

"No, but I think we're about . . . 90 or 100 miles from Reno."

"It's starting to snow." This was bad news for an M5 riding on summer tires.

"I'm slowing to 75." We flashed past a Ferrari. The M5 fishtailed slightly, but held its grip. "Maher, I'm gonna pull back to 65."

"If you have to."

I made a mental list of every Gumball car with four-wheel drive, not including the Porsche turbos and Lamborghini Murcielagos—their OEM summer tires rendering four-wheel drive useless in snow—which left a silver Audi S4 and Rawlings's Avalanche.

"Whooooaa!"

Thousands of people lined the three blocks to the Reno Circus Circus Hotel and Casino. Reno PD officers waved and cheered with the crowd as we rolled alone toward the red-shirted Gumball staff in the distance.

"Maher! There's only one thing to do!" I pulled up to the nearest officer and lowered my window.

He laughed heartily. "Blue-light special?" I nodded in agreement while we held up our police lights. "Sure! Just make a right up there and you'll find all your buddies!"

"*Danke,* Officer!" I said.

The crowd *and* police whooped and applauded as we parked in front of the mobbed Circus Circus entrance—behind a row of at least fifteen Gumball cars amid what looked like every on- and off-duty cop in Reno.

A Gumball staffer walked up to me. "What's your car number?"

"One-four-four," I said. "How'd we do?"

"You're here, aren't ya? Go upstairs and join Max for the party!"

"No," I said to the staffer, "I mean, where'd we place?"

"Oh, I've no idea. You should relax and enjoy the party."

"What about our route cards?"

"Roy!" Maher yelled. "C'mon upstairs!"

"You'll get those after the party."

What appeared to be every Reno resident between 14 and 25, dressed in a variety of official race-team, unofficial racing-style, and bomber jackets— the latter sporting collages of racing *and* military patches—stood behind the ropes and along the red carpet. Girls lifted their shirts, their brothers or (apparently shameless) boyfriends trying to hand us markers with which to sign the girls' pale stomachs.

I tried to keep a straight face as I followed Maher to the doors a hundred outstretched hands, pens, and blank pieces of paper away.

"We're like fokkin' celebrities!" yelled one Gumballer. "Wit a red carpet and all!"

"'Ow old were those girls?" said another.

"Alex, Alex!" Cassius yelled from behind me. "Stop! I need a shot of you walking in!"

The fans craned their heads trying to identify the celebrity upon whom the foreign cameraman trained his spotlight. Then they saw ... me, and questions rained down from all sides.

Do you know Tony Hawk? Where's Ryan Dunn? Is Tony Hawk coming? What about Ryan? Are you friends with Tony Hawk? Ohmiiigod! I love Ryan! Is he here? Is he coming?

"Roy!" Maher yelled from inside. "Let's go!"

"Look for Rawlings," I said.

"Look for food," said Maher.

"Riiiggght over here, gentlemen," said the Circus Circus host, one of the countless staff assigned to the Gumballers now hugging and slapping hands in the roped-off Gumballers-only section of the casino floor. Fans four deep called out to us over the shoulders of security guards beside each stanchion. Max worked the crowd, signing autographs and taking pictures.

The Gumball rumor mill coalesced around the hot-food buffet table.

"—the cycle cop stopped us, but then his radio went off about another speeder going even faster than us! So he took off without giving us a ticket—"

"*Our* cop," chimed in a short bookish driver with glasses, "demanded our camcorder tape as evidence against us and 'the other racers,' so while we were waiting I rewound the tape and recorded over it with us just sitting there."

"Those guys are so fucked," came a voice behind me, "can't believe they took 'em all to jail!"

"Whaddya expect," said another, "after they're racing four abreast across the Golden Gate Bridge!"

A Gumball staffer I didn't recognize brushed past. "Excuse me," I asked him, "have you seen Rawlings?"

"Who?"

"I see," realizing I didn't recognize the staffer for the same reason he didn't know Rawlings—Gumball logistics required *two* checkpoint crews leapfrogging each other.

"Well, what about a tall guy with a goatee and cowboy hat?"

"*That* bloke? One of the first ones in, I think, but haven't seen him in a bit."

"Maher!" I called out, and ran toward his most likely location. "We gotta go, *now*!"

"But they're waiting for everyone to come in before handing out the route cards."

"Look," a Gumballer whispered behind us, "those police guys are taking off."

"You mean that Roy guy?" said another. "Shit, we better go, too."

"Maher," I whispered, "walk out slowly so no one else tries to follow us."

We drove away with our Las Vegas route cards in hand—just as a long line of Gumballers pulled in and parked behind us.

"How much gas do we have?" asked Maher.

"One-quarter-ish. How far to Vegas?"

"I'd say . . . no interstate this leg . . . about four-fifty."

That didn't seem far at all. This was our chance to catch up.

U.S. ROUTE 95 SOUTH
SOMEWHERE SOUTH OF FALLON, NEVADA

We cruised at an eerily silent 115 mph through the frozen desert. We slowed only for the infrequent burst of metallic, authoritative voices from the scanner, during which, in one instance, a pair of Xenons approached from behind at high speed and the Koenigsegg's black BMW X5 support vehicle—filled with passengers and luggage—passed us with at least a 20 mph speed differential, on the right shoulder. We shook our heads at their impatience. I tried not to laugh as flashing lights soon appeared in my rearview mirror, and the local sheriff's Chevy Suburban crossed the solid white line to pass us on the left at 95 mph—this being far more dangerous than an X5 doing 90 on the shoulder. Within minutes the Koenigsegg support crew was parked on the right shoulder, making the acquaintance of that very sheriff.

I would have called the X5 to warn them, but neither of us had their number.

We needed to put some distance between us and whoever had called them in.

I accelerated to 130.

My Polizei Police Evasion Strategy was working perfectly.

We caught up with a Gumball convoy I estimated second from the lead. The Polizei M5 and cars we had not yet matched to their crews repeatedly traded positions in an exhilarating 135 mph dance across the solid white line, all rendered meaningless upon the group's seemingly telepathic exit and stop at an isolated and blindingly well-lit gas station. We were now approximately six hours and 318 miles into Gumball.

I wasn't disappointed to see them refuel their smaller tanks more quickly and disappear south into the darkness. A few minutes' lead was within range of our scanner. They'd make perfect bait, and I needed to learn more about its effectiveness before making a big push. We let Cassius shoot their departure, then followed them—from as far as we could make out their taillights—into the town of Tonopah, Nevada.

A town whose main street's signs read MAIN STREET.

A town with two gas stations, both closed.

A town totally devoid of cars or people, through which we drove at 75 mph.

A town with—500 feet from its outbound city limit—a 20 mph speed limit sign.

Then we were pulled over for going 62 in a 25 mph zone. Our arrest evasion strategy worked perfectly as I charmed the sheriff—who made the leap in logic that we were actually New York City cops without any suggestion from us—and we were let go without so much as a ticket being written.

CHAPTER 12

The M5 sat in the center of three long columns of cars parked door-to-door and bumper to bumper. A bellhop gingerly lifted a colorful, overflowing backpack over each trunk and hood, slowly following a pair of dazed Gumballers unable to find their car, the trio like elderly mice in a maze.

I didn't see any red-shirted Gumball staff, but I saw the one thing I'd been looking for since Gumball started, a silver Porsche 996 GT2 with a Union Jack on the roof. Kenworthy's car.

And there, at the very front of the same row, sat Rawlings's Avalanche.

Based on the prior night's convoy and those who'd pulled into Reno behind me, the cars were in approximate arrival order. But within an hour, once the majority of Gumballers had shuffled out, entered their cars, and the staff had begun handing out route cards, it appeared that parking determined your grid position, and your prior day's convoy-relative position determined your next day's departure sequence.

Every day I failed to advance through the grid, whether by driving or aggressive postarrival parking-spot changes, I'd be treading water.

Rawlings and Kenworthy left first at the head of the right column, followed by many I'd passed the night before, including the silver-and-yellow Porsche 996 turbo X50s. My column, including those at the front who'd arrived in the top ten, were held until even last night's stragglers passed on the right.

I silently fumed while stuck in our midpack departure slot. Maher recounted rumors he'd heard about missing cars and drivers.

The Koenigsegg had allegedly been flatbedded to the local Volkswagen dealer, whose owner, having been awakened before dawn, had opened early to help—the $700,000 Koenigsegg apparently constructed with multiple parts common to the $25,000 VW Golf.

"Maher, I'm in no mood—"

"Relax, we're dressed like doctors. They never lose their calm."

U.S. ROUTE 93 SOUTHBOUND
LEAVING HOOVER DAM

126

We began moving up the grid. Rawlings and Kenworthy—whose face I'd still not seen—had pulled out of the breakfast checkpoint less than a minute ahead of us, then made an inexplicable left turn and exited Vegas by a route whose superiority had eluded my *length-of-red-light-panic-unfold-map-in-lap* study of the shortest exit routes. At least ten Gumball virgins had followed them.

We headed south on Route 93 toward Kingman, a desert road straight, flat, and clear of traffic—perfect for detecting radar, scanner, and CB traffic at maximum range.

134

One hundred and thirty-four miles per hour was a safe and reasonable cruising speed given the road conditions and lack of police-scanner traffic.

We were approximately 250 miles from our next checkpoint—the Phoenix International Raceway.

The scanner lit up:

NV MISC DSPTCH: *"—Four-eight-four your traffic—"*

126

NV MOB D: *"Ten-six."*

119

I thought *10-6* meant "busy," but I didn't want to tell Maher, have him press me (as always) to accelerate, then get caught for being a poor man's know-it-all.

NV MISC DSPTCH: *"...U.S. 93/118 southbound...multiple sports cars—"*

115

One hundred and fifteen was the perfect speed at which to maintain our position while granting us—given a radar or scanner warning—the two to three seconds necessary to brake and slow to within 10 mph of the speed limit, if only I could remember what it was.

NV MOB E: "... 'bout a Ten-nine—"

I had *no* idea what that meant.

AZ DPS DSPTCH: "... *Five-ten* ... *188* ... *southbound—*"

"Someone called in somebody," I said, "see anyone front or back?"

"Clear behind and ... high-speed convoy top of next hill!"

111

"It really is beautiful," I said as we crested the hill, the bright column of cars stretched out before us.

138

One by one the convoyers moved to the right lane as we approached and exchanged waves with each we passed.

141

DING-DING-DING

"Holy shit!" I yelled, and let off the gas. "What the hell is that?"

"*You* should know. It's your car."

125

"I think it's some BMW warning." I squinted to read the message on the M5's dashboard instrument panel, the letters barely visible in the bright sun: *TIRE DEFECT.*

Holy fucking fuck!

Tire failure was the most common cause of accidents after driver error and drunk driving. I had to slow down, but a panic break might blow the bad tire.

"Tire Defect!" I yelled.

119

"Relax," said Maher. "Does the car feel funny? Pulling left or right?"

"No!" I coasted into the right lane.

105

"Well," said Maher, "the tires sound okay, and if there was a serious problem we'd hear it, or feel it."

The cars ahead began to pull away, the cars behind bunching up on our rear bumper, poised to pass on our left. Frankl began his pass.

"Alex, no need to slow down just yet." Our lives depended on the $1,200 worth of armored balloons spinning beneath us almost twice per second, the four Michelin Pilot Sports' 149 mph ZR-rating well exceeded just before dawn that very morning.

The silver Porsche began its pass.

Our tires had to withstand the stress of carrying Maher, Cassius, myself, our luggage, and my Polizei gear—the sum of which was certainly over the

M5's recommended weight—and absorb 3,000 miles of bumps and potholes, resist puncture by nails and spikes, *and* the lateral forces of high-speed cornering at near-race conditions.

Had I set the correct pressures?

90

Tires expand and contract based on temperature. And tires heat up at high speeds. Using that logic, I'd told the BMW San Francisco tech to set them at 42/46, allowing for expansion to the Michelin recommended 44/48, *but I hadn't told him why.* And I hadn't consulted with Maher, despite his superior track-earned knowledge.

Maher would have—should have—made me stop 10 seconds earlier had he thought we were in danger. But Maher wasn't stupid.

He stared straight ahead, deep in thought. "Alex," Maher finally decreed, "if one tire was bad we'd feel it, so either all four are shot, which is unlikely, or it's the system, which is most likely."

"Unless I set *all* four too low, and now they're all about to blow."

"Take it back to 95 so we don't lose these guys."

"You sure?"

"Dude, this car's built like a fucking brick. We'll check the pressure at the next stop."

"You're right," I said. In the prior 17 hours I'd pushed this car harder than I ever imagined possible. We'd averaged 79 mph through traffic and snow to Reno, and over 100 mph—*including* one fuel stop—through the night to Las Vegas.

89

If he was wrong, we'd be killed quite soon, but I trusted him. Enough to risk my life on it.

"Just saw a sign for Arizona," said Maher.

"Switching scanner frequencies," I said out loud, leaning forward to switch scanner banks. "Arizona now active!"

It was time to catch up.

127

The convoy couldn't be far.

Traffic ahead suddenly thickened, red and yellow sports cars interspersed among local cars. "Whaddya see?" said Maher.

92

"Holy shit," I said, braking harder, "what the hell is that?"

Three vehicles sat in the median, one at an odd angle.

The latter, its outline bent and crumpled, was slowly orbited by vague shapes kneeling and crawling around an elliptical ring of debris.

Clothes . . .

51

A green Mitsubishi minivan sat a hundred feet beyond.

"Everyone *looks* okay," Maher said, clearly wanting to believe it. "No one on the ground, and someone's on the phone. I sure hope—"

I finished his thought with telepathic anguish "—it wasn't one of our guys."

My greatest fear wasn't merely that *I* might be killed, but that I might injure or kill someone else. From the moment I chose to lap Manhattan, safety had influenced my every decision. Formula 1 racing school had included accident avoidance. The Manhattan runs had only occurred between 2 and 3 A.M. The BMW 5-Series' crashworthiness was well known. I, unlike some Gumballers, had replaced every critical component—brake pads, fluid, tires, air bags, and more. Commitment to any potentially dangerous pass was made after having weighed the relative location, speed, and intentions of nearby cars—whether Gumball or civilian (with additional weight given to possible civilian panic over our speed differential)—and then only with Maher's consent.

The wrecked minivan—the very possibility that an innocent had paid the ultimate price for what I was part of—ripped this fantasy away.

The accident scene flashed past. "Maher! Gumballers stopped on the right! Do you think we should stop?"

Suddenly, as quickly as we passed Frankl's idling EVO, *Rally Alex* took over. "We can't stop!" I yelled. "*Look* what I'm wearing! I'm dressed like a doctor!"

The scanner lit up. AZ DPS MOB DSPTCH: *"Code Two . . . possible Nine-six-three . . . loc—"*

"What does *that* mean?" I said, starting to panic.

AZ DPS MOB B: *"Ten-four on a—"*

"We need gas," Maher said with amazing calm. "There's—"

"But what if they think we're involved and fleeing the scene?"

"Dude, just pull in here."

I came to a gentle stop at the pumps closest to the road—and exit—just in case. Maher hopped out immediately and turned to me. "Alex, wake up! Where's the tire-pressure gauge?"

I handed it to him, my eyes fixed on the gas station's ramshackle wooden structure, its single long, wide window offering a panoramic view out—and in. Several dozen locals, so far oblivious to the arrival of the

German Highway Patrol and ersatz surgeon lacking even EMT training, were enjoying a quiet lunch at the Sunshine Grocery and Sundries/Diner/Bar/Pool Hall/Game Room Express Mart.

"Maher, I gotta piss, can you get the gas?"

"I'm doing the tires! Piss while you pump!"

Normally, I would never object to making efficient use of the two-foot strip between the pump and the car. In an oft-rehearsed ballet I slid my oil-company-specific credit card out of its special pocket, slid it in and out of the pump, replaced it in its special pocket, then returned the nozzle with one hand and unscrewed the M5's fuel cap with the other. The rapidly rising sound of Gumballers approaching, slowing and turning to pull in *right* behind the M5—thereby preventing stealthy urination—suddenly triggered lightning bolts from deep within my bladder. I jammed the nozzle into the M5—unable to even pull the pump lever—and stumbled headlong toward the Express Mart entrance.

"Hey!" the cashier yelled after the white-coated man running toward the back.

I emerged three happy minutes later, walking nonchalantly as if no one would recognize me. Then, as if in a hallucinatory flashback, I heard from behind the cash register the metallic voices coming from a police scanner.

Everyone at the counter was leaning forward. Everyone behind the counter was listening intently.

"—reporting multiple sports cars with that wreck on 93—"

"Ten-four."

I was almost at the door.

"Hey!" someone called out in my direction. "You, there!"

"Look!" said one of the diners. "Outside! It's them sports cars!"

"Hey!" the cashier yelled after me. "You a doctor? There's been an accident!"

"Maher!" I said, out the door, running toward the first island of pumps. "Maher!" Maher, camcorder in hand, was shooting the Gumballers' arrival. "Mah—" I cut off my impatient summons when I saw the fuel hose pulsing behind him. I dropped into The Driver's seat and fidgeted.

"Slow pump," said Maher.

Disaster loomed. "What about the tires?"

"They're fine!" he yelled over the *thrum* of the Ferraris idling in a row behind us.

I needed the scanner up. I turned the key halfway.

AZ DPS DSPTCH: "—repeat . . . probable Nine-six-two . . . request medical . . . Route 93—"

One of the diners emerged from the door and urgently waved at us.

BINGBING!

AZ DPS MOB C: *"Ten-ninety-seven . . . vehicles fleeing southbound . . . possible hit-and-run—"*

Maher replaced the nozzle. Another diner emerged and conferred with the first. The fuel cap clicked and locked. "Alex, want the receipt?" The diners pointed at us and turned back inside. I started the engine. "Guess not," he said, sliding in and closing the door.

"Sorry," I said, the M5's tires kicking up sand as we pulled away.

The CB radio—which had remained so quiet I'd forgotten it had been on since San Francisco—now lit up: *"Ten-four on them sports cars . . . we got a bunch of 'em here at the Mart right now—"*

"—sorry Mart, come back—"

"—some boys dressed like doctors just peeled out Dale Earnhardt–style headin' south—"

"—can someone maybe get these boys to come back?"

"I *told* you," I said.

79

"Nice," said Maher, "to see you pick up the pace a little."

"Maher," I said, my heart racing, "if we don't get some distance—"

"Cop on the left! Moving!"

AZ MOB B: *"—just spotted another rally ve-hicle southbound 93—"*

"Shit," I said, "he's talking about us!"

Route 93 South was perfectly straight. There was nowhere to hide.

We stared at each other across the median.

His radar wouldn't work until he made a U-turn.

AZ MOB B: *"—can someone confirm if these rally ve-hicles were involved—"*

I craned my head.

Not turning.

"Let's make a run for it," I said. "Maher?"

"Do it."

Then, with none of the reckless humor of the namesake film's drivers, one word came to mind.

86

99

114

126

133

141
Gumball

CHAPTER 13

The Head of the Snake

U.S. ROUTE 93 SOUTHBOUND

SOMEWHERE SOUTH OF KINGMAN, ARIZONA

"Maher, how far to Phoenix?"

"About . . . a hundred and sixty, hundred and seventy miles?"

"High-speed convoy ahead!" said Maher. "Last car is . . . black 550, large antenna!"

Collins. We were close—and getting closer—to Rawlings. Rawlings meant Kenworthy. This was the lead convoy.

I bore right—behind Collins.

133

121

I matched his speed. Collins flashed his hazards in recognition, then waved.

"Maher, I'm gonna hang right here. He knows what he's doing." Maher nodded. This was the first time he'd consented—unless police were in sight—to staying behind anyone. He reached forward and turned up the scanner volume.

AZ DPS DSPTCH: *"—all units on South 93 . . . Gumball rally cars are going through Wikiup milepost 120 still at a high rate of speed, again . . . Gumball rally vehicles at a high rate of speed Thirteen-twenty-six—"*

"That's us," said Maher.

"Wikiup *has* to be just ahead of our convoy . . . how many cars you think?"

"Looks like fewer than twenty cars."

"Which means this convoy can't be more than a mile long, which means we should be right on top of Wikiup *now*, but I haven't seen any signs—"

"Any Gumballers," the CB squawked, *"got your ears on?"*

"Who's that?" I asked as Maher reached for the CB handset.

"Ten-four," Maher broadcast, "this is Polizei, who's this?"

"Hey, Polizei, this is Dennis Collins and brother James in the 550."

"Copy that, Dennis. Any word on bears around here?"

"We heard something about a speed trap in a place called . . . Wikiman? Wikiup? About 15 miles from here."

"Holy shit," I said to Maher. "If Wikiup is 15 miles away, and the lead vehicles are already through, then this isn't the lead convoy. Collins must have fallen behind."

Fifteen miles was a huge gap. Given *no* traffic and *no* police, we *might* be able to catch up with Rawlings's Avalanche, but only if we greatly exceeded his 130 mph top speed. Catching up with Kenworthy would be impossible. His GT2 had at least a 20 mph top speed advantage over the Polizei M5's theoretical 180 mph limit.

EASTER SUNDAY, APRIL 20, 2003
LOEWS VENTANA CANYON RESORT
TUCSON, ARIZONA
GUMBALL + 3

"Don't tell me," I said, hunting desperately for a piece of luggage I was quite sure I'd unloaded.

"Duuuuude," Maher said from his bed, "you should have seen this one girl at the bar last night."

"Katie? I saw her, the one who mooned us."

"Yeah," Maher groaned. "I wish we could fit her in the car."

"Me, too, but we've got a bigger problem. Missing bag of Polizei uniforms. Today's Plan B. Meet me at the M5 in ten."

I'd gotten up an hour early to position the M5 at the start of the grid, and with great satisfaction I walked out through the lobby doors only to find approximately ten Gumball cars forming a single line from the end of the hotel's driveway back to the parking lot. But not Rawlings or Kenworthy.

I sprinted to the M5, closed the door on Team Polizei's Plan B uniform of the day—a Tucson Loews Ventana Canyon Resort quilted bathrobe—then quintupled the parking lot's 10 mph limit and pulled into line—

Fucking silver Porsche cutting me off?

—in *twelfth* place, right behind Kenworthy.

We emerged from our cars.

"It's the policeman!" he said with a boyish grin.

Rob "Lonman" Kenworthy, six-foot-one with a crew cut, looking every bit the rugby player he was, the legendary Gumball veteran, heralded on the Gumball, BMW, and Porsche message boards as the "fastest" Gumballer of all time, The Driver whose car I'd never seen moving, one of the two Gumballers every *other* Gumballer wanted to run with, one of the Gumballers most likely to know, know of, or be known to The Driver, *knew who I was.*

"Hey!" I said.

"Good luck today, Roy!"

He even knew my name.

"Know where we're going?" I asked Maher.

"Heard it's a *BIG* one today!" he yelled, standing through the M5's open sunroof. His bathrobe flapped against my face as we inched toward the start line.

"Maher! Do you see Rawlings from up there?"

"No!"

"Collins?"

"No!"

We moved up to the start line. Maher dropped into his seat to review the route card and program our finicky GPS.

"White Sands Missile Range," he read out loud. "Three hundred and five miles."

"That's not gonna be in the GPS. Near Las Cruces?"

"I *did* hear a rumor we're going to San Antonio."

"San Antonio, Texas?" I looked at the map. "About a thousand miles."

One thousand miles straight across the desert. There would be nowhere to hide from police, and there was only one way to get there.

I-10 EASTBOUND
10 MILES SOUTHWEST OF WILCOX, ARIZONA

One hundred and sixty-four miles per hour.

"High-speed convoy ahead!" said Maher. "White Mercedes SL, silver Porsche, black Mercedes SL, and the lead cars are . . . a silver—" Maher leaned forward as if inches would make it clear. "GT2!" he yelled. "And a red . . . it's the F50!"

"Holy shit!" I exclaimed. "The F50!"

Kenworthy's GT2, the million dollar F50, and Macari's SL55 AMG; the lead convoy.

"Pick it up!" Maher yelled. "That GT2 can do 212, and the F50 . . ."

We became the tail of the world's fastest snake, following its red-and-silver head from the right lane to left and back again—around the occasional truck and civilian—at over 150 mph.

163

DING-DING-DING

Wha—

TIRE DEFECT

Don't panic.

My hands froze on the steering wheel.

158

The road is straight. The shoulder is clear. There's nothing to hit.

My right foot shivered with doubt.

"What do I do?" I yelled. "Do we slow down?"

"I checked the pressures," Maher said calmly, "they're fine. Ignore it. Trust me," said Maher.

146

I needed to make up for even this momentary hesitation on the throttle.

"Nice one catching up," said Maher, "but I still can't believe those guys are right behind us."

"Who?" I looked in the rearview mirror.

Holy shit.

The only BMW X5 in the United States capable of 147 mph was less than one car length behind us and trying to pass.

"Jesus," I said. "A BMW X5 SUV? Those Koenigsegg support guys are crazy."

"What's in that thing? The new 4.8?"

"I think it's a 4.6," I said, eyes darting to the mirror, "engine's similar to ours, newer, I guess."

"But carrying a lot more weight . . . with four people and luggage."

"Maher, we're three and *more* luggage."

"Alex, did you forget Cassius isn't in the car today?"

"Oh yeah, where is he anyway?'

"In our convoy," said Maher, "with Macari in the SL55."

"Dude"—Maher smiled—"the Plan B bathrobe idea was sweet."

"I like to be comfortable. Bathrobe plus a/c is the only way to Gumball."

The X5 driver chose to stay behind us, but his intermittent lunges made it clear he was gauging his top-end acceleration.

"What about Frankl? Haven't seen him since he stopped to help that accident."

150

"Dude," said Maher, "pick it up a little. The F50 and GT2 are getting away."

"Truck on the right, hang on."

I moved left.

"Maher! X5 passing on the right shoulder!" The X5 pulled in behind—Joe Macari's black Mercedes SL55 AMG—cruising with its top down.

"Dude," said Maher, "*now* pick it up so they don't all get away."

Kenworthy and the Ferrari F50 dueled at over 170 mph for the next ten minutes. Maher videotaped the spectacle, smiling.

The red-and-silver pair slowed and moved to the right lane.

155

I moved left and passed the F50. We waved. The F50 crew, both wearing aircraft-style noise-canceling headsets and microphones, waved back.

158

We passed Kenworthy. We waved. He waved back.

We were in convoy with the most heralded veteran in Gumball history. The fact that he'd allowed us to pass—however temporarily—was a gesture of respect.

159

Kenworthy, Macari, the unknown F50 driver, and the X5 formed a single line on our bumper. The convoy formed and re-formed with our every brake light flash warning of *Danger! Police Ahead!* For the next 15 minutes—they passed, we followed, then took the lead once more—the gentleman's handoff repeated in a surreal hour-long ballet of musical cars at one-fifth the speed of sound—*we were the head of the snake.*

"Maher?"

"Yeah?"

"What's that sound?"

CHAPTER 14

Requiem for the Blue Mercedes

It was the wind.

153

The M5 was silent.

The rpms had fallen to zero. The engine had died.

We were in first place. The convoy was lined up on our bumper, Kenworthy half a car length away, ready to pass at my slightest hesitation to stay above 150 mph—the F50, Macari, and the X5 in close pursuit.

"You're going to get us killed!" said Maher.

"I . . . it's not me, it's—"

The steering was locked.

150

The air-conditioning cut out. *Kenworthy passed on the left.* The GPS display was blank. The F50 passed. All was silent except for the wind's roaring struggle—and impending victory—over our zero-horsepower aerodynamic brick.

"Maher . . . Don't . . . say . . . a . . . word."

I turned the ignition off.

133

I waited one second, pressed the clutch down, turned the key back to start, and . . .

The engine restarted. I let the clutch out and hit the gas.

"Alex," Maher said quietly, "that was incredible, nerves of steel."

Now we were the tail of the snake.

"Maher, shouldn't we be worried that our entire car's electrical system just failed, I restarted the car while rolling at a hundred and thirty and—"

DING-DING-DING

"Not again." I sighed, then saw the message on the driver information display: *REIFENPANNE.*

"What does *that* mean?" I yelled.

"What does it say?"

"Reef-en-pane," I said in my best phonetic reading. "It's German. The whole system just rebooted to German!"

"Don't slow down," said Maher, "we'll figure it out."

"Hand me my phone, Maher."

136

"Hello, BMW Roadside Assistance, may I have your VIN number, please?"

"That's gonna be tough right now—"

"Can you speak up, sir? There seems to be a lot of noise on the line."

"Maher, set the cruise control."

141

Maher leaned over and engaged it for me.

"Hello? Sir?"

"I can't get the VIN right now, um . . ."

"If you give me your name, I can loo—"

"Alexander Roy, 2000 BMW M5."

"Okay, I've got it right here. What seems to be the problem?"

I explained.

"That is very odd, to say the least, but I'd be glad to make an emergency appointment for you at BMW Manhattan—"

"That's not going to work." We passed a truck, the loud rush of wind buffeting the M5.

"Sir, are you currently driving? If you are, I recommend you stop the car immediately."

"Have you heard of the Gumball Rally?"

"Gumball? One of your friends in an M3 called us earlier."

"Do you have any suggestions other than stopping?"

"I'm afraid not, but if you know your next overnight stop I can make an emergency appointment for you there."

"I'll call you back."

"Any luck?" said Maher.

"Nada," I said, then shivered with revelatory genius. "Maher! My mom's German! She'll know what it means." I called her home number in Bad Homburg. No answer. I called her cell, to no avail.

142

"Pick it up a little," said Maher, "while you're thinking about it."

"Maher, I've got the craziest idea yet." I dialed again.

"International Information?"

"Can you please connect me to BMW Roadside Assistance in Germany?"

"Please hold one moment."

"Alex, you're right, *that* is crazy."

"But not a bad idea, right?"

"Guten Abend . . . BMW . . . automatische—"

I pressed 0, the international button for "I need a human *NOW*!"

150

"Hallo," said a young German man who had just received the phone call he'd tell his kids about, *"das is—"*

"Guten Abend," I started in what little German I knew. "Do you speak English?"

"Ja . . . I speak some English. Do you haf your car ID code?"

"No, it's complicated. I'm in America right now—"

"You are calling from America? So I give you a phone numb—"

"We have an alarm in German we don't understand, and . . ." I explained our problems to date.

"Ah, *ja,* what model car?"

"An M *funf."*

"Gut car."

"Thanks."

"What does the alarm say?"

"Reef . . . en . . . pane?"

"Reifenpanne?!? Mein Gott! This iz a . . . broken tire! Shtop the car now!"

"It's okay, we had that before."

"Mein Gott! Are you certain alles okay wit there tires?"

"Yeah, look, do you have any other ideas?"

"Ja . . . okay . . . you muzt make a date *für* ze electrical inspection—"

"I really can't do that—"

"But you muszt—"

"Have you heard of the Gumball?"

"Gumball? You are on Gumball now? What are you doing?"

"In kilometers, I'd say we're doing—"

"Two-forty," said Maher.

"Two-forty," I said into the phone.

"Mein Gott! You are in ze front, I hope!"

"We were, but do you have any ideas that don't include stopping?"

"Ah ja . . . nein . . . hmm . . . nein . . . okay . . . nein . . . hmm . . . nein—"

"Anything?"

"Ehh . . . no . . . but . . . please call me if you finish! I give you my name und—"

"Just hang up," said Maher, "and drive."

We had to catch up with Kenworthy—barely in sight, at the head of the snake—before the White Sands checkpoint. We had to arrive *with him,* in a show of endurance, aggression, and commitment. Kenworthy . . . and perhaps . . . the driver of the F50 were my keys to The Driver, I was certain.

Las Cruces was almost in sight, and White Sands was approximately twenty miles beyond. Just far enough for us to catch up. We might not have another chance until 2004.

163

Rawlings was far behind. His Avalanche wasn't capable of these speeds. All I had to do was shake hands with Kenworthy in White Sands.

I-10/US ROUTE 70 EASTBOUND

VICINITY OF LAS CRUCES, NEW MEXICO

20 MILES FROM WHITE SANDS CHECKPOINT

GUMBALL + 3

"Kenworthy's just ahead," said Maher, "running slow."

"X5 pulled over with cops on the right."

"Alex, *that's* the cop the Ho Ho Ho Express just warned us about."

"Thank God for those truckers," I said.

The Ho Ho Ho Express Trucking driver had given us the precise location of every police car for the last 70 miles. Our virtual immunity from capture had become apparent to all in our convoy, which is why they'd let us take the lead even when they could have passed.

Respect.

As good as they were, the convoy was running blind until we caught up and shared what we knew by the only means possible—brake-light flash warnings.

"Maher, remind me at the checkpoint to exchange numbers with *everyone* from today's convoy."

"Maher, you think the Ho Ho Ho Express is still in range?"

"Try his buddy Gilbert."

I reached for the CB. "Hey, Ho Ho Ho Express, come in, Ho Ho Ho Express, or come in, Gilbert, can you hear me?"

"This is Gilbert! Don't think Ho Ho can hear you, blue Mercedes!"

"When," said Maher, "are these guys going to stop calling us the blue Mercedes?"

"Copy that, Gilbert, can we get a bear check?"

"Ten-four, blue Mercedes, standby."

Maher's phone rang. "It's M-Trouble; turn down the CB and warn her about the cops behind us."

"Hey, Gilbert, got a call, gimme five!"

"Copy that, blue Mercedes."

M-Trouble was Alison Cornea in the gray M5.

"Hey, Alison! I've got all the police locations on the I-10 into Las Cruces, where're you now?"

"Oh . . . just leaving White Sands."

"What?"

"We just left White Sands . . . headed for San Antonio with—"

"You're leaving White Sands right *now*?"

We still were eastbound on U.S. Route 70, approximately 10 miles and 15 minutes from the White Sands checkpoint.

"Yeah, we're cruising with a couple of cars."

I spotted a bright red car covered with stickers—across the median.

"Maher! *Why* are there Gumballers headed the opposite way?"

"Alex? Alex?"

Maher peered across the road. The red car disappeared behind a berm.

"Sorry, M-Trouble, I'm back."

"You have to double back from White Sands on 70 to get back to the 10."

"Wait, Alison, how many cars are with you?"

"I guess, five or six?"

Kenworthy was with *us*. The F50 was with *us*. Macari was with *us*. We were in the lead. Something was wrong. Something was very wrong.

"Gotta drive! See you in San Antonio."

A new voice bellowed from the CB. *"Hey, Gumballers, be careful goin' into this missile range! We gotta buncha coppers down there!"*

"Love these truckers," said Maher.

A black truck flashed past in the opposite direction.

"Maher—"

"Dude, isn't *that*—"

"Was . . . that . . . *Rawlings*? Going the other way?"

"Who cares?" said Maher. "We're almost there, and I'm starving."

Maher was right. There was still one more police trap between us and White Sands, and *then* another 600 miles to San Antonio.

Then I had some strategy reassessment to do. A *lot* of strategy reassessment.

CHAPTER 15

The District Attorney's Daughter and the Sheriff's Wife

TUESDAY, APRIL 22, 2003
I-10 EASTBOUND—VICINITY OF MOBILE, ALABAMA
720 MILES TO FINISH LINE
GUMBALL + 5

"Alex, man, I'm really glad you came out last night. I love New Orleans, and you needed to unwind. What happened with you and that girl?"

"Dave," I said, using his first name for the first time since the start, in an effort to convey the gravity of the prior night's events, "her dad's a district attorney. It's best if we just don't talk about it. Don't worry, I'm pretty sure she's over twenty-two."

"That's the part of Gumball no one warns you about. Just make sure my girlfriend doesn't hear about it, or she'll think I was involved."

I-10 EASTBOUND—VICINITY OF PENSACOLA, FLORIDA
ESCAMBIA BAY CAUSEWAY
665 MILES TO FINISH LINE

135

I was glad to have Maher drive. He was 5 percent faster than I was, even at my best. He'd done slightly less than half the driving—I should have given him more.

"Nice one back there"—Maher chuckled—"hitting One-Arm Wes with the Polizei Blue Light Special. You got that on video?"

"The whole thing. I can't believe how many Gumballers have fallen for *that* one, especially in the daytime."

"Dude," said Maher, "look."

There it was—the tall black shape of a truck, antennas raked back.

"Look, Alex, it's your favorite Avalanche." It *was* Rawlings, and we were about to pass him.

Rawlings lowered his window, his hair whipping in the wind, bared his teeth in a huge grin, and gave us the international hand signal for "Rock On."

How did we catch up with him? We'd left the New Orleans checkpoint midpack. Rawlings had been up front.

I thought back to the Tucson–to–White Sands run.

If Rawlings wanted to be first to every checkpoint, and would do whatever it took—within reason—to do it fair and square, and if Collins was with him the whole time, maybe there *was* one other way they could've beaten us to White Sands.

Maybe Rawlings *wasn't* leaving early. Maybe Rawlings was employing *every* single strategy I'd thought of, but with greater discipline and focus. He was leaving at precisely 9 A.M. in first place. He and Collins—*Lone Wolves* paired, cooperating over and discussing navigation, scanner, and CB traffic—weren't pushing past 150 mph as often as we had. They were cruising at 120, conserving fuel, because *that* was the sweet spot of fuel economy vs. time and distance elapsed.

I'd ignored my fuel tables, running with Kenworthy at 150 at nine miles per gallon.

Rawlings had been approximately 25 minutes ahead of us into White Sands—almost *precisely* the length of time we'd spent getting out of Tucson because of our GPS failure and additional fuel stop(s).

And now we'd caught up with him.

Rawlings had left New Orleans approximately 15 minutes ahead of us. We'd inadvertently caught up *only* because Maher had driven a consistent 130 mph, which—although more fuel efficient than 140, was worse than their 120—meant we were going to fall behind them again.

"Maher, Collins is right up ahead."

"Don't say it. Let's run with these two until we need gas."

"That's *exactly* what I was going to say."

120

"Maher, just make sure we pass both of them before we refuel."

"Why?"

"Just do it when we're beyond their visual range."

Once we disappeared, if Rawlings thought there was even a *chance* we might beat him to the Ocala Hooters—the 2003 Gumball's penultimate checkpoint—he might push harder, make a mistake, waste gas, get pulled over . . . *anything.*

I-10 EASTBOUND—VICINITY OF WESTVILLE, FLORIDA
UNKNOWN GAS STATION
570 MILES TO FINISH LINE

"The world's fastest refuel," I said, "starts in . . . ten seconds. I just hope Rawlings and Collins didn't see us pull off for gas."

We stopped, jumped out, and Maher ran to the bathroom. Rawlings and Collins pulled in right next to the M5. I waved and looked at the pump.

Maher waltzed back, took out his camcorder, and walked over to the Avalanche.

"How ya doin'?" he said to Rawlings.

"Ahriiiiigggggght! How 'bout you boys?"

"Just fine," said Maher, walking over to Collins. "How you doing?"

"Real good," said Collins, uninterested.

Amazingly, inexplicably, catastrophically, all three of our pumps finished almost simultaneously. Rawlings and Collins pulled out to the edge of the road, then stopped.

"Dude," said Maher, "they want you to go first."

"Duh, they want us as bait. Haven't you been listening to the scanner? Every cop in the panhandle is looking for us after that 180 mph shit we just pulled."

"Maybe we should take side roads."

"I'll pull out and take it slow, it'll drive them nuts."

75

Then the CB squawked and everything changed.

"Hey, Polizei," said Collins, *"got your ears on?"*

Maher took the handset. *"Ten-four, Dennis."*

"Hey, Richard?"

"That's aaa Teeeeeeeeen-four!"

"Hey, Polizei, you got your fancy scanner up?"

"Sure do!" said Maher.

"And we got ours!" said Rawlings.

"Hey, Polizei, we've got the same as yours . . . let's see if we're picking up the same stuff."

"Pol-eez-eye," said Rawlings, *"what say we all take it easy until we're clear of these coppers, then we'll hammer down!"*

"Ten-four!" said Maher, smiling as he peered ahead for radar traps.

I smiled my happiest smile of the week, and for the next 200 miles we ran with Rawlings and Collins.

We'd joined the world's fastest Wolf Pack, that is, until we got to the Ocala Hooters checkpoint, stepped inside for my favorite cheesesteak, and snapped pictures of the waitresses in their tight orange short shorts. I went to look for our new convoy partners, stopped to watch Kenworthy paint rubber donuts in the parking lot, but Rawlings and Collins were gone.

MANDARIN ORIENTAL HOTEL, MIAMI BEACH
GUMBALL FINISH-LINE PARTY

I waded through a sea of grins, outstretched hands, Gumballers' wives, children *and* even several rally girlfriends who'd made it more than one checkpoint past where their relationships had begun.

Rings of wide black rubber stained the hotel driveway.

I walked out and stood at the center of the circular driveway, surrounded by cars, red, yellow, and orange paint dusted, dulled, and in the darkness nearly indistinguishable from those black and gray, some with Gumball stickers and car numbers partially torn away.

A second police car slid past, its headlights briefly illuminating my M5. Battered. Dented. Filthy. Beautiful.

On the other side of the circle, looming high over the Lamborghinis and Ferraris, sat Rawlings's black Avalanche, as proud and mysterious as its driver.

I *had* come to race, but I had a lot to learn. But I'd run with Kenworthy. I'd run with Rawlings. It was time to face them. We had a lot to talk about. I turned back inside. Girls' laughter cascaded down from the Mandarin Oriental's penthouse deck.

The *private* private private after-party in the Mandarin Oriental's Penthouse Presidential Suite was hosted by Arthur Chirkinian—owner of the Koenigsegg and its 164 mph X5 support car—who, with telepathic wisdom, had invited nearly every Gumballer I longed to talk to.

I had a long discussion with the Koenigsegg's backup crew that had so tormented us in their X5. "One more question," I said quietly so as not to upset Arthur, standing nearby, "but what really happened to the Koenigsegg?"

"It's no secret, mate. Among other things, the clutch went bad into Las Vegas, but Sunday morning VW parts was closed, so he bought a VW Golf, put *that* clutch in the Koenigsegg, then threw the keys back at the dealer."

"Wow," I said. That was an amazing story, even for Gumball.

"There's more, you see, because *that* clutch failed as well, so he had these blokes from Jeff's Auto Repair in Vegas follow him cross country with more parts, and it's a good thing they did because—"

"Hang on," I said. "Did they have to pay them hourly . . . all the way . . . *here?*"

"I really couldn't say, but the car's not actually here yet because of another—"

"Excuse me, Alex?" came the voice of a large man behind me—hopefully not a driver I'd cut off.

"Yes?" I turned.

Rob and Mike—Eyhab's high-speed logistics and support crew—towered over me.

"Alex," Mike said without any emotion, "we just wanted to thank you, in person, before it was too late."

"You're welcome, but . . . what are you thanking me for?"

"For treating us the same, after you met Rob in San Francisco, after you found out the Lambo and the Spyder weren't ours."

Rob nodded in agreement. "Very cool, mate."

"That's it," said Mike, "have a good night." They each shook my hand, then walked away.

Maher approached. "What was that all about?"

"Good guys, just really good guys."

"If you say so. How's your new New Orleans girlfriend?"

"Well"—I sighed—"she wants to fly here and drive back to New York with me."

"And her dad's really a D.A.?"

"That's what she said."

"That's either a really bad idea, or the best guy's daughter to have in the car if you're stopped for speeding. I hear South Carolina's really bad."

"Maher, I swear . . . I *won't* be speeding back."

"I hope you're leaving the Polizei stickers on the car."

"I may never take them off. Any sign of our friend from Texas? Or Lonman?"

"Relax. Rawlings said he was coming, and Kenworthy's off doing his own thing."

"His own thing?"

"I dunno, maybe he's not a party kinda guy."

"All riiiiight!" the voice of Texas announced from the front door. "Anyone got a cold beer?" The white cowboy hat and I converged on the wet bar. Rawlings placed his Gumball Trophy—a metal bust of Burt Reynolds *also* in a cowboy hat—on the counter.

"Hey, Polizei! That was real nice running with you today."

"Yeah, man, where's Collins? I wanted to thank him."

"Awwww, Dennis is probably in bed already!"

"Rawlings, seriously, that was really cool of you and Dennis at Radio-Shack today."

Somewhere in central Florida I'd accidentally kicked out and broken the M5's CB-radio power cable—making it impossible to remain useful to our wolf pack—but, amazingly, Rawlings and Collins had volunteered to pull over with us at a nearby RadioShack. Maher hid the M5 alongside the 550 and Avalanche while I ran inside.

"You check your tires, Mr. Pol-eez-eye?"

My heart froze. "What . . ." I paused, barely capable of speech.

"You should keep a better eye on your boy Dave! Doing donuts behind the Shack with them coppers out looking for us?"

I learned against the bar to maintain my balance.

"Polizei, didja know the three of us were doin' a buck-thirty past some sheriff's wife mowing the lawn? She called him straight up, and that's what brought all that heat down on us!"

I laughed weakly. "I *thought* I heard that on the scanner."

"You know, Alex, you're the only guy besides me and Dennis who came prepared. I mean, when I saw your car in SF I thought you might have more fancy gear than we did!"

"Rawlings, you should have seen my face when I got my first look inside your truck at the start line."

Rawlings handed me a beer. "Here's to running hard! Gumball!"

"Gumball," I said, clinking bottles. "You guys really kicked ass."

"Me and my wife and Dennis just came here to have a good time, but it's really too bad more guys didn't wanna run with us, I mean really run."

"What about Kenworthy and those guys? You don't think they came to run?"

"Sure they did," said Rawlings. "Those boys are mighty quick. But if you wanna get anywhere fast, you gotta get out front before the slower boys start kicking up the beehive! It woulda been nice to see more of y'all run with me and Dennis. It's no fun running alone."

"Well," I said, looking at his bust on the counter, "that's why you got *that*."

"*First* to nearly *every* checkpoint!" he yelled. "Me and Dennis mighta had a little competition if you'd spent a little more time driving than trying not to get arrested!"

He was right. Despite all my strategizing, once I was in the car I'd focused almost completely on what would happen if we were stopped.

It was time for *the* question.

"Richard," I said, leaning closer and using his first name for the first time, "have you ever raced cross-country? I mean flat out, no parties, no checkpoints, no stickers?"

"Ooooh"—he hesitated—"you mean like the *real* Cannonball, like back in the old days?"

"Precisely."

"Polizei, man, now *that* shit sounds dangerous."

"You've," I said slowly, "never done it?"

"Sure would! But somebody's gotta get some boys together who know what the hell they're doing!"

"Yeah," I said. "It's too bad no one's organizing *that*."

"Alex, you hear about another *real* Cannonball going down, we gotta go. I *know* Dennis'll be in. You gotta run against guys you trust, right?"

He didn't know The Driver. Of all the 2003 Gumballers, Rawlings and Collins were the logical picks for recruitment. The Driver would already know Kenworthy from the 2002 Gumball.

Wherever they went, I'd go.

Handsome Dave's exact words used when Rawlings received his bust were "—*first to nearly every checkpoint*—"

The exact words used when Kenworthy received the Fastest Wheels Trophy were *"the hardest driver by a mile."*

Maher and I won the Spirit Trophy—apparently Gumball's greatest honor—for "*doing it in the craziest way*," just like Max had said at orientation only five days earlier, "*because it goes to whoever best embodies the enthusiasm, creativity, and spirit of Gumball.*"

That was probably true. This time.

Gumball really was a rally, a fantastical, amorphous community that coalesced, dispersed, and teleported itself each day, five days a year, between points distant, a surreal universe of which I was a small part, and of which I'd seen a larger but *still* very small sliver of its mythical totality. *The sliver containing those who came to race.* First. Hardest.

Rawlings, Kenworthy, and I had each come for a different race of our own creation, each with different rules, and each of us had won. If only two or more of us played by the same rules, that would be a real race.

This had only been the first battle. I'd earned Rawlings's respect. Kenworthy knew who I was. But if I wanted to find The Driver, I had to push. Harder. Unless, by some miracle, The Driver called before the 2004 Gumball registration deadline eight months away, I'd be back.

"Richard, you know, you gave me a real shock when we saw you coming out of White Sands going the other way."

"Wasn't that funny?"

"How come you weren't stopped by those cops at the White Sands exit?"

Rawlings shook his head. "Man, I was talking to all the same truckers as you! Didn't you hear me warn y'all?"

"Wait . . . that was *you*? You warned us on the CB when you were going the other way?"

"Hells yeah!" He picked up another beer. "Ain't I a nice guy?" Interesting. "So," said Rawlings, "you doing Gumball in Europe next year?"

Kenworthy would be there, as would legends who'd missed 2003—the notorious Kim Schmitz and secretive Peter Malmstrom, names I'd heard spoken in hushed tones but about whom I knew little.

"Dunno, Rawlings. You?"

"Dunno, man, Africa and shit? Sounds dangerous . . . never driven down there, but if you're going, let's talk after this is over."

"Done."

I hoped he would be. Rawlings was a fierce competitor, but if disaster struck and I needed help, I'd trust him.

Eight hours earlier, after another *Reifenpanne,* after he and Collins left the Ocala Hooters checkpoint ten minutes ahead of us, after Maher caught up with them for the second time, after I encouraged Maher to pass and push to the finish line ahead of them, after I told Maher to disregard the fuel gauge . . . we ran out of gas.

Rawlings and Collins passed. I called out on the CB for help.

Rawlings answered, imploring us to get the M5 rolling just one more mile to the overpass, where, sitting on the shoulder by the mile marker, exactly like one of two I'd seen strapped to the back of a black Chevy Avalanche parked in front of the Fairmont in San Francisco—we found a bright red jerry can full of gas.

I reached for the second most important box in my life—an unassuming lit-tle brown cardboard cube sitting on a shelf in my lobby's mail room—and ripped it open before the elevator doors closed behind me.

It was Brock Yates's *Cannonball!* memoir.

Of course Gumball was nothing like Cannonball.

The majority of Cannonballers drove coast-to-coast, nonstop, in 35 to 40 hours, *during which the lead drivers sustained average speeds of over 80mph*—a Herculean feat even today. The 2003 Gumball took five days to cover 3,350 miles—the longest stage a 12- to 15-hour run over 924 miles.

But those few serious Gumballers who *raced*—forced to use every tool and tactic possible to avoid being stopped merely for being stickered—suffered a trial by fire *far* harsher than any Cannonballer. The fraction of Gumballers who finished virtually unmolested by police—among them Rawlings, Collins, and myself—possessed skills and instincts untaught any-where, at any price, and utterly useless anywhere *but on the secret race the Gumball wasn't.*

Were Gumball all there was or had ever been, I'd return ever year until I died, but that Rawlings and Collins existed at all—yearning and hoping for something beyond even the surreal madness of Gumball, that on the final night I felt closer to them than anyone outside my oldest friends, that there were others seemingly like us yet unknown to me—meant I was right.

I wasn't alone.

Hillary *had* to climb Everest, Bannister *had* to run the four-minute mile, and we felt the inexorable pull of a distant, mythological journey across America, a *race* that—whenever people like Rawlings and I met—became inevitable.

Nonstop. No parties. No checkpoints. No bullshit.

If only someone would invite us.

I completed the first page of the book before the elevator door opened on my floor. Within hours I'd learned that racing legend Dan Gurney (whose control of a Ferrari Daytona was described by copilot Yates as that of "a vir-tuoso playing . . . a fine instrument,") set the inaugural 1971 Cannonball re-cord of 35:54, and that this was later shattered when David Heinz and David Yarborough, civilians nowhere as skilled as the F1 legend, set the final 32:51 Cannonball record in 1979.

"Laser and radar jammers remain unproven," Yates wrote, calling the CB network "raggedly unpredictable."

But Maher and I had had a 99 percent success rate in mapping, spotting, and avoiding police, and our two traffic stops occurred *only* because we'd failed to heed our V1.

"The time for Cannonball-style races is over," Yates wrote, citing increased law enforcement, liability, traffic, and urban sprawl. But I was among several Gumballers, all in stickered cars far more conspicuous than the stealthy Cannonballers', who finished with but two tickets—*par with several top-five Cannonball finishers.*

As for traffic and sprawl, in 1999 Yates drove cross-country—*through a snowstorm,* with his son, in a stock Chrysler 300M—in 38 hours, then said 36 hours remained "within the realm of possibility."

There *had* to be a secret race out there.

Had to be.

CHAPTER 16

What You Get for the Statue of Liberty

I waited for the call for months, but it was always Gumballers wanting to go clubbing in New York, or party at Eyhab's London mansion, or invite me to dinner in Paris. I befriended Frankl and Michael Ross—the watermelon-helmeted owner of the 28 whom I'd seen arrested just after the 2003 start—at the L.A. premiere of the Gumball movie that November, and Maher began dating Emma, a six-foot three-inch English model who worked for Ross's girlfriend. My superficial star turn in the movie led fans and Gumballers to call for technical and legal advice, as if my schizophrenic months of preparation only one year earlier made me an authority. Even Morgan called, improbably asking if I would officiate and witness his wedding to Kira that afternoon in New York before they flew home to England. Virtually everyone I asked expressed interest in a Cannonball revival, but none admitted being aware of—let alone invited to—one.

The Driver wasn't going to call. I had to hone my skills on the 2004 Gumball. That's where I'd find Kenworthy, Kidd, Macari, Schmitz, and a new driver whose real name no one knew. A driver known only from online rumors and fan gossip. A driver who—whether or not he understood the true nature of the Gumball Spirit Trophy—had declared the 2003 winner his prime target, the man he intended to defeat at all costs.

A driver who had declared *me* Public Enemy number one.

A driver named Torquenstein.

MAY 3, 2004

PARIS, FRANCE

GUMBALL-2

2300 HOURS (APPROX)

"So . . . er . . . Alex . . . what do you think of him *now*?"

I stood beside George Gurley, the *Vanity Fair* writer assigned to my Royal Canadian Mounted Police Pursuit M5 for Gumball '04.

A candy-apple-red Dodge Viper spun in circles not 20 feet away, its engine revving wildly, its wide tires scrabbling on Paris's famously uneven pavement, chirping and spitting out increasingly large clouds of acrid smoke. The fans whooped, hollered, clapped, cheered, laughed, and shouted.

The driver was approximately five nine, yet looked smaller at the helm of the North Dakota–plated 700-horsepower Hennessy Venom 650R Viper currently spinning in place; he wore a suit of black leather armor, belts and cross straps, matching shoulder pads, and driving gloves lined with spikes that made him appear to be the result of a strange mating between a medieval knight and an S&M club habitué. He completed the look with black-lensed goggles over a face-concealing helmet topped with small red horns.

"So?" George huffed, as we watched the spectacle from behind a large tree.

I looked at the fantastic structure looming above us—built for the 1889 World's Fair, one of the great symbols of Parisian architecture and French culture, one of the most recognized symbols in human history, atop which countless couples had met, fallen in love, and proposed—from which a thousand grand lights shone carelessly upon the sideshow unfolding at its feet.

"They built *that*." I gestured at the Eiffel Tower. "*They* gave us the Statue of Liberty. "We gave them . . . Torquenstein."

FIVE MONTHS EARLIER

DECEMBER 2003

NEW YORK

"You're really screwed," said The Weis, standing before a laptop on my kitchen counter.

"Let *me* see that." I jumped out of the office chair from where I'd been perusing the Gumball forums—hunting for hints of equipment I might have overlooked—and from where, having just discovered a thread about a new and apparently *very* well-prepared entrant, I'd found his website address, www.torquenstein.net, and had read it out loud to The Weis.

"Holy shit!" I exclaimed.

"This looks bad," said The Weis.

"This *is* bad."

"This guy looks really serious. Who is he?"

"I don't know."

The Weis clicked on Torquenstein's car-page link, nodding with grudging admiration at the $200,000 Dodge Viper. He raised his eyebrows—and my heart sank—when he scrolled down to a picture of a lemon-yellow Hummer H2 support truck.

"This *is* bad." The Weis placed a hand on my shoulder. "For *you*."

Torquenstein's equipment list duplicated mine, *and* he was adding my dream support vehicle, replete with tools, spare tires, parts, and emergency jerry cans. His budget for emergency gear, the support car, and entry fees for both it *and* its personnel *had* to exceed $200,000. Of the hundred and fifty or so entrants in the upcoming 2004 Gumball, Torquenstein was the only one I knew of better prepared than I.

Despite my experience—and probably *because* of it—the 2004 Gumball seemed far more daunting than the 2003. The route was Paris to somewhere in Spain, then Morocco (almost certainly in and out via the port city of Tangier), Barcelona (to coincide with the Formula 1 race there on May 9), and ending Cannes, for the first day of its film festival.

Half my gear would be useless. European police-radio frequencies and ten-code vernacular weren't public, my near-fluent French probably wouldn't be sufficient to understand them anyway, and I didn't speak Spanish. European truckers didn't use CB radios. I wasn't sure my V1—despite its instruction manual—would pick up 100 percent of the French and Spanish police radar. In 2003 my Lidatek laser jammer alarm had rung *every* time a late-model LED-brake-light-equipped vehicle hit the brakes, so I'd replaced them with an as-yet-untested Escort ZR3 system. I'd decided to ignore the M5's GPS and install a Garmin 2650, the best mobile unit available. I'd spent $1,000 on European and African DVD map sets, and an external backup windshield antenna.

Contrary to popular belief, European highways—however more suitable for speeding than those in the United States—*did* have speed limits, and although speed limits were often 90 mph or higher and police cars were rare, radar speed-trap cameras were common. I wasn't worried about their shooting my license plates. I'd replaced the front with a $7.93, eBay-purchased, vintage Canadian Northwest Territories, red-and-white polar-bear-shaped collectible plate, last valid in 1973, and the rear with a New York State plate that read INPOL144, valid, suggestive, meaningless, and covered with a Specterguard antiphoto radar reflective shield. In the event we *were* caught by police, my situation would be far worse than back home. European traffic and criminal law were vastly different. I could be detained for days, even weeks, while a magistrate prepared charges. My car could be impounded and auctioned off *before* I was released and could bid on it.

Except for the loss of time and money, speeding tickets would be irrelevant. France and Spain didn't have DMV moving-violation-point reciprocity treaties with *any* American state, and fines could be paid on the spot with a credit card.

. If I hurt or killed anyone—life as I knew it would be over.

I hoped the presence of my long-distance, almost-ex-girlfriend/lover-but-who-was-such-a-good-friend-she-was-still-coming copilot, Amanda Kinsley, would cheer up any cops who might stop us. We'd met in L.A. when she'd seen me wearing a Team Polizei jacket with a bright orange Gumball patch, asked how many I'd done, then volunteered her services. Kinsley, the head concierge at a five-star hotel in Los Angeles, quickly procured voluminous research on European and Moroccan law, geography, projected fuel stops and pump octane levels, high-end tire stores, BMW service centers, *and* the most-likely-but-still-secret Gumball checkpoints.

She was clever, meticulous, excellent with maps, and never lost her temper.

She looked fantastic not only in the RCMP's bright red tunic, jodhpurs, tall boots and campaign hat, but also in Team Polizei's new-for-2004 white leather Svenska Motorvag Polis jackets, *and* in our lightweight-for-summer, black Tasmanian Highway Patrol uniforms.

She couldn't drive stick, but she *was* my first line of defense against a speeding ticket or arrest.

Disaster loomed in Morocco, the quality of its road network eliciting only laughter from U.S. State Department offices in Washington and Rabat, and there were but two BMW dealers in the country—in the capital and the centrally located city of Meknes—in the unlikely event we broke down nearby. The Gumball would pass through for less than 48 hours.

If *anything* went wrong, we'd be stranded.

The Weis patted me on the back. "Relax, what do your little friends online say?"

"Some guys say Torquenstein's going balls out, first into checkpoints, *and* to get the Spirit Trophy at the same time, but—"

"Aliray, did you really think you're the *only* guy serious about this?"

"Well . . . the fans say Kenworthy can't be beat."

"Listen," said The Weis, "this is all meaningless without real rules and time cards."

"But there's a code of honor . . . seriously . . . even if not everyone knows what it is. Kenworthy probably *could* be first every time, if he felt like it, but he doesn't . . . and people respect him as the best."

The Weis walked away, slowly paced around my living room, then took a seat at the bar facing me. "Aliray . . . why are you doing this again?"

"I *have* to show the flag. Kenworthy will be there, and Schmitz."

"And this Rawlings guy isn't going?"

"No," I said. "Hardly any Americans are. Everyone's freaked out about Morocco . . . breakdowns, carjackings, *and* it's an Arab country, but my Moroccan friends said not to worry . . . they love Americans."

"Read BBC.com, tough guy. You *don't* wanna break down outside a major city. The king wasn't elected, and there're some unhappy people in the desert. Have a good time impressing your secret racer buddies."

"The Weis, there'll never be another one like this. Africa? C'mon, you gotta admit it's nuts. I mean, it's way more 'once in a lifetime' than San Fran to Miami."

"Like I said"—The Weis deployed his most disapproving tone—"have a good time."

"I'll be careful . . . everyone loves Canadians."

"You better hope so, because that red jacket and hat make you look like an idiot."

"But no one's gonna arrest me *in Europe* for impersonating a Mountie!"

The Weis, bored with my rationalizations, glanced once again at Torquenstein's website. "So . . . if there's no *winning* per se, and you're just showing the flag, what's the point? What if this *Vanity Fair* guy makes you look like a complete idiot? I mean, you're pretty easy to make fun of, smart guy."

"If I can speak for the intelligent, rational, normal people who do Gumball, and especially if I have a safe, professional drive and get better, I can pitch sponsors for the next one."

"For 2005?" He stared, as if my doing a third rally had never occurred to him. "Aliray, I've said it before, but you really *are* crazy."

Only a very unusual person could or would commit utterly—as I had—to Gumballing as if it were a professional motor-sport event. One had to have time, money, and, most of all, serious motivation bordering on a deeper psychological problem.

Torquenstein appeared to exceed me in all three. And The Driver would be watching.

HOTEL GEORGE V PARKING GARAGE
GUMBALL START DAY
1530 HOURS (APPROX)

The RCMP M5 wouldn't turn over.

Kenworthy rolled past.

If all had gone as planned, we, having parked in approximately twentieth position, would already have pulled out and entered the line of cars slowly spiraling up the ramp, out of the garage, and into the prestart parade, and I, having lived in Paris, could have used my superior knowledge of the eighth arrondissement's streets to cut ahead, advancing up the grid before the flag drop beneath the Trocadero.

Who did I know with jumper cables?

"Kinsley?" I said nervously, sweat rolling off my brow onto the wool RCMP tunic. We both suffered in the heat of a dozen cars idling two unventilated levels belowground. Kinsley was also afflicted by a mild but intensifying flu, and with futile sympathy I saw as she approached—with eager eyes and a forced smile—the unbalanced steps of one trying to delay necessary bed rest.

"Any better?"

"I'll make it," she said quietly. "What's . . . wrong? You look—"

"The battery's dead."

"Alex," she said, my shame reflected in her glare, "with all the stuff we packed, *tell* me you brought jumper cables. Didn't this happen last year?"

I glanced at the police lights on the roof. "Yes," I said with self-directed anger, "and it happened for the same reason. Kinsley . . . I think you have a better chance at getting cables than me, and keep an eye out for Ross or his copilot, Emma; they might only be one level up."

She headed off without a word.

The last car of the main pack passed us by. Except for the occasional straggler and those disabled by more serious problems, we were alone.

CHAPTER 17

The Unluckiest Lamborghini Owner in the World

WEDNESDAY, MAY 5, 2004
AUTOROUTE A63/N10 SOUTHBOUND
5 MILES TO SPANISH BORDER
GUMBALL + 1
SOMETIME BEFORE DAWN

I was exhausted. Kinsley's flu was worsening. We'd run out of gas. We'd gotten lost. George and Julian had slept through virtually the entire ordeal.

"Kinsley, how far to Madrid?"

"Garmin says . . . 300 miles."

My phone rang, startling me. "Team Polizei," I answered.

"Roy! It's . . . we . . . south . . . police—"

"Can you speak up? Who is this?"

"Cops . . . took the lot . . . black Lambo . . . ahead three . . . threatened—"

Then I lost the signal. "Couldn't hear a thing," I said, "just 'cops' and 'Lambo.' Here's a gas station, let's be safe this time."

Kinsley and the others stayed in the car while I inserted my Visa card into the pump. We were far behind the main pack. Maybe even last.

Nine hundred miles hadn't seemed that bad—10 to 12 hours with no navigational mistakes—but every stressful hour spent lost was an emotionally and physically debilitating fatigue multiplier. I had no backup driver.

Something pattered against the metal awning over the pump. *Rain*—the enemy of speed.

Suddenly a high-pitched engine flared behind me. I turned and stared, stunned, as a bright red Gumball-stickered Porsche 996 turbo pulled up to the neighboring pump.

Somehow, someone in a *very* good car was behind us.

Two women stepped out, a redhead peering around the pump and waving.

"Alex!!!" she yelled. "Oh my God, it's *great* to see you!"

"M-Trouble?" We ran toward each other and hugged. "*Nice* car," I said, "but I didn't see you in Paris!"

"It was a mess back there, but the car? Joe sold it to me!"

"Macari?"

"Yup! It's been a tough leg. I heard the police stopped a lot of cars before Mas-du-Clos—"

"Wow," I said. I guess two girls in a red Porsche can get away with almost anything in France. Have you seen Kenworthy or Torquenstein?"

"Hardly seen anyone, but you know Rory in the black Gallardo? At my last gas stop he told me the police stopped him so many times that if he's stopped again, they're taking the car!"

"Permanently?"

"That's France!"

"M-Trouble, *that's* what you get for Gumballing in a Lambo with temp plates."

We both turned our heads at the sound of an oncoming car. It *sounded* like a sports car, but the whine of its engine and the growl of its exhaust approached too slowly for it to be a Gumballer. A pair of bright headlights appeared beyond the gas station and entrance. A low black shape cruised past *very* slowly.

"Alison, was that a—"

"Black Gallardo? Guess who!"

There was only one thing to do.

AUTOROUTE A63/N10 SOUTHBOUND
2 MILES TO SPANISH BORDER

I had to catch him.

91

I was pretty sure the speed limit was 130 kilometers per hour, about 80 mph. The Gallardo *had* passed the station *very* slowly.

110

He couldn't get caught. The police would take his car. All he had to do was make it to the border.

126

"Kinsley, how far to the Spanish border?"

"Garmin says . . . 1 or 2 miles."

I spotted a pair of rear running lights ahead, close to the ground.

"Kinsley, camcorder ready?"

"It's on."

George stirred. "What's up, Alex?"

"We're chasing someone down."

"Cool."

There he is . . . at 81.

I matched his speed—the driver clearly desperate to save his brand-new, paper-plated Lamborghini Gallardo from seizure and the outright loss of $175,000.

And he was *so* close to escaping France.

"Everyone get ready."

Team Polizei's original raison d'être was the avoidance of tickets and arrest while racing, and the new-for-2004 installation of grille-mounted lights and sirens *had* proven very effective in cutting through Parisian rush-hour traffic, but I'd long believed that in the unfortunate event we fell behind, such gear, if used on other Gumballers in a *Polizei Shock-und-Fear Strategy,* would allow us to pass Gumballers who would otherwise never allow it.

It was inconceivable that I would ever do this to a friend, but to someone I *didn't* know, someone fearful of losing his brand-new Lamborghini cruising at or under the speed limit, in a tail-between-his-legs saunter to the Spanish border, only a mile or 2 away, where he would certainly accelerate to 150 mph or more, I had absolutely no choice.

81

The Gallardo was now three car lengths away.

"PA system's on?" I asked Kinsley.

"PA system is on."

The Gallardo was now two car lengths away. I signaled Kinsley to flip down and activate the visor-mounted yellow lights. I pressed the steering-wheel tunnel switch for the white strobes concealed in our headlights. The Gallardo's brake lights came on.

"Awwww yes!" Kinsley squealed.

"We got him!" I said.

"Get him to *stop,*" George said in an uncharacteristically aggressive tone.

I reached for the public-address system's handset, and in what little French I could remember without laughing, ignoring all rules of grammar, in the most authoritative voice I could muster, I said, *"ARRETE LA VOITURE . . . A LA DROITE."*

Whether the driver understood or not, the Gallardo slowed and moved onto the right shoulder.

"Awww," George said with great satisfaction, "that's so beautiful."

"Yeesssssss!" said Kinsley.

The Gallardo came to a stop. I stopped the RCMP M5 one car length behind him.

"ARRETE LE MOTEUR DE VOTRE VOITURE."

"Try to get them out of the car," said George. "That would be funny."

How can he *not* recognize a blue M5 covered with stickers? I shook my head. *"ARRETE LE MOTEUR."*

"They don't speak French," said Kinsley.

I heard someone shouting. *Was the driver calling out at us?* I lowered my window.

"—don't speak French!" came a faint voice from the Gallardo.

"It's Eubanks," said George, referring to Chris Eubanks, the retired boxer.

I reached for the handset. *"METTEZ LES MAINS SUR LE VOLANT DE LA VOITURE."*

"Should I go to the side of the car?" asked Kinsley.

"SORTEZ LA VOITURE ... A GAUCHE."

"I don't speak French!" the driver yelled.

I pressed the PA switch, and in what little German I knew said, *"SPRE-CHEN SIE DEUTSCHE?"*

"No!" the driver yelled.

Kinsley and I giggled while George and Julian tried to contain themselves behind us.

There was still one *more* thing I could do, and in my best ever impression of a French gendarme *trying* to speak English, I said, *"TURN OFF ZEE ENGEENE OF ZEE CAR."*

The driver didn't comply, but he *did* fumble with his visor, clearly looking for his car documents.

"PLACE YOUR HAND BRAKE."

"Oh, man," said George.

"ZEE DRIVER PLEASE STEP OUT OF ZEE VEE-HI-KUL!"

The Gallardo door opened to reveal a gorgeous beige leather panel, now being spattered with rain.

"Yes!" said Kinsley.

A tall slender thirtysomething guy stepped out, documents in hand, wearing a green shirt and track pants, looking exactly like the young banker-on-vacation I presumed him to be. I thought I'd seen him with Jodie Kidd at the prestart party, but the darkness made it hard to be sure.

He started walking toward us.

The driver crossed in front of our lights and toward Kinsley's window. *"PLEASE BRING YOUR DOCUMENTS TO ZEE CAR."*

He must be close enough to see our stickers. He hesitated. Kinsley lowered her window. *Doesn't he see our red Mountie jackets?* He advanced once again, approaching her window just as we burst into uproarious laughter. *"YOU HAVE BEEN CAPTURED BY GUMBALL 144!"*

"You," he said upon seeing the camcorder in Kinsley's hand, beginning to grasp the magnitude of the situation, any relief at our *not* being gendarmes outweighed by shame and anger, "are such a fucking loser."

"I'm sorry," I said over my passengers' laughter. "What's your name?"

"My name is . . . *blow me.*"

"I'm sorry," I said, "really, man, I'm sorry."

"You're not sorry, motherfucker." He angrily stormed back to his car while I cackled along with my passengers.

Once this story got out, I was sure no one would try to outrun a cop for the rest of Gumball 2004. Alternatively, if Gumballers thought the flashing lights behind them were mine *and* they made a run for it—there was no telling the legal ramifications.

I'd done my part to ensure the safe driving of all Gumballers.

When we arrived in Madrid—after befriending the *real* Spanish police at our next gas stop—we learned that the overnight checkpoint was 370 miles farther, in Marbella.

I couldn't believe I'd driven it alone. George and Julian had slept through most of it. Kinsley, despite her worsening condition, had remained awake. By the time we lay down for a preparty catnap, after driving 1,283 miles in something like 17 or 18 hours, I thought I might be in worse shape than she was.

We staggered through that night's party drunk on DayQuil, then collapsed in bed. I stared at the ceiling and listened to Kinsley breathing laboriously beside me.

I sorted through the rumors I'd heard at the party, during which Gumballers—having driven 24 hours or more—continued to arrive.

We'd been lucky. French police roadblocks had stopped dozens of Gumballers, seized multiple cars, stranding many who'd had to hitch rides in what few cars had more than two seats, or fly to Marbella. Numerous drivers had paid 750-euro fines—some more than once—for the crime of driving while Gumballing, a euphemism for having stickers on an expensive car.

Several cars were immobilized after their drivers filled them with diesel.

A Saudi-plated, million-dollar, Gemballa-modified Porsche Cayenne turbo—hand-waxed by a team of four the night before departure—had broken down.

So had a million-dollar red Ferrari Enzo, as if that were a surprise.

But one rumor kept me awake.

CHAPTER 18

I Can't Believe the King of Morocco Did That

FRIDAY, MAY 7, 2004
HOTEL MANSOUR EDDHABI MARRAKECH
PARKING LOT/PREDEPARTURE STAGING
GUMBALL + 3
0850 HOURS

We were precisely halfway through the 2004 Gumball. King Mohammed VI *had* lifted all speed limits and traffic laws for the 48-hour duration of our visit. We'd arrived in the port of Tangier 17 hours earlier. To my relief, George and Julian chose to escape the RCMP M5's cramped rear for rides in other cars—taking their luggage with them.

Departure was in 10 minutes. I'd warned Jim, our quiet, fortyish, shaggy long-haired English TV cameraman of the day, not to be late.

"Alex, *tell* me you fixed the GPS."

"It wasn't broken," I said. "I'd loaded the wrong map set."

We were in approximately thirtieth position. *Kenworthy was farther up. So was Torquenstein.* Today was the day I caught them.

"Here comes Jim," said Kinsley, "*right* on time."

HIGHWAY P24
NORTHEAST SUBURBS OF MARRAKECH
282 MILES TO FEZ CHECKPOINT

"Livestock ahead!" Kinsley screamed.

I veered left into oncoming traffic—narrowly missing the donkey-driven vegetable cart—then jerked the wheel right *just* before colliding head-on with a horse-drawn cart.

"Jesus!" I yelled. I wiped my brow with the sleeve of my blue NYPD uniform shirt. *"That,"* I exhaled, "was the closest one yet. I can't believe no one's hit an animal."

"Yet! Look, *there* they are!" Kinsley pointed at the Gumballers ahead, fighting through traffic like snakes surging through a pipe. I downshifted to third, lunging forward and around a dense group of donkeys, horses, bicycles, mopeds, motorcycles, stray dogs, and commuters in dusty hatchbacks.

A trio of mustached Moroccan police—all in pressed royal-blue uniforms, double-breasted jackets, light blue shirts, black ties, shiny boots, bright white belts, shoulder straps, and hats—enthusiastically waved us on.

I was driving 74 mph in a densely populated urban area. Legally.

We were moving up the grid.

Kinsley leaned right in her seat. "Traffic circle ahead!"

77

"Keep those warnings coming! We don't need a North African *Bonfire of the Vanities*!"

HIGHWAY P24
APPROXIMATELY 100 MILES NORTHEAST OF MARRAKECH
LATE MORNING

The convoy's tight columns uncoiled, lunging and fighting two and sometimes three cars abreast—one column against thankfully infrequent oncoming traffic, forcing locals onto the left shoulder, the other onto the right shoulder when debris didn't force quick reentry into the one legal lane.

"More livestock ahead!" Kinsley yelled.

121

We exchanged waves with a Moroccan farmer cradling a small dog in one arm.

A pair of gray-clad Moroccan police stood back from the right shoulder, repeatedly thrusting their long white traffic gloves toward the horizon.

Toward Fez.

The Gumballers ahead accelerated as traffic thinned, yellow fields stretching far off to both sides.

125

"Wow," I said, "these guys are really booting."

"You gonna stay with them?"

"Sure."

We'd moved far up the grid, but Kenworthy and Torquenstein were still ahead.

129

"Watch out," said Kinsley, "left, on the left!"

Jim's long, black hair, and pale arm loomed large in my left rearview mirror—he was hanging out the window, shooting the black 360 Spyder one car length behind us in the left lane, poised to pass.

Suddenly a car appeared to the 360's left—on the *LEFT* shoulder—passed the 360, and veered right toward us, still accelerating, turning in too tightly, the car beginning to spin—

"Kinsley! Hang on!"

—Just *6 feet ahead of us,* flashing past our front bumper at a 90-degree angle before it rolled into the field to our right.

"Oh my God," said Kinsley, looking back at the long geyser of smoke and dust.

I pulled over on the right shoulder, a long line of Gumballers stopping behind me, and we ran to where the car had come to rest.

Gumball no. 57, the white-and-orange-striped Reyland Cosworth—a highly modified, race-prepared, 700-horsepower, 194 mph–capable Ford Escort with a roll cage—lay on its side, several hundred feet off the road, luggage and debris strewn in long colorful ellipses across the field. The Cosworth was the only *pure* race car on Gumball. Its crew even wore track-grade neck-protection devices—which might have been why this hadn't been the first time I'd seen them make a risky pass like this. I'd tried to give them a wide berth anytime they came close.

Dozens of Gumballers surrounded the car as we approached. The Moroccan police arrived within minutes.

There was nothing for us to do. We stood among a crowd of silent Gumballers watching emergency personnel tend to the copilot lying prone, blood streaming from his nose. According to the police, he'd been unbelted and thrown from the car. He'd apparently suffered no more than a bloody nose and one or more broken ribs.

The driver, a lanky Englishman with a single line of blood running down his pale, shaved head, stalked the scene, ensuring no one stole any of their personal items lying in the field.

I knew it had been his fault. As far as I knew, this was the first-ever major accident on Gumball, and although I was relieved their injuries weren't serious, *everyone* was lucky to see them out of the rally. He'd almost killed us.

I held Kinsley close. "We'll take it easy from here on."

We joined a long slow line of Gumballers pulling away from the accident. Laggards who came up quickly upon the accident slowed, then joined our pensive convoy. No one needed to explain.

HIGHWAY P24 NORTHBOUND
MIDDAY

"Kinsley, any idea where we are?"

The road gently dipped as if on its hind legs, then lifted its neck, its spine curving upward into the Atlas Mountains, the asphalt rising and curling around its golden cliffs—their rare split unveiling dark green patchworks planted in the yellow desert, far below.

"Look who it is!" Two black coupes—a Bentley GT and a BMW 850— sat parked side by side. "We *have* to stop," said Kinsley, "and take a picture."

The GT-Car no. 09 . . . belonged to well-known veteran Michael Ross.

The 850 belonged to Mark Quinn, a gentleman Gumballer of the highest order, a veteran of 2003 I'd chatted with but overlooked in my pursuit of Kenworthy and Rawlings. Quinn was a handsome, understated, fiftyish London real-estate developer who, had he not been so quick to flash a childlike grin, resembled James Mason at his peak.

They waved as we skidded to a dusty halt.

"Mr. Quinn," I said, "it's good to see you safe."

"And *you*, Mr. Roy, and you."

"You know," I announced to all, "I still can't believe the king of Morocco—"

"I know," said Ross, "but maybe you should take a moment."

Quinn nodded, looking out from our perch. Kinsley wiped her nose and inhaled the crisp, cool, fresh mountain air.

We stood and looked out over the green, gold, and blue horizon, grateful for our first-ever quiet, motionless minutes together.

HIGHWAY P24 NORTHBOUND
APPROACHING KHENIFRA
APPROXIMATELY 100 MILES TO FEZ CHECKPOINT
EARLY AFTERNOON

134

Kinsley sighed. "Guess you got over that accident."

"Too fast? I can slow down."

"The road's decent . . . be my guest."

My phone rang. It was Julie, Max's wife, Gumball's Number Two.

"Alex, Alex!" she yelled from a windy convertible. *"Can you hear me?"*

"Barely! Julie, I tried to call you! There's been another accid—"

"I know about the Porsche!"

"Kinsley"—I cupped my hand over my phone—"did anyone call you about a Porsche crash?" She shook her head and shrugged.

"Julie, no! A red 360 hit a tractor and—"

"Alex! Listen! No more speeding! We're kicking people off who speed—"

Then the signal cut out.

HIGHWAY P1 EASTBOUND
135 MILES EAST OF FEZ
APPROXIMATELY 65 MILES FROM NADOR PORT FERRY
LATE AFTERNOON

A red speck appeared in my rearview mirror.

"Kinsley, when we left Fez, how close was Torquenstein to being ready to go?"

149

"Omigod, did you *see* him standing on top of his car, throwing stickers at the people until the cops arrived?"

"No, but it sounds like a classic Torquenstein move. Did he look ready to go?"

"No," said Kinsley, "but I think I saw him eating lunch when we arrived."

"Holy shit!" I yelled. "You *saw* him with his mask off?"

"I didn't see *him,* but I saw his wife and some people wearing those Torquenstein shirts, at a table . . . near the bazaar."

"Wait, was his mask on the table? He must have been one of them! What did he look like?"

"Sorry, Alex, I didn't know it was that important to you."

I hadn't seen Torquenstein at the Cosworth accident, which meant he'd been ahead, maybe even running with Kenworthy . . . but Kinsley saw him in Fez, which meant that even once we'd slowed *after* the accidents, *I'd almost caught up with him in Fez,* which meant we'd been making *great* time, despite the accidents.

I shouldn't be proud of this.

Red speck closing the gap, quickly.

135

An unidentifiable animal darted across the road.

"I'm slowing, Kinsley, the road's starting to suck anyway."

120

"Those lights." She pointed. "Is that a gas station?"

"I don't know . . . we're really low now. Not enough to get us to the ferry in Nador. If we miss it, we're out of Gumball."

I slowed to enter the station.

Red speck approaching fast.

If Torquenstein was back there, I was seconds from losing the enormous lead I thought I'd had. I checked the mirror one last time before turning into the station.

Torquenstein's red Viper roared past—a second's rush of wind kicking up prior customers' gas receipts—and disappeared over the hill.

LOCAL ROAD 19 NORTHBOUND
40 MILES FROM NADOR PORT FERRY

"Kinsley . . . I see a lot of people up ahead." The sun had just disappeared behind the mountains.

"Oh, please no," she said.

Someone in a black Gumball jumpsuit stood atop a small rise a hundred feet from the left shoulder, a crowd of locals gathered beneath him. A truck had stopped on the right, as had a police car and official-looking white van.

I stopped, got out, and approached one of the Moroccan bystanders.

"Who was it?" The man shrugged. "The driver! Where is the driver?"

"The driver?" he said in French-accented English. "The driver is dead or in jail."

I stood on the median stripes, paralyzed, at the exact point where the car had left the road. Then I walked the car's path. The tire treads pointed diagonally left off the road and into the dirt, debris scattered along a pair of long shallow trenches leading several hundred feet up the low rise.

A gray-clad police officer approached. *"Monsieur!"* he said sternly. *"Vous parlez français?"*

"Oui," I said sheepishly, *"mais—"*

Someone had been killed. I knew it. I felt it as I had the morning almost exactly three years earlier, when I stood in the shower longer than I ever had—ignoring the ringing phone until emerging naked to answer the fifth call—and was told my father was dead.

"*Oui,*" I said to the officer in uncharacteristically faltering French, "*je parle français . . . mais . . . j'ai oublié comment . . .* I've . . . just forgotten   "

The officer looked at me, clearly a New York City police officer, on vacation. In uniform.

"You are American?" he said in excellent English.

"Er . . . yes?"

"Allahu Akbar, we could use your expertise, monsieur," he said. "Do you know the men in this car?"

I peered over his shoulder at a single large piece of red debris lying halfway toward the wreck. The crowd separated. I spotted the front half of a red Viper.

I'd caught up with Torquenstein.

MONDAY, MAY 10, 2004
CARLTON INTERCONTINENTAL HOTEL BANQUET HALL
CANNES
GUMBALL FINISH PARTY

"And this year's winners of the Gumball Spirit Trophy are—"

Gary Lutke and John Docherty—the crew of Gumball no. 112, the "General Lee"–liveried vintage orange Citroën 2CV, possibly the cheapest, oldest car in the rally—won, and they deserved it. Although their car's maximum speed was 72 mph and the engine rattled like a loose chain saw in a metal box, they completed the route with no tickets, no accidents, and no complaints.

Adrian Brody, who in his white Porsche turbo had briefly fallen for my Blue Light Special in Spain, claimed "victory" after leaving Barcelona early to guarantee his first-place arrival before the film-festival crowds.

Kim Schmitz, after taking a shortcut *through* a crowd of pedestrians on the Cannes boardwalk, also claimed "victory."

Kenworthy, who *had* led in first-place stage finishes, was in jail, but expected to be released within 48 hours.

Team Polizei received the Gumball Style Trophy.

Despite the rumors of his death, despite the chase-car video showing his tire blowout and three midair flips, Torquenstein was alive.

I'd forged a new and potentially important friendship with Ross. I was tired, and unsure if I'd ever hear from The Driver unless and until I made a spectacular display of competitive aggression. But that would have to wait another year.

Someone tapped my shoulder from behind. "Excuse me . . . Alex?"

I turned and faced a short, boyish-faced Gumballer roughly my age, tired but friendly eyes peering out from the bandage around the top of his head, around his neck a white makeshift sling in which one arm rested, a dangling hand holding the sunglasses he'd just removed.

"Hi." I paused. "Wait . . . Torquen—?"

"Hey," he said quietly, "I'm Jerry."

CHAPTER 19

The Bed of My Enemy's Avalanche

FRIDAY, MAY 14, 2004
NEW YORK CITY

"Alex, Rawlings is definitely coming."

It was Handsome Dave, aka David Green, now cofounder of the Bullrun, a six-day rally from L.A. to Miami. I *wanted* to enter, but the cost, logistics, and stress of doing two rallies in one summer had seemed impossible until—

"*Rawlings,* Alex—"

"Tell him *I'm* coming. *Tell* him."

"Kinsley, are you sure you won't lose your job for this?"

She didn't answer.

Her employer, the Ritz-Carlton Marina Del Ray, offered a near-perfect solution. Guests who booked a suite received a complimentary courtesy car during their stay, specifically a Mercedes E, S, or SL500. All were five-liter, V8-engined, which would be perfect, and although the $90,000 SL was but a two-seater, I *could* make the sacrifice. Suites' daily rates began at $550, *far* below the cost of actually renting an E, S or SL500 for the same period.

My perusal of the hotel's courtesy-car contract made it clear neither the Ritz-Carlton Corporation nor Mercedes-Benz had ever dealt with the likes of Team Polizei, or the document would have included mileage restrictions, *and* it would have specified *to which* Ritz-Carlton the car had to be returned.

Marina Del Ray was half an hour from the Bullrun start line, in Hollywood. The Ritz-Carlton in Miami Beach, was 3,000 miles away. Bellhop jackets wouldn't be a problem.

"The Ritz Merc is a terrible idea," said Vegas "Matchmaker to the Stars" Mike. Mike had a heart condition, and although we'd only convoyed together briefly on the 2003 Gumball, as soon as I heard he'd checked into a Miami hospital the day after the finish, I got his number from Maximillion.

"I don't forget things like that, Alex. Things like that make it clear who your friends are. I tell you what, why don't you fly here, pick out one of my cars, and take that on Bullrun."

"*Here* where?"

"Vegas," said Vegas Mike. "Trust me, I've got something you'll like."

"Mike—"

"Call me Jesse."

SATURDAY, JUNE 5, 2004
HOLLYWOOD, CALIFORNIA
MANN'S CHINESE THEATRE
BULLRUN START LINE

"Herr Roy!" said my *Neue Master Co-Piloten* Nicholas Frankl, Three-Time Gumball veteran and 2002 Gumball Spirit Trophy Winner, Three-Time Hungarian Olympic Team Bobsledder, automotive journalist, semiprofessional race-car driver, man-about-L.A., and son of Andrew Frankl. Frankl senior was founder of *Car* magazine and, according to Brock Yates's memoir *Cannonball!*, veteran of the last Cannonball Run in 1979. Nicholas and I briefly met on the 2003 Gumball, again at the 2003 Gumball L.A. movie premiere, and again at the end of the 2004 Gumball in Cannes.

Nicholas's skills and pedigree made him *precisely* the type of recruit I'd pick were I The Driver. Frankl or his father might *already* know him, which is why Nicholas *didn't* Gumball the way I did—he considered it a vacation.

This chapter of my quest would have two prongs—beat Rawlings, and earn Frankl's respect. I needed to succeed at only one and my phone would ring. I was sure of it. It might even be Frankl himself, or his father. Twenty-five years had passed since the last Cannonball, and it would make perfect sense if a secret successor race stayed in the family.

"Herr Roy! Come now for a first-stage strategy discussion now, *bitte*!"

Frankl's staccato speech was normally delivered in a confidence-inspiring English accent, but wouldn't for the next six days.

"Herr Frankl, you would like zee first leg?"

"*Ja*, I vill use zee geography learned from lifing heeeer, *Herr Kapitaaaan!*"

Frankl and I settled into Vegas Mike's/Jesse's brand-new, $150,000, obsidian-black, Renntech-modified, twin-turbocharged, 612-horsepower, 197-mph-capable Mercedes-Benz *StuttgartAutobahnVerfolgungGeschutzActhung-Polizei* CL600. The dashboard was a mass of black plastic centipedes intertwined, Velcroed, cable-tied, and taped down to the black and gray leather. Mike had insisted I leave *everything,* including stickers, in and on the car when I returned it.

Any damage was my responsibility.

"Herr Roy! I still can't believe you haf installed all of zee equipment from zee M5 in our new Interzeptor!"

"It vas most difficult, Herr Master Co-piloten, but it is a big battle coming, no?" I didn't know how much longer I could keep talking like this.

"*Ja!*" Frankl laughed, drying the tears running down his face. "Herr *Rowwwwlings* does not look very confident!"

"*Nein!*" I burst into laughter. "Rowwwwlings is *nicht macht* happy *mit* Team Polizei!" We'd brought a box of tissues for just this eventuality, one-quarter of them already damp and crumpled in both sides' door pockets.

"Frankl," I said, trying to calm down, "can we speak English for just one minute?" He nodded, his chest heaving. "Frankl . . . Krispy Kreme's sponsoring Bullrun . . . and donuts are the international gift of Polizei friendship—"

"Roy, don't say another word."

With one of the rear seats designated for Ollie, our TV cameraman, and the other for Helga the Au Pair Love Sexy Inflatable Sex Doll, there wasn't much room for the seven boxes of Krispy Kremes we needed in case of a police traffic stop.

"I think der Krispy Kremes vill be fine in her lapppp, Herr Kapitaaan!"

I adjusted my uniform in the CL600's window—a white summer Polizei shirt with rank chevrons, Team 144 badge, and nameplate, useless but cool-looking blue-tinted bubble goggles dangling from my neck, black police pants with blue highway-patrol stripes, NYPD-issue black leather motorcycle boots and duty belt, and a Motorola belt radio with coiled-wire handset clipped to my left shoulder.

"Frankl," I said, "it's time to talk nav."

Rawlings was parked at the very front of the hundred-odd Bullrun grid, arrayed three lanes abreast on Hollywood Boulevard, thick crowds of fans packing the sidewalks to both sides. The Polizei CL was two cars behind him. Paris Hilton sat on the bed of my enemy's Avalanche, posing for photographers until Handsome Dave handed her the Bullrun start flag.

"Systems check?" said Frankl.

"*Eine* moment," I said, restarting both Garmin 2760 GPSs, the Uniden BC520XL CB, V1, Escort ZR3 laser jammers, the as-yet-untested Uniden BC796D scanner, and both backup cell phones. "*Alles gut,* Herr Frankl."

Paris dropped the flag.

PAHRUMP RACEWAY
BULLRUN LUNCH CHECKPOINT
PAHRUMP, NEVADA
58 MILES TO LAS VEGAS CHECKPOINT

"*Herr Roy! Herr Rowwlings* did not look pleased mit our *First Place Position!*"

"No," I said as Rawlings drove away, "he didn't."

"You see, Roy? Rawlings is totally beatable. Now can we eat and celebrate our *vikktoreee?* By the way, your driving is not as bad as I thought . . . perhaps with some practice you might be mediocre!"

"*Danke schön,* Herr Frankl."

"*Now* that we've beaten your little nemesis in a proper race, can we put on some fucking music in the car?"

"Only if it's clear to him we're *not* racing that day, or we'll never hear the scanner."

"*You* figure it out and let me know the rules of your funny little competition. Just remember that you can win whenever you feel like it, *if* you're focused, *if* you're prepared, *if* you don't make mistakes, my *Kapi-taaaaan!*
"Maybe if you're nice I'll take you out on the track sometime."

"Just not in Mike's car."

"The CL's not appropriate. *That's* what all those Ferrari lawn mowers and washing machines are built for, *Herr Roy!*"

Frankl stepped into the lunch tent while I watched Rawlings's Avalanche disappear in a dusty haze. The Vegas overnight checkpoint was 40 minutes away. After our treacherous, police-infested, 270-mile desert run from Los Angeles, if he wanted to take his route card, skip lunch, immediately turn around, and race to claim the day's second, less meaningful checkpoint, he could have it. He knew what it meant. He knew the difference. He and I had never discussed rules.

We didn't have to.

U.S. ROUTE 93 SOUTHBOUND

40 MILES SOUTH OF THE HOOVER DAM

"Herr Kapitan, I respect your desire to impress me with your driving skill, but driving a hundred sixty miles per hour is not the way to do it."

"No?"

"Anyone can drive *this* car *this* fast in a straight line on a perfectly flat desert road. You could drive 200 and I would still think you're terrible. Of course, this is only possible for a long duration because of your expert programming of the scanner, and for that I *do* commend you."

"Thank you."

165

"Roy, seriously, we could catch up with Rawlings easily if we maintained a steady one-thirty."

"So, Roy, you're telling me that based on what we've heard, you're *quite* certain that there are no more police cars between us and Kingman. It's a notoriously bad place to speed, you know."

"Trust me. Why don't you call the guys behind us and tell them it's clear up to where we are?"

"*Dummkopf! You* forgot I did that five minutes ago? They're not far behind us, and almost got caught by a cop *you* didn't pick up on the scanner!"

"Frankl, I *promise* you the scanner works. Here, I'll reset it."

I let off the gas, leaned forward to double-check the scanner settings, disabled and reenabled the Arizona police-frequency channel bank—

158

BRAAAAAAAAAAAAAAAAAAAAAAAAAAAAAAAAAAAAA

—and shot past a police car hiding behind a bush in the median.

"Good job, Roy. Now you better hope he's more interested in the bright red Ferrari behind us than our Polizei Interzeptor."

Distant, tiny police lights flashed in the rearview mirror. "We're toast, Frankl, I'm sorry."

"*You're* toast, moron, for relying on this scanner more than your eyes."

"Frankl, the next exit is too far for us to make a run for it. Do you think I should be respectful and just pull over and wait?"

"That's *two* mistakes, Roy, because if you even wanted the option to make a run for it, you shouldn't have slowed from 160 to 90. Do you think he possibly could have caught up with us? And if this fancy scanner worked as well as *you* said, you could have run for it and known if there were any more cops ahead!"

I shook my head. "Too late now, here he comes."

"He's pulling us over, but it looks like we have more lights than he does!"

I pointed at the green/green dash-top flasher unit. "Pull *that* one down, now!" I slowed and stopped onto the right shoulder.

"Roy, be polite, it usually works, and don't laugh."

"I won't laugh if you won't. Leave the scanner on until he gets out . . . I wanna hear what he says about us. And pull out the car documents."

"You mean the ones I put in the air-conditioned center armrest along with these nice chocolate bars and Red Bull? Better drink it now, honey, so you'll have energy to fight off your new boyfriend in jail tonight."

The scanner lit up.

AZ DPS MOB B: *"Thirty-three southbound . . . got a black Mercedes, see the word* Bullrun—*"*

"He's running our plates," said Frankl.

AZ DPS MOB B: *"Boy, Union, Lincoln, Robert, Nora—"*

"So," said Ollie, who rarely spoke, "tell our viewers what the tactic is now."

Frankl turned to the camera. "The tactic is *Herr Roy vill be punished for this crimes!*"

The officer got out of his car. "Frankl, here's my emergency bail money. You *will* get me out, right?"

"Yes, Captain, even *I* would miss the likes of you."

"Hey, Officer?" I said from the backseat of the Arizona Department of Public Safety cruiser in which I sat uncomfortably cuffed, hands behind my back. "Do you think I'll spend the night in jail? I've never spent the night before."

"Maybe," he said, smiling at me in the rearview mirror, "but you won't be lonely . . . we just pulled over your buddies in that red Ferrari and a BMW back there."

Macari and McCloud. I was moving up in the world.

THURSDAY, JUNE 10, 2004
U.S. ROUTE 19 SOUTHBOUND
VICINITY OF PERRY, FLORIDA
185 MILES TO TAMPA CHECKPOINT
BULLRUN + 5

"Don't play stupid, Roy, you're only curious because you want to know more about Cannonball, and you think that because you're getting a little superficial fame for being good at rallying, you know anything about what it's like to Cannonball. Let me tell you, all this fun we're having racing around in police uniforms, driving for 6 or 7 hours then having a nice dinner and going to a party . . . Gumball, Bullrun, these are *nothing* like the original Cannonball. Rallies are supposed to be *fun,* that's why people pay all this money. How many of these guys can you see driving cross-country nonstop for 35, 40 hours? They'd be crying after hour 10! Crying! Think about it, here we are, driving around with stickers all over our car calling attention to ourselves even when we're getting gas. We get to sleep every night for at least a couple of hours while the police look on the Internet and plan how to stop us the next day, and we play these little games with the scanner and CB.

"Roy, you and Rawlings are the only ones so serious about it. I really enjoy our *Polizei Stra-teg-eez,* but I have a mind to turn off the scanner and turn on the radio. I had quite good fun rallying before I met you, you know, and I never had any of this stuff."

"What about your dad?" I asked, pausing before the question I'd waited on all week. "The Yates book said he did the '79 Cannonball, but what about after? There had to be guys who wanted to keep racing."

"You read the book, Roy, . . . there was too much publicity, it became impossible to continue Cannonball with all the press tipping off the authorities to the start. Think about it . . . if the police know where and when everyone is leaving and there are only a few possible routes to Los Angeles, the whole thing is pointless. It was no longer underground, so they stopped it."

"Surely, Frankl, there *had* to be Cannonballers who wanted to go out again. But if there was a race like that, a *real* race, totally secret, would you go?"

"*Of course* I would go, but only with a few people I trust so it won't get all fucked by some *idiotem.* If you knew how to drive, then we could start something."

"What about Rawlings . . . and Collins?"

"If Rawlings could keep quiet about it, sure. You could invite Collins, too, if you trust him."

"I do."

"Well, get cracking, *Mein Kapi-taaan*! Let me know when you've got it all set up!"

"Frankl, how'd your dad do in '79?"

"He came in last."

FRIDAY, JUNE 11, 2004
SEBRING INTERNATIONAL RACEWAY
LUNCH CHECKPOINT
171 MILES TO MIAMI FINISH LINE
FINAL DAY BULLRUN 2004

"Kicked yo' *ass* again, Mr. Pol-eez-eye! What's your excuse this time?"

Rawlings—having stood to get the attention of the hundred-plus Bull-runners eating barbecue trackside while waiting to take their cars out—sat down in a flurry of high fives to finish his burger.

I ignored those staring and pointing at me as I approached his table, pulled up a plastic chair, sat beside him, and explained.

How our car had been sabotaged. How the air had been let out of our tires. Again.

"Wait," said Rawlings, "you're not making this shit up?"

"Look at my face."

"I can see you're upset, but we're all friends here, but, man . . . I'd be *mighty* pissed off if somebody laid a finger on my truck!"

"I know, I know."

"Well, you woulda have to have beaten me here *and* Miami to win it for the Pol-eez-eye. I reckon best you coulda done was tie with me, so let's just shake hands and call it."

"You're a good man, Richard."

"*Richard?* Hell! You never call me that! We must be getting too friendly. Better not let anyone see us talkin' too long." I stood up. "Don't worry, Alex, we'll find out who did it, and I'll even help y'all kick his ass!"

"Thanks, man. I'm gonna go watch Frankl do his thing."

"Now excuse me while I finish my burger, I gotta do an interview after where I tell 'em how much y'all suck!"

"Fear not, *Herrr Rowwwwlings*! I shall have my vengeance next year!"

"Hey, Alex." It was Vegas Mike, still not entirely recovered from food poisoning that had plagued him all week. "I heard what happened. Good thing you checked the tires, or you, my rims, *and* the CL would have been toast."

I nodded. He patted me on the back.

"Why don't you take out the CL? It'll cheer you up some more . . . when you're done, I'll let you take out the Murcie."

Oh my God.

As lucky as I was to be able to afford to enter *this,* my third rally in two years, as lucky as I'd been to have Mike lend me a $150,000 car on a handshake, the mere possibility of driving a $300,000 Lamborghini Murcielago *on a track*—in its domain—had seemed inconceivable.

"Mike . . . you'll let me . . . take your Lamborghini on the track?"

"Alex, I totally trust you, but there's one catch."

"Don't go over 100?"

"You *better* go over a hundred, because I told that girl back there you're my personal, ex-military, professional high-speed escape and evasion driver, and that you'd take her for a ride . . . you know, since I'm not feeling well."

He waved at a slender, tan five-foot nine-inch brunette—her flat stomach exposed between a tight white baby T and black low-riding sweatpants—who smiled and waved back.

"Alex, Michelle over there *really* wants a ride."

I wasn't a race-car driver, nor had I ever claimed to be. All I was, and had ever expected to be, was a long-distance endurance driver. *That* was what I'd prepared for since my father first spoke of Cannonball, The Driver, and the Wall—the unbroken 32-hour barrier between New York and Los Angeles. Gumball and Bullrun were my research, school, proving grounds, and—I was increasingly convinced—recruiting grounds for The Driver and his associates. Everything I'd done, bought, tested, and learned in 9,000-plus miles of rally driving had been in *that* context, toward *one* goal.

Find The Driver. Climb the Wall. Break 32 hours.

I considered myself a pretty good semiprofessional driver, a B- looking to move up at least one increment per rally. I knew I was too cautious, too scared. Driving well required practice. Driving fast required discipline. Driving fast and well required instincts I needed to hone.

The 6.2-liter, 12-cylinder, 580-horsepower Lamborghini engine roared behind us like a pack of caged lions peering at a pile of raw meat just beyond their reach. Its acceleration pressed my lovely passenger and me back in our seats, squeezing high-pitched squeals from her. Comically wide tires gripped through turns that would have spun or flipped my M5. The Audi-derived four-wheel-drive system allowed me to take turns far faster than I thought possible. I gained confidence and completed yet another, faster lap, until I entered the first turn at 130 mph, spun, and hit the wall.

CHAPTER 20

Whatever It Costs

My quest—having once merely chipped at my dwindling (and not so great) fortune—had become a wrecking ball. If only I gave up my ludicrous quest, then normal life—alien to me since the morning of my father's death—could resume. I returned to Europe By Car for the first time in a month, and with teary eyes Alfred lifted me off the ground in a first-ever-between-us bear hug. The entire staff made a point of saying how glad they were to see me safe, although Genia, my ever tough-loving godmother scolded me in heavily Russian-accented English for being *stupidstupid,* then hugged me as if I'd never left.

Perhaps my quest *was* over. The Driver would never call now, and I had a $30,000 debt to pay.

"I'm delighted hear from you, *Mein Kapitan,* but you better not ask me to help cover the Lambo damage."

"No, Frankl."

"So how much do Murcielago front ends cost these days?"

After trading friendly insults, Frankl surprised me when he said, "Now go dig into your Polizei gadget budget and find a way to pay our friend in Vegas. I *do* admire you for being a man about it. A lot of people would have tried to weasel out of it. You're almost a grown-up, which is quite rare these days!"

"You told him *what*?!?!?"

The Weis, now expecting a son, was the last person I wanted to tell. "The Weis . . . I . . . I told Mike I'd pay, whatever it costs."

"You're not crazy, you're stupid. Just plain stupid. Did you sign anything?"

"I gave him my word."

"Oooooooooh, Aliray's word counts for something now?"

"I hate you."

"I hate you, too. How much do you owe this . . ."

"Mike," I said. "The Weis, I've got thirty thousand reasons not to tell you."

"Holy shit! Thirty Gs . . . wait . . . that car runs about two seventy-five. You know something, you might actually be the luckiest idiot in the world, since it *was* your fault. Poor Aliray, there goes your 2005 rally budget. Maybe it's a reality check. You're thirty-two now, you're not a kid. Wake up and think about what you're doing with your life."

Maybe he was right.

Handsome Dave called a few days later.

"Roy! How are you, mate? Gotta get back on your feet, man! The world's best race drivers have all had a few spills."

"But they didn't have to pay for the damages."

"I'm sure a guy like you has some tricks up your sleeve."

"Why are we talking?"

"We're planning another Bullrun—"

"That's like asking a one-legged solider to get back in the trench."

"—in September, London to Ibiza. Three days, a perfect little trip. Bring the M5."

"It's not going to happen. I can't ship the M5 in time, and I can't afford to ship the M5 in time. I need some rest."

"All right, Alex, but it won't be the same without you. Malmstrom is coming—"

"I can't." *Malmstrom.* But there was no way.

"Very well. I'm calling Jesse next. I'll let you know if he's in a better mood."

My phone rang again fifteen minutes later. "Hey, Alex," said Jesse/Vegas Mike, an anvil suddenly chained to the phone I struggled to hold against my ear.

"Jesse, man, long time no speak, I've been waiting to hear from you."

"You got five minutes?

"For you? Of course. I'm ready for the address, and I'll FedEx the check today."

"That's exactly what I wanted to talk about. You see, Alex, I like you. I've noticed something really interesting about you. You *always* answer the phone, even from restricted numbers. When you're involved in nightlife in Vegas, people *always* want something. People *always* answer the phone when they want something, but they *never* answer the phone when *you* need something. People who always answer the phone have nothing to hide. That's how you know who your friends are. After you crashed the Lambo, the first words out of your mouth were 'I'll pay for it, whatever it costs.' That meant a lot, and now you're answering the phone. I know you saw my name on the caller ID. That means you're my friend. I don't gamble money, I gamble on people, and I was right about you.

"So, Alex, here's what I'm saying. We both agree you owe me this money, and we both know the damage is about thirty grand. Thirty grand might mean shit to a lot of these rally guys, but I know it's a lot of money for Alex Roy. So I'm gonna make you an offer.

"Because I consider you a good friend, I'm gonna put the accident on my insurance, and all you have to cover is the deductible. I'm gonna give you four conditions, and if you break them, I won't be mad, I'll be hurt, and you can't imagine how I'd take that. First, if anyone ever asks about what happened between us, you tell them. Any asshole who comes along and says I screwed you, you tell them the truth. We're friends, and friends don't screw each other. Second, after you put that check in the mail, I never want you to bring it up again. We'll never stay friends if you're always feeling guilty about me going easy on you and I don't want that. Third is I want you to get back out there and drive again. Everyone loves the German police shtick, and it wouldn't be the same next year without you. I'll even lend you the CL again. Fourth is that I want you to be my copilot on the Bullrun Ibiza in September. I'll pay for it, whatever it costs."

A few days later, while surfing the rally forums at work, I saw a post directing people to a new discussion thread:

GUMBALLING OLD SCHOOL—These Gumballers aren't so tough . . . check out the trailer for this doc about the real guys back in the day: www. 32hours7minutes.com.

I clicked on the link. A rapid montage began, CB-radio chatter over vintage in-car film footage. *"Hey, you westbounders up there, I've got a sports car coming—"*

Then two seconds of black-and-white aerial footage of a car on a highway.

"—doing about 95 miles an hour!"

Four numbers flashed on-screen: *1983.*

Then a bearded man in his fifties, interviewed quite recently, said, *"We were able to cross the country in as many hours as our pioneer forefathers had taken in weeks."*

Then another graphic. *2,874 miles.*

Then Bobby Unser, the retired racing champion, appeared and said, *"To go from New York to California in 32 hours? It's unbelievable."*

I sat paralyzed until the trailer ended.

A secret race in 1983? Thirty-two hours, 7 minutes? My quest was not nearly over.

Googling director Cory Welles returned nothing. I e-mailed him asking when the film would come out, then left my office without saying good-bye. I walked home in a daze. I began logging the 70 hours of in-car video I'd taken in the prior fifteen months. I had more to learn before I drove again.

Cory e-mailed me a few days later. He was two years into compiling historical footage and interviews with the drivers, and needed money to complete the film. I asked for the prospectus, which arrived by FedEx the next morning. I ignored the thick legal documents, and began reading two items more valuable to me than a winning lottery ticket. The one-page plot summary read:

> October 15, 1983. The sun is setting, the gas is topped, and it's time for one last run in the most outrageous road race in American history. Formerly the Cannonball Run, the U.S. Express gathers the best of the best, to speed nonstop from New York to Los Angeles, in a race where the only rule is there are no rules. These real-life, 32-hour outlaws drive over the limit and under the radar with one thing in their sights: becoming the fastest humans to ever cross the continent. Irreverent and gripping, this feature documentary chronicles the last great American outlaw race.

There was a photocopy of a twenty-one-year-old newspaper clipping showing two men, Doug Turner and David Diem, trophy in hand, standing in front of a Ferrari 308, *winners of the 1983 U.S. Express . . . new world record . . . 32 hours, 7 minutes.*

There was only one way to learn more before the film came out. I e-mailed Cory asking to meet in person as soon as possible. I was ready to underwrite the film's completion, whatever the cost. We set a meeting for September 18, twenty-four hours before I would leave for London to face Malmstrom.

Six weeks earlier I'd faced catastrophe.

I didn't believe in coincidence or divine intervention, but once again it seemed the stars had aligned in my favor, the sky clear of portents, until Vegas Mike called on September 2 to say he couldn't make it . . . because of his heart condition.

CHAPTER 21

Cory Welles's name flashed on my caller ID, the number preprogrammed in anticipation of his arrival from L.A. that afternoon and our first, casual meeting that night at a local lounge.

"Hey!" said a young female voice.

"Who's this?"

"It's Cory! Who else would it be?"

Cory's . . . a . . . woman.

I didn't know why I was surprised. Strangely, irrationally perhaps, in the haze through which my quest advanced, I figured Cory Welles—the person who might hold the key to The Driver—passionate about cars and the history of such races, willing even to lose money on a project dear to his heart, had to be a *man.*

"Alex, you were expecting a guy?"

"To be honest, yes. I'm really sorry."

"This always happens. Where we meeting up?"

"I'll text you the bar's address. How will I recognize you?"

"Don't worry, I'll recognize you. If not, I'll be the hot one."

She stopped me *after* I'd walked past her and doubled back.

Cory Welles was thirty years old, stood five-foot-two, had a Farrah Fawcett mane of dirty-blond hair, a passion for yoga, a brown belt in two forms of martial arts I'd never heard of, and no patience for bullshit. She knew one of the drivers who'd set the 32:07 record and who, along with her father and stepfather, had invested her life savings to make this movie.

She was one of the most beautiful and fascinating women I'd ever met.

"Alex, you have no idea how many tough-guy car people e-mail me about this movie. Seriously, everyone and their brother says they've done it, or done better, or come close, or that it's all bullshit."

"Is it?"

"No. I heard the stories growing up. It all sounded so crazy, so one day I asked my stepdad's friend Doug if it was true."

"Who's Doug?"

"Doug Turner. As in Doug Turner and David Diem. They're the ones who set the record."

"Wow," she said, surveying the floor full of electronics I was inventorying before my flight to London. I'd left everything out until the last minute specifically so she would see it *before* I saw any footage. "I didn't know you were that serious about this rally thing."

"I'm one of the few."

"How many other guys are like you? The Gumball site makes it seem like a bunch of guys partying."

"I'd say . . . there're about five or six."

She pondered that for a moment, then set up her DV deck to show me the footage.

"This is really rough," she said. "What you're about to see are interviews with some of the drivers, and some aerial footage. The guy with the beard and glasses is Rick Doherty, he was the organizer."

She hit play, and for the next 20 minutes I memorized every name I heard and saw. I sat in frozen silence when it ended.

"So what do you think?" she said.

"How much money do you need?"

MONDAY, SEPTEMBER 27, 2004
IBIZA, SPAIN

"—and then," I said over the crackling Ibiza–to–Los Angeles connection, "Malmstrom invited me to spend the weekend at his château north of London."

"Hang on," said Cory. "*You* beat a Ferrari F40 halfway across Europe?"

"London to Ibiza."

NEAR THE END. Dad in 1999, one year before he passed away.

MY FIRST CAR WAS A PORSCHE. Mom holds me in the Targa in late 1971.

MY FIRST ACCIDENT AVOIDANCE CLASS. And first tow.

MY FIRST RACE. The instructor has already fled in fear.

THE 356. *I inherited my love of fast cars from Dad, shown here with his Porsche 356 in the late 1950s.*

THE TARGA. *Mom with Dad's Porsche 911 Targa in early 1971. She'd been a stewardess in the swinging sixties.*

THE POLIZEI BMW M5. *The M5's Gumball 3000 debut in 2003 in San Francisco. I'm wearing the vintage 1950s Chaparral racing outfit.*

MY ENEMY'S AVALANCHE. The Chevy Avalanche of fierce competitor Richard Rawlings, sporting twin spare gas cans, parked in front of San Francisco's Fairmont Hotel before the start of Gumball '03.

YEEEEEHAWWWW! Rawlings celebrating Bullrun 2004 victory.

MAHER. Team Polizei copilot, Dave Maher, at the wheel during Gumball '03. Maher was an experienced track racer—I had a lot to learn from him.

HEART ATTACK TIME.
Driving 140 mph with the "tire defect" warning flashing during Gumball '03.

THE HEAD OF THE SNAKE.
As seen in the M5's mirror, McCloud's Ferrari F50 is on the left, Kenworthy's Porsche GT2 on the right.

MEIN GOTT! *We found out from BMW Roadside Assistance in Germany that Reifenpanne was German for tire defect. Proof we didn't imagine it.*

OUT OF GAS. Maher is amazed that Rawlings has left one of his spare jerrycans for us in Florida. Tough competitor—good guy.

GUMBALL! Team Polizei made its mark as Maher and I won the coveted 2003 Spirit of the Gumball Trophy. Note the attractive fake gold Gumball chains given to us upon arrival at the Miami finish line.

TORQUENSTEIN, I PRESUME? With Jerry "Torquenstein" Reynolds and Eric "Dr. Gruene" Ward.

THE MOUNTIES ALWAYS GET THEIR MAN! Amanda Kinsley and I amused the Madrid police during Gumball '04.

OUR EVASION UND ARREST AVOIDANCE STRATEGY IS KAPUT! The Arizona Department of Public Safety demonstrates how real police slap on the iron bracelets during Bullrun USA '04.

GUT CUFFS. Die macht legendary Nicholas Frankl praises the quality of American metallurgy prior to my visit to the inside of the paddy wagon.

VEGAS MIKE. And his yellow Lamborghini Murcielago, prior to my smashing it into the wall at the track during a Bullrun USA '04 pit stop.

"THAT'S MY SON!" Mom cheers Team Polizei at the Gumball '05 start line in London.

ATENCIÓN! *The M5 sporting Spanish Guardia Civil Contra-GumballVenganza Interceptacion livery in London prior to the start of Gumball '05.*

ROSS AND NINE. *Michael Ross and Jon "Nine" Goodrich discuss potential damage to Ross's Bentley after the traffic cone incident during Gumball '05.*

SPENCER. *Spencer Bourne and his Porsche 996 Turbo Race-spec X50.*

SCHTAVEN. *Steve Jennions, kept us up to date on Spencer's every move.*

MORLEY. *Oliver Morley was secretly working with Spencer to beat Team Polizei to Rome.*

SPENCER ON LEFT! *Spencer passes us in heavy traffic on Rome's Circonvallazione Tiburtina.*

FIRST PLACE. *Team Polizei is first to arrive at the Gumball '05 checkpoint in Vienna.*

POLIZEI MAKEOVER. *The last minute selection of Ross's Bentley over the M5 for Gumball '06 meant a quick and dirty installation of the necessary Polizei gear.*

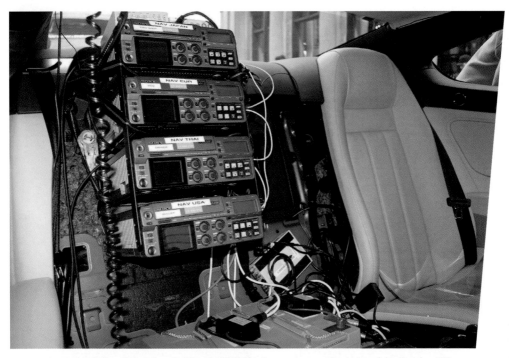

NO ROOM TO SPARE. *Cohosting the Gumball '06 TV show meant trading one of the Bentley GT's rear seats for four professional DV decks . . . and the two extra car batteries required to run them.*

LAST MINUTE PLANNING. *Master pilot Michael Ross and I at the Gumball '06 start line on London's Pall Mall minutes before departure.*

OUT OF TIME. *Maggie and I at the Gumball '06 finish line party at the Playboy Mansion in front of Ross's Bentley.*

MAXIMILLION COOPER. *Gumball 3000's ringleader— with his ubiquitous sunglasses.*

NUMBER 2. *Julie Brangstrup, Max's wife, with Koenigsegg owner, Arthur Chirkinian.*

LONMAN. *Rob "Lonman" Kenworthy— the most respected Gumballer of all time.*

MALMSTROM. *Gumball legend Peter Malmstrom refuels his Ferrari F40 while I shamelessly brag about beating him.*

MACARI AND KIDD. *Joe Macari with supermodel and professional race car driver Jodie Kidd.*

EYHAB. *The ever upbeat Eyhab with friends Rob and Mike.*

THEY WERE GIANTS. *1981 U.S. Express winner Mike Digonis and 1982 U.S. Express driver Steve Stander share their wisdom with Nine and me at New York City's Classic Car Club.*

IF BALLS WERE CASH, SHE'D OWN WALL STREET. *The unstoppable Cory Welles checks the M5's front bumper camera.*

ESCAPE FROM NEW YORK. Another day of staring at Garmin's MapQuest route planning application

SPARE. Rolling the M5's front spare down New York's Astor Place mere hours before the final cross-country run.

HIGH PRESSURE. The enormity of our task finally got to the normally unflappable Maher.

ABOUT TO CROSS THE RUBICON . . . *Or at least the Hudson as I punch out on the time clock.*

POLIZEI AIR. *Pilots Paul "The Weis" Weismann and Keith "The Captain" Baskett.*

CHESS, POLIZEI STYLE. *Hiding from the cops in the shadow of an 18-wheeler in Oklahoma during the final cross-country run.*

WINKING AT THE POLICE. *The M5 (left), with one headlight out, approaches the police cruiser on the Santa Monica Pier, and . . .*

passes by it without any trouble. Incredible.

31:04. *We did it—and I couldn't believe it.*

"Driven by this Malmstrom guy, who's one of the best? And then he forgave you for insulting him and—"

"Invited me to his country house for the weekend."

"And *how* did you beat him?"

"F40s suck in the rain, I sat on his tail all the way through a storm to Paris, and I just happened to know the city a little better, but that's another story."

"Well . . . congratulations," said Cory, with whom sharing details of my first unequivocal victory was but an ulterior motive. "The Express guys are mostly friendly now, even those who haven't seen each other for years. Good to know your guys are the same way. They sure don't look it in the videos online. Thanks for your check, by the way, it really means a lot. You wouldn't believe how many people waste my time just so they can see footage."

"You're welcome. I'm curious. I googled 'U.S. Express' and didn't find anything. I also tried the organizer, Richard Doherty, and Diem and Turner, and there's basically nothing about them anywhere."

"Why do you think I'm making the movie?"

"All right, then, if the race ran from '80 to '83, why did it end? What came after?"

"Nothing. After Diem and Turner set the record and it got in the news, a lot of the guys were freaked out about press. Doherty thought someone else would pick up the reins in '84, but no one did."

"Cory, you say a lot of the Express drivers were former Cannonballers?"

"Doherty was . . . and a couple of others."

"And Brock Yates knew about Doherty organizing this?"

"Yeah, and he tried to stop it."

"And you've interviewed Doherty at least once, recently. Does he know if anyone else tried to organize a similar race . . . later? Recently?"

"Dunno, but he was definitely worried about copycats. Everyone was scared someone would get killed on another race that might let *anyone* in, and then everyone would be screwed."

"What happened to the other events?"

"There was the *Four-ball*, and another one, but none as big as the Express."

I tried to sound nonchalant, but there was no avoiding the question. "So . . . when *can* I see more footage, or at least learn more about the Express, especially since you can't fit everything you've got in 90 minutes, right?"

"Alex"—her voice hardened—"*no one* gets to see anything until I'm done. *No one.* I'll be done when I'm done, and that goes for investors, too."

"Cory . . . I totally understand, and I'm glad my investment's in safe hands. Let me ask you this, then, how long before there's more to see? Three months? Six months?"

"Call it a year. This isn't some street-racing video. If anything changes, I'll let you know."

One year meant . . . September 2005. I couldn't let a year pass without showing the flag.

Unless the phone rang before the January cutoff for the 2005 Gumball, *I'd have to go out again.*

But it didn't. I had to do something spectacular.

Part IV The Golden Age

CHAPTER 22

I Think Those Priests Were Lying

Now one of the world's few four-time rally veterans, I was on the periphery of an even more exclusive group, among whom respect was accorded by a loose set of rules: Leave on time. Push safely. Pass with respect. Help stricken drivers. Finish well.

Although I had abided by all of these, I remained best known merely for my Team Polizei antics. The Polizei/Rawlings war had unfolded out of sight of the predominantly European veterans. Their respect couldn't be bought with fragmentary anecdotes.

Then Gumball unintentionally gave me a gift of incalculable value.

Every 2005 Gumball car would be a equipped with an ALK "CoPilot" GPS-enabled cell phone. Gumball's motivation was to help non-GPS-equipped teams find the checkpoints, an unbelievably real problem given most teams' failure to purchase even paper maps. But no one given a CoPilot, least of all Gumballers only hours from the kickoff party, was going to read the instruction manual. Expecting them to master its use on the inaugural 835-mile (London–Prague) endurance stage was like expecting a high-schooler to make sweet, beautiful, successful love—on his first try—to a Czech porn goddess.

I knew that no GPS was 100 percent reliable, especially on Gumball, and *especially* one programmed by topographers ignorant of the necessity of plotting routes *around* potentially finish-rank crushing interchanges and mobile police roadblocks. Plotting these on the fly, at 100 mph or more, required a navigator as familiar with the GPS as he was with his wife or girl-friend. My solution was to custom-program my top-of-the-line, Garmin 2650 GPS with multiple routes into and out of each checkpoint, using the BMW and CoPilot units as backup.

Although the mass distribution of CoPilots would slightly diminish my navigational advantages, this would be offset by my knowing *precisely* everyone else's route, and therefore where the police would ambush them, allowing me to bypass them and escape.

All this was minor compared to the CoPilot's other function. Each CoPilot would transmit Gumballers' locations to a moving map on ALK's website, allowing anyone to follow their progress in real time. Although Gumball's intention was to help fans follow the action live, they had unintentionally created the perfect method of tracking departure rankings and start and finish times.

I was ready for a merciless demonstration of everything I'd learned. I knew I was more than Team Polizei. Now I could prove it.

THURSDAY, MAY 12, 2005
TRAFALGAR SQUARE HILTON, LONDON
GUMBALL-2

"I always wanted to make love to a priest," the concierge whispered into her phone downstairs.

"It's very noisy in the lobby," I said with sincere incredulity. "Can you repeat that?"

"I *said,* Mr. Roy, that I want to make a love to a priest, since I was a little girl in Poland." However convenient her response to my request for custom-made, same-day church vestments in my size, I couldn't say that I'd ever wanted to make love to anyone—not even a gorgeous, six-foot-tall, sin-ready Polish girl—while dressed as a priest. Nine, the logical copilot for Team Polizei's impending 150 mph assault on Germany and Eastern Europe, poked his head out of our suite's bathroom. "What's she saying?"

"My dear Paulina," I said, ignoring Nine, "then I'm *sure* you know where to find some priests' outfits right away."

"Aliray," said Nine, "with the shit *you* get away with, I'm surprised *everyone* on Gumball doesn't bring a fake police car."

Much to my surprise, Team Polizei's London arrival had been greeted by dozens of fans asking for autographs and pictures beside the M5 now stickered as—in a tribute to the Spanish authorities' anti-Gumball operations in 2004—a *Barcelona Contra-Gumball Venganza Guardia Civil Interceptación Policia M5.* Gumball's highly enthusiastic fans, to whom I felt closer than many drivers, had deigned to add Team Polizei to the pantheon of legends like Kenworthy and (ahem) Schmitz. Although I was neither the best driver nor in the best car, Team Polizei seemed to have struck a populist, perhaps even anti-establishment, chord. Given how many months I'd spent scouring eBay for uniforms and gear I couldn't borrow or cobble together, I was flattered and grateful, which was why, upon spotting a copycat fake Italian Polizia Lamborghini Gallardo in the hotel garage, I was within an hour of burying Team Polizei forever. If the Polizia team wore full uniforms, half my backup plan was already in the M5's trunk. The other half was minutes away.

"So, Aliray, if we switch up, what's our new team name, Vatican Motorsports?"

I pulled out my notes from an online English-to-Latin translator. *"Sanctus Urbs Altus Volo Templum Sanctimonia."*

"What does *that* mean?"

"Holy City High-Speed Church Chariot."

"We're going straight to hell."

"Any better ideas?" said Nine on the cab ride back from our unsuccessful visit to the tailor across from Westminster Abbey.

"Oh yes. Oooooooooooh yes." I explained my plan, after which he didn't speak until we arrived back at the hotel.

"Good luck with this one, Aliray."

"Paulina," I said, stepping up to the concierge desk, "I need you to call another church . . . and say that two American bishops lost all their luggage."

"You are soooo bad." She winked. "Perhaps I should have them send someone here for the fitting?"

"Aw yeah," said Nine. "Now you're talkin'!"

"An excellent idea," I said.

Paulina pulled up a list of numbers on-screen and reached for the phone.

"Maybe," said Nine, "they can messenger over a catalog of all the fancy outfits they wear, and we can pick out something special."

"Nine, you're not concerned about . . . you know . . . blasphemy?"

"You think the big guy upstairs is gonna punish a nice guy like you for dressing like a priest after all the other crap you've done?"

"How about his nonpracticing Jewish best friend?"

"Alex," said Paulina, smiling at me, phone in hand, "so I shouldn't tell them you're not Catholic?"

"See you at the bar," said Nine, waving at Ant and Pete—emerging rally legends raising their pints on the far side of the lobby.

"Hang on, tough guy. Let's see how ballsy those Lambo guys are. Tell everyone that we're terrified of wearing *our* uniforms. Spread the word that the police have already threatened us about it."

"Wow, smart guy, it's like you're some kind of psychologist or something."

"Cute. Paulina, will you just please send the catalog over to the bar, unless anyone official looking brings it, in which case please tell him we're very, very ill. Nine, ready for your homework?"

"Can't I just get a drink and relax?"

"Not yet. We're looking for Mark Muss and Seamus Conlon, new guys who've prepared more than anyone. They've got a *lot* to share with us about Eastern Europe they're not telling anyone else. I've invited them to convoy with us. And look out for—"

"Aliray, I thought this was supposed to be fun."

"This *is* the fun part. Work starts in the car."

SATURDAY, MAY 14, 2005
WATERLOO PLACE, LONDON
GUMBALL START LINE
LATE AFTERNOON

"Aliray, is it always like this?!!?"

We'd been standing astride the Policia M5 for over an hour, posing for pictures with hundreds of fans who, out of the thousands ringing the pre-start staging zone on Waterloo Place, had pushed their way through the crowd and called out my name from behind the barrier tape. We invited them through in pairs, smiling and shaking hands with as many as possible until engines began firing up across the street at the start line.

"Not like *this*," I said. "There's gotta be . . . five thousand people right here!"

"At least! I saw a lot more around the corner."

"You see my mom?"

"She's waiting *right* at the desk where they give us the cards."

We handed out every spare Polizei 144 T-shirt and cap we had and got in the M5 for the customary last-minute systems check. The crowd cheered as Nine hit the switch, our siren's *WHOOOOOP* echoing off the surrounding buildings, then he switched on the red-blue and green-yellow police lights I'd installed front and rear. Dozens of camera flashes lit up in my rearview mirror. Not only had the mechanics who'd double-checked my car at BMW Battersea come—with their children—to see us off, so had several of London's Finest. They were very impressed with the bright orange jackets I'd bought online—to which I'd affixed fake Spanish police badges and patches—all agreeing they were far more authoritative (and visible) than any *real* uniforms, including their own. To my surprise and the crowd's delighted clapping, a bright-yellow-jacketed officer removed his hat, pulled off its silver London Metropolitan Police badge, and placed it on my dashboard "for good luck, mate." Nine asked a bobby-hatted duo to estimate the crowd size, their guesses ranging from ten to fifty thousand, all debate ending when their commander summoned them for the flag drop—the same commander who, after Maximillion's earlier orientation briefing, told the assembled drivers to be careful beyond the city limits. The cheering Gumballers—with a twisted understanding of what this meant *within* the city limits—nearly carried him out on their shoulders.

"Mate," said the copper, pumping my hand, "me and the boys want you to show these poncy wankers. Cane it. Do it for *us*." His eyes hardened as he looked over my shoulder, switched back to cop-on-duty, and began barking at fans trying to sneak under the tape.

I turned to Nine. "Cane it?"

"It's a British thing, smart guy. It's gotta mean drive balls out."

"Duh. Funny that he wants us to represent, I guess . . . the police worldwide?"

"I wouldn't believe it if I hadn't seen it. Crazy. Are all European cops that cool?"

"Not in France. I hear the Belgian parliament wants to make an example of Gumball, but I speak French, so we should be okay. Germany I don't know, but it's got to take a lot to get stopped there. Austria's probably the same. I've got my mom checking the news; she'll call if she hears anything. Muss says Eastern Europe is like the Wild West . . . just bring cash."

"Thank God you did, but you wanna know our most serious problem?"

"Well, Nine, you know what my dad always said."

"Bad news first."

"Okay, what's the new problem?"

"*You* think you've got it pretty good in NYC, with your cute little girlfriend and loft parties, but you're a total loser there compared to London. Alex Roy and Polizei are household names here. The least you can do is move here and take advantage of your minor celebrity before it runs out, or you get too fat."

"Can we talk about serious problems?"

"This *is* a serious problem. Everybody saw you on last year's Gumball show with Kinsley, and the few hot chicks who come up to us think the two of you are still together."

"So? We've both got girlfriends. Nothing's secret on Gumball."

"What I'm saying is, aren't there any chick fans that, you know, maybe if we're single again and come back to London . . . I mean, pretty much ninety percent of the Polizei fans are guys."

"Look." I lowered my window. "Here comes a cute girl right now."

"Finally! We have any hats left?"

I removed my sunglasses as the young, pale woman ran up to my doorsill.

"Oh my God!" She giggled. "Team Polizei! You guys are complete morons and I love love love it! Can I have your autograph for my little brother?"

"My pleasure," I said with a smile. I signed her copy of the 2003 Gumball DVD with my face on the cover, then she kissed me on both cheeks and ran off.

"Gotta say it, Aliray, your mom sure looks hot in that Polizei jacket."

I sighed, slowly pulling the M5 up to the start line. Ingeborg, my sixty-one-but-looked-forty-and-acted-twenty-five mom, stood beaming, waving her arms just beyond the mass of newscasters and cameramen waiting to interview us before we took off. Nine hit the lights. Cheers erupted. Disembodied arms—cameras in hand—reached out from the crowd to snap our picture in a kaleidoscope of flashes, a chorus of goodwill: "Go for it, Roy!" "Show those tossers!" "Go Polizei!"

"London *loves* Aliray." Nine laughed. "It's the exact opposite of New York!"

I read my mom's lips as she leaped in the air. "Ali! Ali! I love you! I love you!" Although she wasn't the only female within earshot expressing such feelings, she was suddenly surrounded by journalists wanting to know the identity of the pixieish woman with the platinum-blond crew cut and black leather Polizei jacket. "How do you know Alex Roy?" said one as I rolled up to kiss her good-bye. *"That's* my son!" she screamed. "That's *my* son!"

I reached for the PA handset. "Mom!" My voice blared over the crowd. "I love you, too, just don't read the paper for the next five days!"

CHAPTER 23

The Coefficient of Danger

AUTOROUTE E40 EASTBOUND

APPROACHING BELGIAN-GERMAN BORDER

500 MILES FROM PRAGUE CHECKPOINT

"Aliray, are we going to be driving this fast the whole time?"

"We're only doing 145."

"Like I said, are we going to be driving this fast the whole time?"

"We've only been doing it for half an hour. Any news from Schtaven?" Schtaven, aka Steven Jennions or Steve J, was our inner circle's representative in London, a half-English, half-Norwegian, sixty-two, bald, importantly stomached, car-loving banker-cum-explorer who—having honeymooned with his dreadlocked, stunning obsidian goddess wife, Ester, in Syria, and having just returned from a guided vacation of North Korea—considered staying up overnight to report news from the CoPilot Web page but a minor favor.

"Nothing since he said we're tied with Ross. For first."

Our second hour at 150 or more inspired a highly unscientific analysis of the actual danger we faced. I concocted what I called *The Danger Coefficient* (DC). I guessed the average NASCAR driver, in a thirty-six-race season including practice, probably drove 15,000 miles—with a safety cage and onboard active-fire suppression—on highly prepared tracks, with hospitals less than 15 minutes away by choppers on standby. Assuming this represented a DC of ten, Gumball's 3,000 miles meant our DC was two ... *until* factoring our relative safety deficiencies. High speeds over potholes *had* to triple our DC to six. Civilian traffic doubled it again, to twelve. Time and distance to medical help? Double again, to twenty-four. Lack of roll cages, harnesses, and HANS devices? My guesses ended when I realized Gumball—at least the way I did it—was at least five times more dangerous than NASCAR.

It *had* to be. Thank God Nine was there to take over once I got tired. But that would make it six times as dangerous. At least.

"Hey, Aliray, I don't think I can drive."

"Are you sick?" We were approximately 500 miles into an 835-mile stage, and although our absurdly, criminally high sustained cruising speeds—far higher than in the States—would shorten its duration, safety demanded we switch seats soon. Nine was an experienced Porsche Club driver, far better on the track than I. Without him, my plan was doomed.

"I'm not sick, I just . . . look, I knew we were gonna drive fast, but I didn't know it was going to be like this."

"We're doing 165. Light rain, no traffic. The road's straight and perfect."

"Listen, if you wanna win this thing, I *know* you're going to take some risks that I'm just not willing to take."

"You mean like *this*? You've got veto power. Do you feel unsafe?"

"Not at all. Alex, I may be better than you on the track, but what you're doing right now . . . is incredible. I can't believe it. If we didn't have the camcorder, no one would. As long as you feel good, you drive and I'll be the world's best copilot ever. Unless you need me to take over, I'd rather you run as hard as you can."

Nine still felt guilt over an incident I'd forgotten. Three weeks after the M5's purchase, at the end of its second day of testing, with Nine at the wheel and summer tires between us and the icy driveway to The Weis's country house, a 15 mph skid ended against a tree. My first question was whether everyone was all right. I never expressed any anger, even upon receipt of the $10,000 damage bill. The tire decision had been mine. My faith in him had never wavered, otherwise I'd never have invited him on Gumball.

"Nine . . . are you sure?"

"I'm sure."

Eight-hundred-odd miles was nothing compared to the 1,270-mile Paris–Marbella stage from 2004. I could finish it alone.

"Then keep a close eye on me. If I'm about to make a mistake, start yelling."

"Just punch it, Chewy."

"In that case, 170 it is."

AUTOBAHN A6 EASTBOUND
APPROACHING SCHWANDORF, GERMANY
170 MILES FROM PRAGUE CHECKPOINT
EARLY MORNING

Ross's headlights flashed twice in my mirror. I pulled to the right as his Bentley passed at 185 mph, its 6-liter, twin-turbocharged, 12-cylinder engine emitting a high-pitched whine similar to a 747 at takeoff.

"I really don't give a shit about high-end hardware, Aliray, but that does sound pretty cool."

"Me neither, but yeah, it does. Ross is probably the only Bentley owner on the planet who actually runs his car the way they're supposed to. Everyone else is going to dinner—"

"Hang on. Schtaven reports . . . He says we're in the lead, cane it, order him an extra steak when we get to Prague, and overnight it to him."

Nothing could stop us—

"Nine, what's that in the road?"

—unless I made a mistake.

The Bentley's rooster tails obscured our view of whatever had caused him to brake. Hard. Construction cones appeared out of the mist just ahead of him—the left lane suddenly closed—and he squeezed past a civilian jalopy just as the road narrowed to one lane. Water burst up from beneath the Bentley and civilian as they ran over a piece of debris I barely avoided by jinking left.

"Nice one!" Nine yelled. "What *was* that?"

"Some moron hit a cone and left it there."

We pulled over behind Ross, just past the construction zone.

"Nine, we've gotta get that debris off the road before fifteen Gumballers get killed." There were at least seven medium-size pieces, but each required a separate near-suicidal sprint in front of thickening civilian traffic.

"Back to Ross," Nine huffed as we ran back. "I'll start calling everyone we know. Where the fuck are we?"

"Just past the B85 turnoff. Use my phone. Call Jodie Kidd, Muss, and Ant and Pete. Between them, it'll get to almost everybody."

By the time we reached the white-shirted Ross, he was already prone in the mud under the Bentley. "Tire puncture," he said calmly. "Be so kind as to bring my jack and spare, and we can sort this right away. I brought a full-size for just this eventuality."

"Of course he did," Nine said as we unpacked the spare. "This guy's like James Bond."

"We brought one, too."

"Yeah, but you're more Austin Powers."

We had no more than five minutes to fix it were we to maintain our lead. Within three, a loud crunch to our rear announced the arrival of a previously unseen Aston Martin DB9. They pulled over and took a cursory glance under their car before getting back in. Even from 20 feet away it was clear they were leaking oil. Nine ran to warn them, but they left seemingly unconcerned.

"Brand-new DB9"—he shook his head—"and these guys don't care. I'll bet you Taco Bell they don't make Prague."

"Only someone with Ford stock would take that bet. I can't wait to see them stopped with a dead engine. That's gotta cost twenty grand."

We were about to mount the spare when Ross spoke up from under the car. "We have a problem. Fluid leak, not oil, but potentially serious. Pass me the duct tape, then we'll mount the tire and be off."

By minute four, multiple high-pitched engines flared behind us, a blue Lamborghini, a silver Porsche, a black Ferrari, and Loretta all stopping to help. I was little surprised and greatly delighted to see Jodie Kidd, her copilot and boyfriend Aidan Butler, Muss, Seamus, and two Gumballers I didn't know gathered around us on the shoulder. The black SLR kept going, as did another five cars. They were correct in assuming nothing more could be done.

Our unheralded, superhuman, nearly 700-mile run halfway across Europe had been for naught. I'd known enough disappointment in the past to remain quiet over my anguish. With the privilege of convoying with Ross came responsibility. Every car that passed while I stood by was another brick in the foundation of Ross's trust. This was the Gumball spirit for which I'd received the trophy in 2003. I had to live up to it.

We taped the leak and mounted the tire, thankfully urged our reluctant friends back on the road, and then Ross turned to me. "A quick pace won't be possible for the remainder of this stage, alas. Mr. Goodrich has volunteered to ride with me in case anything goes wrong. We hope you will safely deliver Lady Emma to Prague."

"I'm not a lady," she quipped. "I mean I am, but not by title."

"As you wish," Ross said to her, then shook my hand. "Go, Mr. Roy. We'll make it up tomorrow."

"You needn't worry, Mr. Ross, about either task." I returned to the M5, started the engine, and made a mental note to ask Nine why he and I adopted—only when talking to Ross or Emma—a faux-English accent and cadence. With great sadness I watched the Bentley disappear in the rearview mirror.

"Are you okay?" I cautiously asked my new copilot. We'd had drinks and dinner many times among friends, but this was my first time alone with the stunning girl pursued by so many. Her looks had been invisible to me since first noting Ross's paternal concern, back when she began dating Maher in 2003. Now given the instruction to deliver her safely, I thought of nothing but.

"Yes . . . yes." She stared straight ahead. Even with the seat all the way back, her long legs barely fit under the glove box. Despite her composure and six feet, three inches, she was still a twenty-two-year-old girl who'd just survived her second accident on Gumball. I dared not ask her to perform any of Nine's duties.

"Alex . . . thank you for letting me have a quiet moment."

"You've got another hour or two of quiet, I think."

I proceeded, in an effort not to upset her, toward the border at 120. "Don't slow down because of me, Alex. I'm over it."

"Are you certain?"

"Alex, you should see how Michael drives."

"As you wish!" I accelerated to 140 and soon caught up with Ant, Pete, and Jodie Kidd at the tail of at least fifty cars waiting at the Czech passport control. I looked at Emma, who immediately read my mind, and we slowly advanced to cut the line. I was about to instruct her as to location of the siren controls when she blurted, "Oh Christ!"

"What? What?"

"I left my passport in the Bentley!"

"Emma, stay calm, okay . . . let me think . . . do you promise to do exactly as I say?"

"If Jon trusts you—"

"Emma, take my camera, get out of the car, and start snapping pictures of me, the car, the border police, and every Gumballer who passes by. Start by standing on the German side, then as I drive through, slowly start walking to the Czech side. There's tons of fans. Look, even the police are taking pictures. No one will notice. Get out now."

"Are you sure? Smuggling is quite a bad offense, I think."

"You a law student?"

"Well, I do intend to go to law school—"

"Then study immigration. Emma, would you prefer for us to wait for Ross?"

"I suppose not."

"Then trust me. I impersonate cops for a living!"

No one noticed our ruse, except the Czech border guard who demanded a picture with the girl whose terrified expression—two heads above his smile—would become apparent only when he developed the roll of film in his camera.

We drove in silence toward Prague, where several thousand fans awaited our arrival in front of the Hotel Carlo IV finish line. A pair of young crew-cutted fans ran up to my window.

"Alex Roy!"

"Americans!? What are you doing here?"

"Dude! Can we get your autograph? We just got back from Iraq and drove all the way here from Ramstein Air Base to meet you!"

"That's better than me coming to Iraq to meet *you*! Come by the bar for drinks in thirty! If anyone stops you, tell them you're my pit crew."

We rolled up to the checkpoint official. Amazingly, despite our ordeals, we were eighth in. Ross and Nine arrived several hours later, just in time for the lunch I ordered them.

"Screwed up again, Mr. Polizei?"

"Roy's not that good, is he?"

I wasn't at all fazed by the passing insults from Gumballers I didn't know. Team Polizei's table in the hotel restaurant became the most efficiently organized command and control center outside of NASA Launch Control, with ours far more comfortable. While other problem-addled Gumballers stood on the hotel steps trying in vain to reach the local Ferrari or Porsche dealer on a Sunday afternoon, Ross's call to Bentley London reactivated a mechanism of English logistical prowess unseen since the days of empire. By one o'clock the owner of Bentley Prague had canceled plans with his family to repair Ross's transmission-fluid reservoir. A new clutch was already on a plane from the UK for Loretta, the black Lotus driven by Muss and Seamus. In order to improve the M5's performance by saving weight, I shipped my dirty laundry home and my clean clothes to the subsequent checkpoints in a schedule perfectly synchronized with my proprietary knowledge, which Muss was about to expand.

"Now listen to me," said Muss. "Tomorrow morning Seamus and I will park Loretta beside your M5. Ross, you park behind Alex. Seamus will call Jon and give you instructions out of the city."

Ross intuited why. Nine didn't. "I thought you lived in Budapest. How do you know . . . holy shit! You didn't—"

"Alex," said Muss, "you want to tell him?"

"Nine, these two psychopaths called every hotel in every city until they figured out exactly where the checkpoints were. Seamus here was the one who recommended the midway checkpoint in Croatia. Two weeks ago they drove the *entire* route in real time as practice. They know the shortcuts into and out of *every* place we're going."

Ross grinned more joyfully than I'd ever seen.

"The only problem"—Muss looked at Ross—"is that you don't have the highway toll stickers to stay with us. The cops are pretty strict about having them."

"Actually, I was lucky enough to procure several sets from my local sources, just in case a friend was in need."

"Fucking James Bond," said Nine. "*All* you guys are out of your minds."

"Thank you so much," said Muss, "and cheers to you, Michael."

"Mapping the shortcuts was a real military op," said Seamus. "No one using GPS stands a chance. These CoPilots are crap except for the tracking function."

"It's too bad," I said, "the CoPilots would rock if set to Gumball speeds."

"Gentlemen," said Seamus, "just make sure to turn yours off when we approach Vienna and Budapest. We don't want anyone following us in via our shortcut."

This *very* strategy had lurked in my mind since the prior night. I couldn't wait to put it to use. If only the Bentley was repaired in time. If only Loretta didn't break down again. If only I didn't make any navigational mistakes. If only everyone stuck to the plan.

Gumballers were still arriving—more than 24 hours after departing London—as I awaited U.S. Army captain Jacob Wallace, an Apache helicopter pilot two weeks back from Iraq who was certainly braver than all of the Gumballers put together. Wallace greeted me as if I, too, had survived a hail of ground fire, and over my first alcoholic drink—a single beer—since my going-away party in New York, I outlined my highly unusual request. He thanked me for the honor and immediately set off to get some sleep.

Ross returned from the Bentley dealer, optimistic all would be ready by dawn, to join Nine and me for dinner. Muss and Seamus had had to bribe the nearest garage owner to open (and stay open overnight) for their clutch replacement. Having been awake for nearly 37 hours, we all agreed to skip the official Gumball party and retire early. Half-drunk Gumballers orbited the bar island, stopping to lean on our table for support—some more than once—in the belief *we* knew where the unofficial party was later that night.

Ross knew, of course, but he wasn't telling anyone, not even me.

MONDAY, MAY 16, 2005
ROUTE E461 SOUTHBOUND
APPROACHING AUSTRIAN BORDER
51 MILES FROM VIENNA CHECKPOINT
LATE MORNING

"Aliray, I *can't* believe those army guys got up at four A.M. to block anyone from parking in front of us."

"Nine, I can't believe we left midpack and are now in the lead. God bless Muss."

"I can't believe we passed five Czech police cars at 120 mph with our lights and sirens blaring and not one of them stopped us. And that cop actually standing in the highway? Did he really think we were gonna stop for a guy on foot?"

"My BlackBerry's vibrating Nine, see who it is."

"It's another one of your exes with updates from CoPilot's site. She says three cars approaching the Austrian border, in the lead. Gotta be us."

"Better be, here's outbound passport control. If the Czechs are gonna arrest us, this is their last chance. *Don't* say a word." I slowed down to the speed limit for the first time since leaving London. We were 50 feet from safety, then 20, then two officers stepped out and blocked our path with hands raised. One approached my window, pausing when he saw our black Policia uniforms, our bright badges glinting in the sun.

"Your license plate . . . you are from New York?"

"Yessir!" I offered him our passports, which he ignored.

"This is . . . police car from New York or . . . *Španělsko?*"

"From . . . er . . . *Spa-nels-ko*. For a movie."

"Very cool, man! You may go!"

I slowly pulled out. "That was . . . surreal, even by my standards."

"That *was* the strangest thing I've ever seen," said Reynolds.

Nine giggled. "*Spanelsko* . . . nice one. So I guess we *are* first."

"You never know. Let's not get cocky." A few hundred feet away a crowd of uniformed officials stood at the Austrian passport control. My mother's online scan of that day's Austrian papers suggested they would be tougher than the Belgians. There was nothing to do but proceed at 20 mph. Several officers raised what appeared to be guns.

"Holy shit," said Nine, "are they pointing . . . wait . . . are they pointing—"

All but the officer approaching my door were . . . taking pictures. I stopped as they clustered in front of the car, camera-toting fans running from beyond the booths to join them. I handed over our documents and with my first-ever I-know-we're-gonna-make-it grin said, *"Guten Abend, Herr Offizier!"*

He chuckled and handed them to his mustached commander, who pocketed his camera and waved me out of the car.

"You are Alex Roy? From der Team Polizei!"

"Ja?"

"Bring your copilot friend! Ve must haf a picture altogether!"

Fifty miles and sixteen successfully jammed police laser guns later, we arrived in Vienna. Thousands of cheering Viennese lined the streets leading toward the Hofburg Imperial Palace, where thousands more were held back by the local Polizei—they, too, waving approvingly—as we squeezed through the arch into Josefplatz Square. I reached for the PA handset and greeted them in the only Spanish I knew.

"Hola de la Policía de Barcelona!"

Then my heart stopped. Beyond the edge of the crowd swarming our car, alone on the far side of the square, sat a gleaming red Ferrari 360 Spyder I hadn't seen since London. Nine and I ignored the microphones and cameras pointing at us and stared at each other. A Gumball checkpoint staffer emerged from the crowd.

"Who the hell," Nine asked him, "are *those* guys?"

"They skipped Prague," said the staffer, "which makes you first!"

First. It was the proudest moment of my Gumball career, and yet gloating over what only a mere handful might recognize for its actual significance would have been in bad taste. "No one cares about first, though, right Aliray? Because it's not a race—"

"It's a rally," I said, "and now we get a twenty-minute break, but we leave immediately if and when the tenth car arrives."

While Nine, Ross, Emma, Muss, and Seamus enjoyed the hot buffet and cash bar in the Hofburg's colossal, high-ceilinged, quadruple-glass-chandeliered dining hall ringed with white columns and gold inlays, I stood by the windows—and listened for engines.

"That's ten!" I yelled. "Saddle up!"

"Remember," Muss said over predeparture handshakes, "the Hungarians won't give a piss about us speeding, but no matter how fast you *want* to go, no one can navigate there faster than Seamus and I. Don't lose us, you'll regret it!"

"Alex, listen, you wanna be first, *be* first, but if you wanna be a man, let Muss and Seamus take this one. It's their town." Nine was right.

I let off the gas. Ross took our hint. We entered the track grounds, the din of thousands clapping upon hearing our engines rising even louder upon sighting the black Lotus in the lead. "Lo-ret-ta!" they cheered. "Lo-ret-ta!" more cheered as we arrived in central Budapest an hour later, parking in second place beside the Lotus from which Muss and Seamus emerged beaming.

Team Polizei's Gumball 2005 standings were now eleventh, eighth, first, second, and second. Three top-five finishes meant a strong but not insurmountable position. The Hungaroring-to-Budapest leg was only 12 miles—no veteran would consider that a major stage—but six major ones still remained. Everything was going according to plan.

But it was not to be, for Ross broke down twice more in Croatia on the way to Dubrovnik, and wouldn't be able to resolve his recurring rim and tire issues until after that night's ferry delivered us to Bari the next morning.

Late that night Ross and I stood freezing on the ferry's bottle-strewn deck, the horde of Gumballers still awake having migrated to the shabby interior lounge behind us, their laughter audible even through the hatches sealed against the wind whipping through my Polizei traffic coat. Among the hundred-odd cars aboard—their sum total value probably greater than the vessel pitching in the Adriatic beneath us—Ross's was one of at least a dozen with a major problem, but we were the only ones not passed out or too drunk to have borrowed every available cell phone in a last-ditch effort to reach a suitable Bentley mechanic in or near the port of Bari. One of the few operable slot machines inside began playing an annoying electronic melody. Cheers ensued. "Bar's fucking closed?" someone yelled. "Bribe the captain!"

Ross turned to me, yet another generous Gumballer's phone against his ear, and I saw sadness in his eyes for the first time. "Mr. Roy, I think it's time we have a serious chat."

"I've still got two more phones to try."

He shook his head and led me to the railing farthest from the noise. "Alex, I appreciate all you and Jonathan have done to help, far more than I could have expected from nearly anyone. I shall never forget it, but I also know how much it means to you to place well this year. I've done the calculations on the remaining stages. It's too late for the run to Taormina, but *from* Taormina you may still fulfill your desire. I want you to proceed without me."

He raised a hand to stop me from expressing my gratitude.

"Alex, there are several very serious drivers here ... drivers we've ignored in all our excitement, drivers intent on this illusory 'victory' you so cherish. You must totally commit to finishing first or second no less than twice . . . or you might as well slow down and enjoy this costly little vacation with our friends inside."

"I understand."

"Then understand that this racing nonsense exists only in our minds, and that one must never let one's ego override a safety decision. Today, Wednesday, doesn't matter. Tomorrow, the Thursday run from Taormina to Rome, I shall not ask. I'm telling you. Be safe."

CHAPTER 24

Total War: The Battle of Rome

The 2005 Gumball had a clear winner, at least according to my totally unofficial calculations of what veterans and fans would consider legitimate. My determination was quite a surprise to all but the winners and the second-place team, *so* close was the margin. After hours of battle over hundreds of miles, the struggle over the final minutes—and the respect concurrently built upon it—can bind temporary enemies more closely than longtime friends.

The 2005 Gumball was the last on which the core group of veterans faced off before retirement, marriage, children, and/or dispersal among other, more secretive events. Were their feats known beyond fragments shared among Gumball fans, they might rightfully take their place among racing's greatest legends. Every Gumball is filled with intraconvoy skirmishes and interconvoy sprints, but an all-out assault on a daily stage, let alone a serious commitment to winning a majority of stages—as I made in 2005—is extraordinarily rare. For two or more such Gumballers to race head-to-head, as Kenworthy and Schmitz did in 2004, is even more so.

One of the greatest such battles in Gumball history has so far remained virtually unknown beyond me, Nine, and the crews of the two other cars.

This is the true story of the Battle of Rome.

THURSDAY, MAY 19, 2005
HOTEL SAN DOMENICO PALACE
TAORMINA, SICILY
305 MILES TO NAPLES LUNCH CHECKPOINT
0815 HOURS (APPROX)

"Dammit!" I yelled, sitting up in the long, wide bed I shared with—one standard male Gumballer's arm length away—Nine, in a pointlessly romantic cliff-side suite overlooking the Mediterranean, typical of those given the other 113 Gumball teams, 97 percent of them male. My bucolic slumber had been interrupted by the most fearsome, terrifying sound in the catalog of race-intentioned Gumballers.

"Mother of God," he groaned, facedown into his pillow. "What time is it?"

"Engines in the parking lot! Move! Move! Move!"

"Holy shit!" Nine jumped up and ran around the bed—having forgotten he was still wearing his prior night's outfit—and stopped as he rounded the corner to the bathroom. "Aliray, you actually slept in your bishop's outfit?"

"No time for jokes! Meet me at the car! People are leaving!" I stripped off the black floor-length frock in which I successfully asked dozens of people to kiss my hand before the hotel manager suggested I go to my room before the townspeople *"cumma to get you Gumballa peoples!"* I'd had no alternative since the hotels in Prague and Budapest shipped my dirty clothes ahead and my clean clothes home.

I now put on my thrice-worn, oil-soaked, uncomfortably hot, yellow-striped, black polyester police pants, then my black driving boots and last clean shirt—a bright yellow Policia Bicicletta Polo. I sprinted downstairs to the tree-lined parking lot, one of two in which cars had dispersed due to the impossibility of placing three-hundred-odd Gumballers in any one of Taormina's old, convention-unfriendly hotels. I didn't know what time we were to convene in Taormina's main square to receive route cards, but the absence of the two cars Ross had warned me about—and the metallic chorus echoing down Taormina's narrow streets—signaled catastrophe.

I started the engine, booted up the electronics, and waited—sweaty, panicked chills running down my damp seat back. Nine burst out of the hotel and threw his bags into the trunk. The lot had but one apparent exit, a one-way cliff-side road leading not *up* toward the town square but—according to the Garmin—nearly two miles *down* toward Messina before the turn—via a small, winding road—back to Taormina, undoubtedly putting us at the rear of the grid. I circled the lot, but the only other road, taken the prior day from the square to the hotel and *into* the lot—its international "Do Not

Enter/One Way" sign no deterrent to someone like myself—was blocked by an enormous tree-trimming truck.

My mind raced, then I read his. "We can't leave until eight-thirty, it's cheating. Muss said the next checkpoint's Naples, then Rome. We'll wait, listen for cars taking off, *we* leave, then you call everyone we know until you've got the exact checkpoint addresses. All the fans watching the online tracking . . . they'll know we didn't cheat."

We synchronized our watches to the Garmin, *its* clock synchronized to the seven orbiting GPS satellite signals it was receiving at 100 percent power.

Nine spun his head around to scan the lot. "Where's that black CLK? And the blue Porsche turbo?"

"The guys Ross warned us about? Gone. The black SLR guy's at another hotel."

"Aliray, the next two minutes are gonna be the worst of our lives. I don't know how you can stay calm, I mean, it would be so easy to cheat . . . just turn off the CoPilot transponder, sneak out, then turn it on later."

"Yeah, but Team Polizei stands for the rule of law."

"One minute," said Nine, eyes following the nameless crew of a silver Porsche convertible—wisely parked in the shade 50 feet away—lower the top, apply suntan lotion to their pale arms, then inspect the car. "Check it out . . . we're about to race outta here, and they're checking for bird shit."

Engines began wailing in the square, the two men's heads turned up to listen, then, as my M5's engine flared, in my rearview mirror I glimpsed both spin toward us with shocked expressions, a flurry of leaves and dust in our wake.

VIA GIUSEPPE LA FARINA—NORTHBOUND
CENTRAL MESSINA, SICILY
APPROACHING CARONTE FERRY LOADING ZONE
0925 HOURS (APPROX)

"Ferry in sight! Text Schtaven for our position! How many cars did we pass on the way here?"

Nine spoke as he typed. "I saw . . . that silver Porsche with the solar-powered thingie on the roof . . . a gray Aston . . . and a black 911. Wow, already? Schtaven reports . . . we are in the lead!"

"Copy that. Sirens and lights, please. We're still in Italy . . . so blue-red." Messina's morning commuters were conveniently law-abiding, obviating the need for the right-wheels-on-the-sidewalk passes necessary during our brief passage through Bosnia two days prior. An inconvenient red light I chose to obey—*one* block shy of the ferry office—inspired Nine to get out and sprint ahead to buy a ticket. I changed my mind regarding the sidewalk, called out over the PA for him to clear it, and made one final loading-position improvement pass. I stopped in front of the thirty-odd civilian cars just as the ferry personnel began beckoning us up the ramp. I handed Nine one of our two rolls of police crime-scene tape, nodded at his disbelieving stare, and got out. Together we sealed off the loading area laterally across the middle of the growing mass of waiting cars, drivers behind the tape watching in bewilderment as those in front followed our Policia M5 up the ramp. Arriving Gumballers, stuck behind the frozen civilians, cursed and yelled at us (and them) as the ramp was raised—the ferry only three-quarters full—and we headed for the mainland.

"Nine, at times like this someone really should call the police."

Nine reached for the vibrating BlackBerry. "Hang on . . . Muss reports Naples checkpoint canceled due to crowds. We're going straight to Rome."

I reprogrammed the Garmin. "That's 434 miles. The ferries leave every fifteen to twenty minutes . . . so that's our lead over everyone waiting back there."

"What was that line from the old *Le Mans* movie? What the team captain says to McQueen at the end?"

I knew this by heart. *I want you to drive all-out, I want Porsche to win Le Mans.*

"Aliray, *I* want *you* to drive all-out, I want *BMW* to win Gumball."

"All-out, with a strong lead from the get-go, it's gonna be impossible to beat us."

"Bad karma, man."

"All right. Impossible . . . unless we break down."

AUTOSTRADA A3—NORTHBOUND
UPPER ARCH OF THE ITALIAN FOOT, VICINITY OF CASTROVILLARI
286 MILES TO ROME CHECKPOINT
1230 HOURS (APPROX)

"Thank God that's over." The first 50 rain-drenched, construction-mired, single-laned miles after the ferry might have been disastrous, but with both shoulders closed no one would be able to pass the numerous trucks. The roadwork ended in the vicinity of Vibo Valentia. We made several 130 mph sprints, interrupted only by sparse traffic through which we cut with feisty use of our lights and sirens.

"It's not over," said Nine. "Slow down before pieces start falling off the car. You wanna duct-tape the Valentine to the visor before the suction cups pop off the windshield?" The phone rang between his thighs. "Schatven's actually calling? He knows we can barely hear him."

"Either our lead is incredible, or—"

"Steve J!" Nine yelled. "How you doin', man?" Schtaven's distant, metallic voice droned uninterrupted for nearly 60 seconds, during which I accelerated to 125, we covered two miles, and I took several unusually risky peeks at the Garmin's screen. The most likely news was that Naples had been canceled due to public outcry over Gumball's historic run from Bari to Taormina, which meant *we* were to be the first car hitting the inevitable roadblocks on the way to Rome. There were three methods of escape: (1) take a parallel route, (2) slow down and wait for a large convoy to pass and saturate the authorities' limited resources, or (3) accelerate to maximum speed and try to pass ambush points *before* they were set up.

No parallel Autostrada was in range.

We were at least 45 minutes ahead of the second car.

Gumball's projected arrival in Rome was 6 to 10 P.M. Our ETA was 3:35 P.M.—an extraordinary lead even by Gumball standards, which left me no choice.

Full attack. No mercy.

The speedometer passed 130, our speed actually lessening the bumps, however dangerous it was to risk a tire blowout over one we'd approach too quickly for me to react. Jerking the steering wheel would kill us. I passed 135 in the psychotic belief it would bring me closer to hearing Schtaven's report.

Nine spoke for the first time in nearly two minutes and four and a half miles. "Yes, Steve! I got it, but are you sure? Okay . . . text from now on, just keep those updates coming! Bye!"

"What is it?"

"Only 135? We need to pick up the pace *now*!"

"I knew it! Where's the first roadblock?"

"Roadblock??? Somebody's closing on us!!!"

"What? That's impossible!"

"Aliray, *go*! Pick it up!"

"But the roadwork . . . the rain . . . it's . . . impossible. Who is it?"

"He doesn't know, he's refreshing the Web page every thirty seconds. He's sure *we're* in the lead, *one* car's closing on us, and everyone else is in or just getting out of the construction."

"Jesus, we've averaged almost a hundred for the last hour! How fast is he going?"

"Schtaven's gonna calculate it and text ASAP."

"How far behind are they?"

"Halfway between the construction and us."

Fifty miles. I knew basic math from school, but I was not skilled in the more obscure and now essential discipline of Rally Math. Four and a half rallies into my career, I still had to mumble through the calculations. We were now under 280 miles and three hours from Rome, almost two and a half hours ahead of police expectations. With luck, any roadblocks would be set up *right* after our passing any given ambush point. I might even be able to accelerate their deployment and set a trap for my pursuer. Just one extraordinarily (even by Gumball standards) audacious pass near a busload of nuns or soldiers on leave would encourage calls to the police. Their Alfa Romeos—unable to catch us—would then snare our pursuer.

"Aliray, you're talking to yourself. Just *drive*. Updates are coming."

"Copy that, sorry . . . 140 it is. Can't do more until the road gets better."

Nine then said something totally unexpected, a sentiment spoken for the first time in 2,338 miles. "Yes, Alex, you can. Do it. Push."

AUTOSTRADA A3—NORTHBOUND
ANKLE OF THE ITALIAN BOOT, VICINITY OF CASALBUNO
235 MILES TO ROME CHECKPOINT
1300 HOURS (APPROX)

"He's still closing . . . holy shit! Schtaven says he's halved the distance!"

He'd halved it in 130 miles. I wasn't angry. I wasn't scared. I was amazed. In the 50 miles since learning of our anonymous foe, I had repeatedly sprinted as high as 150. My determination—my obsession—with winning my first-ever head-to-head duel was far greater than the fear that had so dominated my decisions in the past. I was a different man. I was a better driver, with greater limits, and I was now up against the threshold at which the slightest mistake would instantaneously kill us both. And Nine wasn't trying to stop me. But *that* wasn't what amazed me. It wasn't that anyone was better than I was—I could name ten Gumballers with greater raw skill. It wasn't even that the mystery driver was sufficiently better to close the gap between us at *some* point prior to Rome. I was amazed at the *rate* at which he was closing. To have narrowed the gap, after the roadwork, on the 100 miles prior to Castro-villari (now 53 miles behind us), he had to have averaged at least 120 miles an hour. *In the rain.* It could only be a high-performance sports car with all-wheel drive, either a Lamborghini Murcielago or Porsche 996 turbo, driven by a skilled driver of aggression and purpose matching or surpassing my own. Among the three cars Ross warned of, there was only one it could possibly be, driven by a man about whom I knew nothing other than a name.

"ETA!" I barked. *"What's the ETA to intercept?"*

"Schtaven's working on it."

"Our average is moving up . . . 101! If he's *still* closing, with all the slow parts, he's gotta be running that Porsche into the 170s!"

"How do you know it's a Porsche?"

"It's the blue Porsche with the white stripe! Spencer something with a *B*, semipro track guy, old-school Gumballer. Had a Ferrari in '04, Ross said he's one of the best!"

"Like Kenworthy best?"

"Maybe. I thought he was one of these mattress-testing playboys. Boy, was I wrong."

"You've never been more wrong in your life."

Schtaven's calculations suggested that unless I dramatically increased our average—which would require consistent speeds above 160, nearly impossible given traffic and road conditions—we'd be intercepted in the vicinity of Battipaglia, approximately 50 miles ahead. Not intercepted. *Passed.* Even 140 was difficult to sustain, and yet Spencer was greatly surpassing my theoretical safe limit.

"You wanna pick it up more, Aliray, be my guest."

"One forty-five it is. Ask Schtaven if he can speed up the reports. And ask him to look up Spencer on the Gumball site, and check to see if his team number matches the CoPilot icon."

"Approaching Battaglia," Nine said 20 minutes later. "Schtaven confirms it is Team 35, Bourne, S., UK, Porsche 996 TT, Race Spec, X50. Codriver unlisted. He reports car still closing, but at a slower rate, and congratulates you on finding your manhood."

"He said what?"

"Team 35, Bourne, S.—"

"Niiiine! The *last* part!"

"Well, he actually wrote . . . 'it's nice to see you stick your cock out.' "

"Nine, write back that I expect to see him out here in his thousand-horsepower Supra lawn mower next year, or else."

"You're doing this next year? Are you insane? Isn't *this* enough?"

"We'll see. ETA to intercept?"

"He says . . . our new higher speed has now slightly delayed the intercept, but that he's no more than ten or fifteen minutes behind."

"Time for the police lights. Hit the front white strobes, that'll clear traffic ahead, *and* the rear red-blue! Italian drivers are like New York cabbies, they *always* follow emergency vehicles. *That'll* slow him down."

"You know this guy at all?"

"Spencer? No, but it's gonna drive him crazy. Get out the binoculars, eyes open to the rear. We have to keep talking to each other no matter what happens. Things are gonna get complicated *real* fast."

AUTOSTRADA A3—NORTHBOUND
MIDSHIN OF THE ITALIAN BOOT, APPROACHING SALERNO
170 MILES TO ROME CHECKPOINT
1335 HOURS (APPROX)

"Five minutes or less!" Nine yelled, turning again to sit on his knees facing rearward. "Can't see shit with the binocs at these speeds!"

"See *anything* blue??!?!?"

"Not yet." Nine flipped back into his seat. "Schtaven's refreshing the Web page now . . . he says . . . the icon's *right* on top of us!"

My eyes darted to the rearview mirror every few seconds. I had begun breaking my own safety rules—weaving through thickening traffic—and had collected a tail of the few locals in Alfas and Mercedes who thought they could keep up. A blue speck appeared in the mirror. "Is that—"

Nine, concerned over having to remove his seat belt every time he turned around, pointed the binoculars at his visor mirror. "Blue car approaching fast!"

"Dammit! Construction!" A line of orange cones sealed the shoulder, blocking the type of pass I would never make—but Spencer might. We were seconds from a close-quarters battle among local cars conveniently staggered *just* far enough apart for *one* car to weave between them, but whose proximity made passing the lead duelist impossible—unless he made a mistake. "Which side is he on?"

"Right lane! Stay left!"

Spencer, emerging from behind our two-car tail, hesitated upon spotting us. I accelerated to close the gap with a silver Fiat two car lengths ahead on the right. The small blue shape in my right-hand mirror quivered as if attached to a monstrous rubber band stretched between us. Then, the tension suddenly released, the Porsche flared in size—exhaust howling over the wind's deep roar—and catapulted toward us until disappearing in my blind spot.

Until five seconds earlier the arrival of *Team 35/Bourne, S. (UK)/Porsche 996 TT (Race Spec) X50* had remained an Outside Context Problem—an event so far beyond my ability to understand, adapt to, and mitigate its consequences that, rather than seek a new solution, I pretended my current plan would succeed. Having for the second time mercilessly applied will to ambition—my goal in sight, victory in reach—I refused to acknowledge the single-minded purpose implicit in Spencer's approach.

Beat Roy.

I genuinely believed, halfway into my fifth rally, after one accident and the Ibiza victory, that my ever-improving driving skills, combined with a Herculean investment in logistics and intelligence, made me unbeatable. Unless I made a mistake.

But, since leaving Taormina, I hadn't made any mistakes. Spencer wasn't part of the plan. It was far easier to believe he would never arrive, or didn't exist.

My vain hopes disappeared in the gust against which the M5 shuddered, Spencer's car materializing beside us in a blur of rain-sheared metal so blue it glistened purple as water sprayed up from its wheels. In the seemingly eternal half second we ran even, my car's reflection flashed in its side window, as if a single frame had been accidentally spliced into a film about the Italian countryside, shot from a train.

The Porsche's surge continued, Spencer miraculously sliding into the gap between our front right corner and the plodding Fiat's rear left, *precisely* one Porsche-911-length away. The turbo's high-pitched wail rose even as its blue-white tail narrowed in the distance, until, as if on a divine pendulum, it returned, its turbo eerily silent. He was trapped behind two trucks cruising side by side at a legal 93 mph.

I braked one irresponsibly short car length from his bumper, then fell back three. Nine released the door handle and wiped both hands on his thighs. "I need a cigarette," he panted. "That guy's really good, Aliray. At least you gave it a shot. Let's have a Twix hors d'oeuvre first. You deserve it."

My eyes remained locked on the blue bumper ahead. I wasn't fighting a car. Without Spencer, it was no more than a glamorous hunk of metal.

"Alex. Allllex!?!" Nine waved the Twix before my face. "So . . . I guess you're gonna give him this one?"

I was beatable. He was beatable. Anyone was beatable, but whether *I* could beat Spencer in the 165 miles remaining to Rome, or to the Monaco finish the following day, or even next year, would remain unknown unless I committed to transcending everything I thought possible. Who I was—and would be—depended on it. Spencer was a better driver, in a better car. I was better prepared, my will tempered steel. His worst mistake would be a wrong turn. Mine would be fatal.

I had to see. I had to know.

"No, Jon, not yet." I stared at Spencer and his codriver's heads bobbing in discussion. The left truck accelerated and moved right, but Spencer unexpectedly chose not to exploit this potentially brief opportunity. Given the increasing traffic, this immediately buttressed my battered but now resurgent, more powerful determination.

"Nine! *Look!* He's got a mechanical problem, or . . . doesn't that car get, maybe, twenty-two on the highway?"

"I see where you're going with this. Where do you get twenty-two?"

"Right. Fuel economy on Gumball is half what manufacturers say, or worse. He's getting ten, I *know* it. Text Schtaven! How big is a 996 fuel tank?"

"Seventeen gallons," Nine said without hesitation.

"Oh, *reeeeeeaaaalllly?* And *how* do you know *that?*"

"We're all the same when chicks pass out."

Spencer's range was no more than 170 miles. We were 300 miles out of Taormina. He had to have stopped once. He was now perhaps 40 miles from his second refuel, or, if he was getting *less* than 10 MPG—

"He's pulling off?! Aliray, no matter what The Weis says, you *are* a genius."

"Distance to Rome?"

"About . . . 165, what a coincidence! Guess old Spence here's gonna need *another* fuel stop before Rome, unless he wants to run out of gas two blocks from the hotel!"

"Don't celebrate yet," I said. "We need one more stop, he *might* need another."

"So Mr. Fuel Economy Strategy's *not* gonna give him this one?"

"Oooooohhhhhhh noooooooooo!"

"Let me guess, you've got a plan for this, too."

"Oooooooohhhh yeeeeessss! Three, in fact, and only two need to work to beat him. You know the first one. Get ready for sirens. Eyes open for choppers. Don't worry, we can outrun them."

"Oh . . . maaan."

Clear roads favored the faster, better-handling car. Traffic favored one with lights and sirens. Virgin asphalt favored a lower, stiffer car. Rough pavement favored a bigger, heavier car. The lower the frequency between GPS instructions, the less relevant the CoPilot's small display and weak amplification. The more complex and frequent the GPS instructions—especially in the cramped, noisy environment of a car speeding into one of Europe's largest cities—the more critical our Garmin's large display and external speaker.

If only I kept Spencer in sight, close enough to exploit advantages potentially worth as much as three minutes, every mile closer to Rome improved our odds of victory.

Racing is chess.

If only I didn't make any mistakes.

If only he made one. Just one.

"Tollbooth ahead," I said, suddenly recalling my father's road-trip rules. "Wallets in the armrest. Combine and sort our bills. It'll save time."

"And our asses won't hurt."

We needed gas. We would be invisible to Spencer for the three and a half minutes it took to refuel his car, however long was necessary for his co-driver to urinate inside (if he was too cultured for Team Polizei's pumpside stealth evacuation), and as long as it took to catch up. Would seeing us stopped at a pump satisfy his ego and slow him down? Or would it embolden him?

"Nine, next major gas station *on* the road. A big one."

"Esso coming up, one mile . . . Angionia Est, 145 miles from Rome."

"Prepare for the world's fastest refuel. I'm only putting in enough to get there. That's worth maybe one minute. Get your orange jacket on and stand by the road while I pump. Make sure he sees you. Smile and wave, like it's all fun and games."

Spencer flew past the instant the pump spit out my receipt. "Perfect timing," I said, gently pulling out of the station to save gas, "now let's see if he slows down. We need to pass him before he starts kicking the beehive on the last stretch. Watch for Autostrada A1, that's where the roadblocks are gonna start. Forget choppers and cars. Only cycles can catch us."

We covered the 22 miles to the A1 in nine minutes.

"Averaging 140 won't be enough, Nine. If I sprint up to 170, maybe—"

"Schtaven reports . . . Spencer slightly ahead, just hit 197, but averaging 150ish."

"That won't last once traffic builds. Setting cruise control at 150."

Rome was 124 miles. All was not lost.

"Heads up!" I yelled when the V1 beeped before the Caianello exit. Nine pointed out three Polizia Stradale motorcycles stopped on the right. Spencer had either slowed down, or 150 wasn't enough to get their attention. I slowed to 100. "What does it take to get arrested in this country?"

"Stop pussyfooting, we're a hundred miles out. Schtaven sends congratulations . . . we are now running even, about seven miles behind him."

"So he's three or four minutes ahead?"

"Just drive, Dr. Hawking."

Scattered showers—having no effect on Spencer—forced us as low as a hundred. Accelerating back to 150 burned additional fuel. Nine stopped reading me Schtaven's reports, then the reports stopped altogether.

"Alex, there's no shame in second, not against this guy."

I wasn't ready to concede, but my pessimism grew with every mile during which the phone remained silent. The rain cleared near Frosinone, 53 miles from Rome. I prayed for everything Gumballers despised. I could evade police, I could eviscerate traffic, but I couldn't match Spencer's 170-plus cruising speed. I was losing.

Nine lifted his vibrating phone, then furiously began typing.

"Bad news first," I said.

"Spencer's car disappeared from the tracking. I'm asking where. Maybe he had an accident. If anything happened, we have to stop."

"If anything happened to him, I'm never doing this again."

The sky ahead turned purple and gray. Spotting light beyond the murky deluge, I accelerated into it; pattering droplets became thudding sheets, the car cast in shadow before we could remove our sunglasses. The car fishtailed ever so slightly, Nine's hand moved to the door handle, then suddenly we burst out into the sun blinded, vestigial water stretching against our windshield in luminous streaks.

"Sorry, Nine, I—"

"No prob—" Nine's head snapped right. "There he is!!! At the gas station!"

"What?!? At a pump? Or broken down?"

"Gas!! They must have killed the CoPilot battery and plugged it in! So when they turned the car off, but . . . wait! We're still 45 miles from Rome!"

"So . . . he's only getting a hundred twenty miles per tank! Six miles per gallon? I love it!"

"There's your three minutes! I don't think they saw us! Cane it now!"

"This is . . . insane." Our forward police lights flickered against the rear plates of what few cars didn't pull aside as we bore down at twice their speed. I was blind to everything except the next car ahead, then the next one, and the next one.

"Don't look back!" Nine giggled. I looked. Our rear flashers had attracted a delightfully slow tail of locals waving in encouragement. I couldn't wait for Spencer to meet them.

"*Alex,* eyes on the road." Nine raised the phone to his ear. "No, Stevie, that's *our* siren! What? Yes! Got it! Bye!" The sky darkened again. "Aliray, Schtaven reports Spencer's icon active . . . he's moving!"

The Garmin spoke, inaudible beneath the rush of wind. "Nine! Max volume! Repeat instruction!"

RAMP RIGHT 15 MILES.

Nine reached for the CoPilot. "Already at max, but can't hear it!"

"If we can't, *he* can't. We need to make this turn before he catches up."

Water sprayed from cars' tires ahead, making 120 our safe limit. We had eight minutes to turn, then seven, then Nine yelled, "Spencer closing!"

"We *have* to make that turn without him seeing us."

RAMP RIGHT 12 MILES.

Six minutes. Nine and I tightened our seat belts and peered into the mirrors. "I see him," we said simultaneously and with unexpectedly calm resignation.

"Once he passes," said Nine, "he might still miss the ramp."

Spencer inched closer, blocked by traffic increasingly reluctant to recognize our sirens. Nine switched from *Wail* to *Air Horn*. "I guess Romans are smarter than other Italians?"

"Or they don't care."

Nine waved as Spencer passed. His codriver waved back. The traffic began to clear. Rome was 26 miles. Polizei territory. My territory. I'd driven these roads with my father. Muss had confirmed our Garmin plot. The three-lane-wide A1 gently banked right. Spencer, confident in his car's superiority, broke the first rule of racing. He stayed in the outside lane. I moved inside and broke Team Polizei's first rule of rallying. I pressed the M5's *Sport* button, increasing power but annihilating fuel economy. Both of us would enter Rome on fumes.

"Alex, if you're gonna do this, now *you* have to follow *my* instructions."

"Tell me what to do." Nine didn't speak, he pointed. We passed 150. Spencer crawled away at 155. Rome was 21 miles. Spencer bore down on local cars, braking and passing at full throttle, breaking the second, third, and fourth rules of racing. Conserve energy. Minimize steering inputs. Conserve fuel. I read Nine's outstretched arm. Use the whole road. Nineteen miles. The turbo wailed but pulled away in slow motion, unable to escape the tether of my tenacity.

"Road closure!" Nine barked as a diagonal line of cones cut rightward across all three lanes. "Roadblock at the gas station?"

"They'll need guns to stop us." Nine killed the lights and sirens just in case. Spencer disappeared beyond several trucks funneling into the service area. I accelerated too late, three trucks and two cars between us and our prey. We passed them on the ramp shoulder at 90. With no police in sight, Nine relit the lights and sirens. We barreled between the busy pumps at 60 before being blocked by yet another truck on the exit ramp and losing 30 precious seconds—an eterrrrrrrnity in race time—before getting back on the A1 and accelerating to 140.

RAMP RIGHT 2 MILES.

"Can't see him," said Nine, "and can't hear the CoPilot. He's gotta be doing one-eighty. Think he'll miss it?"

"At those speeds, maybe, but I'm pretty sure English people know *Roma* means Rome."

"Two-hundred-and-seventy-degree left coming up, Aliray, max speed one hundred. Watch for cars!" Thankfully, the exit turn for the A24—the final highway stretch before entering Rome—was totally devoid of civilian traffic. "Wow, he must have taken that at 120. Schtaven reports . . . he made the turn, and we're losing ground."

"C'mon, c'mon," I muttered, my skin pressed against the damp headrest as I accelerated to 145.

"Tollbooth ahead! Blue Porsche two lanes left! He's third in line! Right lane's clear!"

"They don't teach *Toll Strategy* in Porsche driving school. I'll bet you White Castle he doesn't have change." Nine reached into the armrest. We waved at Spencer, still two cars behind us at the booths when we pulled away in the lead.

RAMP LEFT IN 9 MILES.

This was Spencer's last chance to exploit his speed advantage. All I could do was minimize it, but two lanes of moderate traffic held us below 120.

"Schtaven reports . . . our icons are right on top of each other!"

"There's *no* way he could get through this traffic unless he took—"

"A pro like that wouldn't risk the shoulder. We might win this one."

RAMP LEFT 7 MILES.

We heard the Porsche before we saw it, slowly advancing past us on the right shoulder at 125. "Sorry, Aliray, but it looks like we're gonna lose this one after all."

Spencer moved off the shoulder into the right lane, accelerated, and disappeared.

"Nine! More air horn, I gotta have more air horn. And I thought *we* were crazy. Romans have absolutely no respect for the law."

RAMP LEFT 2 MILES.

"Right median!" Nine yelled. "He's stopped!"

"He's confused! He can't hear his CoPilot!" We passed the stationary Porsche at 100, three civilians trailing us in tight formation as I weaved with increasing aggression. I slashed into the right lane and accelerated toward a tunnel where the shoulder on which Spencer now approached would disappear.

"Jesus!" said Nine, staring into the right-side mirror. One second before striking the steel barrier narrowing on our right, Spencer slotted into the short gap between our bumper and the nearest trailing civilian. Our exhaust rumbled through the cavernous tunnel, the Porsche turbo's wail searing even through our sealed windows.

RAMP LEFT 500 FEET.

Spencer tailgated us out of the tunnel, we crossed the Rome city limit and turned left onto the ramp for the Circonvallazione Tiburtina. Two lanes of thick traffic split as I forcibly created a third, intermittently lunging forward until an enormous bus in the right lane blocked our merge.

"Nine! Distance to checkpoint?"

"Two and a half miles. What's your plan, smart guy? Now he's gonna follow us in and pass us fifty feet from the goddamn hotel!"

On the tree of possible outcomes I'd nurtured for almost three hours, this was the first unanticipated branch. In the split second during which I pondered a preemptive countermove, a gap opened left of the bus. Blue flashed in my peripheral vision. I was barely able to pull in behind Spencer without being hit by a tailing Alfa who'd switched loyalties.

ONE-QUARTER MILE RAMP RIGHT.

"So speaks the Garmin"—I giggled—"and no word from the CoPilot. Watch."

The Romans, utterly unimpressed with the bright blue, UK-plated Porsche now in the lead, failed to provide the narrow swath previously accorded our Policia M5. I tailgated as if being towed, our conjoined cars advancing in the left lane at no more than 10 mph until—

FIVE HUNDRED FEET RAMP RIGHT.

"Nine, *watch.*" The traffic lightened as we approached the exit. Spencer accelerated to 40. I waited for his car's nose to pass the point of commitment— the shoulderless ring road depriving him of his usual strategy, albeit in reverse—then *I* made the sharp right no longer available to him. "Good-bye, Mr. Bourne."

"Hope this isn't another Team Polizei long cut. Schtaven reports . . . icons moving apart, equidistant from finish line. Do your thing, Aliray, and we can win this."

"I've made mistakes, but I've never been called dumb. There's gonna be cops all over, so only hit the lights and sirens when I tell you!"

Two miles. Twenty blocks. Roman jaywalkers, twice as ambitious as New York's, were half as hard to spot at 60. Our inter-waypoint average, 135 20 minutes earlier, fell to 97, then 81, then 24. One mile. Roman red lights, half as well hooded from the sun as New York's, were twice as easy to run without guilt—especially when following similarly minded taxis.

TURN RIGHT.

"Via Giovanni Giolitti!" Nine yelled. "North, yes! Turn here! Half a mile from the finish!" I quarter-turned, spotted three police cars one block north, then continued west on Via Alfredo Cappellini. "Make your next right! Spencer's . . . our icons are too close to tell! Next right!"

"Okay, Magellan!" The next perpendicular street, Via Filippo Turati, went one way. South. One block west on Capellini would deliver us to Via Principe Amedeo, which ran north to the finish line, but at the intersection at which we were now stopped, a bright red-and-white sign indicated Capellini's directional reversal.

"Nine, we could run straight down this one block with the lights and sirens."

"It's illegal."

"So?" We and Rome survived, we turned right onto Amadeo, northbound, then—

"Nine! Is every one-way street in Rome only two blocks long??!?!"

"We're still a half mile away . . . Spencer's approaching the finish!"

"Wait! Look! Is this . . . a hospital zone? Yesss!!! Air horn! I gotta have more air horn!" I turned right, right, left, and nearly ran into a small white van blocking Via Enrico Cialdini's single lane. Nine gave them a blast of air horn. "Nine! Stop . . . is that . . . is that an ambulance?"

"Aliray, *no* country uses trucks that shitty." The first of three frail old women stumbled out its side door, a paramedic emerging from the building to hand them walkers. "Oh no, oh man—"

"A wheelchair van." I sighed. "A wheelchair van. I can't believe you airhorned a wheelchair van."

"Er . . . maybe we should back up?"

"Nine, this is a one-way street."

"I can't believe you just said that."

"What if another wheelchair van comes up behind us?"

"*Grazie!*" Nine called out, and waved at them as the van pulled away. "*Molto grazie! Molto grazie!* Termini Train Station ahead! Turn left! Eight blocks to finish line!"

"Cops on the right! Where's Spencer? Should I make a run for it?"

ONE QUARTER MILE BEAR LEFT AT ROUNDABOUT.

"Alex . . . he's five blocks from the finish! Rome cops don't care—" Our tires chirped before he could finish, the cop at the Alfa's wheel waving us on and yelling *"Pronto! Pronto!"* as we slipped through yet another crowd of jaywalkers.

FIVE HUNDRED FEET BEAR LEFT AT ROUNDABOUT.

"He's one block away!" Nine called out. I barreled into the Piazza Della Republica traffic circle, bore left—*against* counterclockwise traffic—to pass a bus, and spotted the Hotel Boscolo finish line 150 feet beyond the cars approaching us head-on four abreast. Nine ignored the phone ringing with what could only be bad news. I turned 160 degrees right, into the legal traffic flow, and grabbed the PA microphone to unleash what little Italian I'd studied for just such an occasion. *"PRONTO! PRONTO! ATTENZIONE! AVANZA! AVANZA!"*

I sped to the outside lane, cut left perpendicular to another bus that would have killed us both had it screeched to a halt 12 inches farther, accelerated between two cars merging from the right, then turned right into the finish line parking lot, nearly killing a gorgeous miniskirted tourist who, in the belief we actually *were* the Barcelona Guardia Civil, ran in front of our car yelling "Guardia Civil?"

"I think we're second," said Nine, looking around for the blue Porsche. I spotted Ross and Emma waving from the deck of the café overlooking the finish line, but I couldn't make out their expressions. A Gumball staffer ran up to Nine's window, and in breathless unison we asked the dreaded question.

"What number are we?"

He looked curious as to why we were asking. "You're . . . number one."

We cheered and hugged, nearly tearing our seats off their rails. I was glad Spencer didn't see us, for when he arrived I owed him humble thanks. Without him I'd never have seen. I'd never have known. After I wiped my head with a towel brought by one of the hotel staffers watching in amusement, I requested two bottles of champagne and parked at the end of the hotel driveway, perfectly positioned to leave first the next morning. We joined Ross and Emma on the deck. Nine and I each drank three large bottles of water, then, at 3:45 P.M., with no blue Porsche in sight precisely 15 minutes after our arrival, our reeking clothes forced us to request the bill.

"Per favore," I asked the concierge on the way upstairs, "please ask the valet to leave space next to the Guardia Civil BMW for a blue Porsche. He's a legend, and this bottle is for him."

"Who shall I say it is from?"

"He'll know."

OVERLOOKING GUMBALL FINISH LINE
1630 HOURS (APPROX)

"Vous êtes fous!" said our new and unexpectedly welcoming friend Greg Tunon, who switched to English upon seeing Nine's confusion. "Jon! How you and Alex Roy drive today is crazy. I know about this, I know about crazy."

The down-to-earth, forty-going-on-fifteen Monegasque entrepreneur with messy graying hair and a furtive grin—one-half of the black Mercedes CLK team Ross warned of—had invited us to his table to watch the cars arrive. Based on the beehives I'd kicked up along the A1 and A24, we prepared for a lengthy predinner dinner.

Little did we know the honor we were being paid, greater even than Ross's convoy invitation. Greg and his tall, goateed co-driver, Remy "Kalbas" Gelas, were the most secretive of Gumball legends, having achieved the highest-ever recorded speed by a team *not* arrested for the feat (224 mph), in Morocco, in Greg's $1 million yellow Ferrari Enzo, subsequently disabled by a defective brake caliper that exploded through the top of the front fender. Greg, well known among manufacturers of such cars, had the car recovered by plane at Ferrari's expense, after which the brake system was redesigned, as per his suggestions, in the world's most expensive vehicular recall. Allegedly. Kalbas was Greg's Nine, and they were accompanied by a Peugeot support van driven by Anna, Greg's olive-skinned, sky-blue-eyed Russian girlfriend of such beauty she resembled Kira Morgan seen through a prism, and Chris, his "sister" of equivalent beauty yet diametrically opposed Nordic appearance.

Greg stretched his arm around Anna's long neck and raised his glass. "We drink to the crazy Polizei. Amazing what you did today, Alex. Kalbas also like the big pass you make in Bosnia, very aggressive. We watch all your moves since London, last year also. Tomorrow we make the big push to Monaco, because the Gumball is finished next to my house. Maybe you drive with us, but I do not think the M5 is fast enough."

"Come, Alex," said Kalbas, "I show you what *we* bring inside the car." Greg's Mercedes was not the $70,000, special-order, 362-horsepower CLK55 AMG I'd suspected, but a CLK-DTM—one of one hundred ever made, a $300,000, 582-horsepower, street-legal race car—the interior fitted with several items even *I* didn't recognize. "Alex, look how nice, these gyrostabilizer binoculars. They attach to the windshield like so, then I spot police at several kilometers. We are going 260 kilometers per hour, and I can see police, cool, we pass at 90! For next time we consider putting night vision also . . ."

The DTM was parked in third position, beside Spencer's Porsche. Kalbas saw my eyes dart inside the 911's interior and scan its bare dash. "Spencer"— he nodded—"he is good, no? Yesterday he race us very hard from Bari to Taormina, almost 500 kilometers! We come in first, but we beat him by five minutes only. Amazing how you beat him, really, Alex Roy, in this BMW. Greg and I could not believe it."

"It was very close."

"Ten or 15 minutes, still! You push your car to the limit, no?"

"The M5 *definitely* had more," said Nine.

"Maybe a little," I said.

"Aliray, don't get me wrong, you were incredible, but I think you coulda gotten five percent more out of the old girl."

"Even so," said Kalbas, "Spencer did not look so happy when he arrived."

"Do you know him?"

"This Spencer? Not so much, only the face, but he is a good driver. We respect him, he respects us. We don't need to know more, yes? Now we know you and Jon, you are okay with us. When we get to Monaco, Greg and I take you out with the girls. You will enjoy this time."

Nine elbowed me on the way back to the table, giving me a sly smile as we sat down—the smile of *we've made it*. Ant and Pete arrived soon thereafter, then Grimaldi and Hagen, Muss and Seamus, and a gray Aston lent—by the factory, allegedly—to The Drivers of the burgundy DB9 I'd predicted wouldn't make it to Prague. While my back was turned, the black SLR—the third and final car Ross had warned of—parked directly in front of the M5. A Mercedes mechanic knelt beside the $500,000-plus car, cables dangling from the dashboard to a laptop propped against his knee. The owner, a tall, redheaded Englishman, stood beside the open engine bay yelling into his phone.

"Guess I owe you Taco Bell," said Nine. "Who's the SLR guy?"

"He's the prick who got us all kicked off the Paul Ricard track last year . . . the last checkpoint before Cannes. We're all doing laps, he shows up in his Bentley, breaks the rule about not passing the pace car, and security-boots *everyone*."

"*Mais oui,*" said Kalbas, "this is Oliver Morley. Someone say he races in the Ferrari Challenge Series, and is quite good." Kalbas shook his fist. "He drives hard, he is a professional."

"Not that day," I said. "He pissed off a lot of people." I waited until Morley finished his call, then walked over and introduced myself with a forced smile. He looked me up and down with contempt before turning back to his car. I hesitated, shocked at this unexpectedly vicious welcome. "Hey,

Oliver . . . I'd really like to go refuel. I don't suppose you might consider . . . moving your car when you're done? With your repairs?"

"Riiiiight"—he snickered over his shoulder—"so you can leave early again?"

Up until that moment I'd only ever had opponents. The instant Rawlings dismounted his Avalanche, we were friends. Kenworthy and I had laughed over beers. Torquenstein and I had shaken hands. Ant and Pete, my technical peers, had always been gentlemen, as had other veterans. Even Spencer and his codriver had waved. Oliver Morley was no mere opponent. Morley, whose experience was of an order of magnitude greater than mine, his SLR 20 percent faster and ten times costlier than my M5, had just uttered the single most offensive accusation possible between veterans. He could easily have verified I hadn't left early. He knew he could probably beat me in a head-to-head duel, and yet he was denying me the checkpoint refuel I might desperately need to keep up, if not win. Team Polizei, the longtime underdog, had acquired a fearsome new enemy at precisely the wrong time.

I returned to the table to discuss stage rankings with Nine. Two checkpoints remained for the final day. Gumball driver psychology guaranteed that whoever took Florence would immediately leave for the Monaco finish. We had taken Vienna and Rome. Greg and Kalbas had taken Taormina. Rumors suggested Spencer had taken Prague. Michele and Ivan had taken KRKA Park in Croatia. Muss and Seamus had taken the Hungaroring and Budapest. To win, we needed to take one or both final checkpoints, or pray none of those in contention took either. Nine looked at my notes and shook his head.

"Nine, bad news first."

"Well, the good news is, if it rains, the SLR is screwed—"

"If it makes it out of Rome."

"Let's hope it does, Aliray, otherwise *we're* screwed tomorrow morning."

"On the flip side, that CLK-DTM's a death trap if it's wet out."

"While you were pissing off Oliver, Kalbas was telling me"—Nine's eyes widened in admiration—"about he and Greg doing Paris-Dakar a coupla times, and the Baja 1000, and about a hundred other races."

Dakar. Baja. These made Gumball look like go-karts at the amusement park.

"Aliray, rain may slow them down, but it won't stop them, and it won't stop Spencer."

"All right"—I paused—"but it will slow down the GT3000 guys, their GT2's rear-wheel drive just like Kenworthy's. Spencer can't improve his navigation overnight, and I know the south of France better than anyone except

Greg. He and Kalbas probably know every cop from Ventimiglia to Monaco, so our only hope's that Morley doesn't get in the way of our taking Florence."

Greg and Kalbas would take Monaco. It was inevitable, and they deserved it, just as Muss had deserved Budapest. We'd earned second no matter how we placed that day. We might even have earned first overall, but more importantly, we'd gained the trust and respect of the legends who wanted nothing but an exchange of phone numbers and a spare seat if they broke down. Ross had already suggested we team up if Nine didn't return in 2006. Grimaldi invited me to Miami, Muss and Seamus demanded I see the real Budapest, and Schtaven, Frankl, and The Weis called upon our arrival in Monaco, their inability to congratulate me without a prerehearsed, counterbalancing insult *almost* as predictable as our having spotted Morley on the Autostrada shoulder several hours earlier, yelling into his phone, standing beside his black Mercedes-MacLaren SLR with its orange-striped hood open, its black paint gleaming in the sun somewhere between Florence and Monaco. There was no way to be sure exactly where, because although I took it easy on the final 250 miles, we were going too fast to stop, and as Nine pointed out, his phone *did* seem to be working. Besides, Nine and I had after-party plans with Greg and Kalbas, and it was rude to be late.

It was the Golden Age.

Little did we know it was the tail end.

Part V The Driver

CHAPTER 25

The Sherpa From Dallas

TUESDAY, SEPTEMBER 20, 2005
NEW YORK CITY

I was lost. The call I'd awaited after Gumball never came, and the victory I so craved—Rawlings's defeat on that summer's Bullrun—had proven Pyrrhic. He broke down and fell behind, I grew complacent, and meticulous newcomer Marek Harrison slipped past me to take first place. And everyone at the finish party knew it.

There was nothing to do but wait. If Cory didn't have the answers, there probably was no Driver, and never had been.

"Don't get all shy on me!" he said in his signature Southern cackle. "I know where y'all live, so get your ass ready! I'll be there in fifteen!" He was never late.

"Aw yeaaaahhhhh!" Rawlings hollered before I fully opened the door. "Alex Roy! Mr. Polizei himself! Wassup!!??"

"Wow ... I ... what a surprise!" We both grinned, he at my most un-Polizei sweatpants and T-shirt, I at how—if I hadn't known better—the man before me appeared on his way to a country-western S&M party in the West Village. Frenemies far from past fields of battle, we hugged in the foyer.

"Aw"—he turned to someone just out of sight in the hall—"isn't Alex just a sweetheart when he ain't Mr. Polizei?" The man stepped forward and offered his hand. I recalled meeting him briefly at the Bullrun Lingerie Party in Vegas.

"Rory," he said, introducing himself, "how you doing?"

"Damn!" Rawlings said as he surveyed my Japanese-style loft's living room, "I sure hope you got some cold beers somewhere in this place!"

"Saving them up just for you."

"Nice sword collection!" He placed a hand on my chrome-plated antique .30-caliber machine gun. "But *this*! You're an interesting guy, Alex. You might need to bring this along next time, *if* you wanna stop me from kicking your ass after what happened this year!"

"I don't think I'll need it . . . you know I play fair."

He turned to me and raised his bottle. "Cheers to that, Roy, but you *will* need it when you see what I got planned for ya!"

"So," I said, "what's the special occasion?"

"Weeeellll," said Rawlings, "Rory here's with Spike TV, and they've been talking with Andy and Dave about doin' something with Bullrun for '06, then we all got talkin' about me doin' my own show, then I started thinkin' about this 32:07 movie you're doin' with Cory."

"How's that going?" Rory asked, then took a conspicuously long swig of his beer.

"It's going, but Cory's in charge, I'm just an investor."

"C'mon," said Rawlings, "is it true? Somebody did New York to L.A. in 32:07?"

"Sure is," I said. Rory shook his head in disbelief.

"And"—Rawlings thrust his bottle toward me—"*you've* got proof?"

"Hells, yeah."

"And you've seen it with your own eyes?! Pictures? Video?"

"Not the finished movie, but a lot of footage, and The Driver interviews."

"Riiiiiiiiight." He and Rory glanced at each other.

"So what's up, guys?"

"Here's the deal, Mr. *Pol-eez-eye* . . . I'll bet you twenty-five grand I can beat you cross-country, mano a mano. Straight up, no bullshit. Just you and me."

"You're kidding."

"Tell you what. I'll betcha fifty grand I'll beat you *and* do it in 25 hours."

"Richard," I said for the first time, "you can't be serious."

"Fuck yeah, I'm serious."

"I'll ignore the fifty grand, since 25 hours is totally impossible—"

"If you *know* I can't do it, then take the bet! You scared, Mr. Police-man?"

"It's not *you* I'm scared of. I might consider doing it, on *one* condition, because there's only one way to get away with it."

"Bring it on!"

"Just the two of us, all stealth, no press, no TV, nobody knows."

Rory shook his head. Rawlings looked at me like *I* was crazy. "Alex, the Bullrun boys are all pumped to shoot it for Spike TV, it'll be sweet! We'll get choppers, a party at both ends—"

I raised my hand to cut him off. "That's the worst idea of all time."

"You *are* scared!"

"Yeah, scared of having guns pulled on me, scared of being arrested at the finish, scared of going to jail! Are you nuts?"

"Come on," said Rory. "Andy and Handsome Dave are ready to do it."

"Of course they are," I said. "Their asses aren't on the line."

"All right, then," said Rawlings, "you think about it and let me know."

"Oh, I'll do it, on my conditions. *You* think about *that.*"

"Ain't got nothing to think about."

I lay down and watched the shadows of the overhead fan blades' slow rotation across the ceiling. Twenty-five hours. Rawlings couldn't have read *Cannonball!,* and he obviously knew nothing of what I'd already learned about the Express from Cory. This would give me a huge advantage, *if* I accepted. He also believed I was the second best illegal endurance driver in the United States, after him, of course. I was flattered. I was terrified. His offer was the only alternative to the gradual, seemingly inevitable end of my quest, but it wasn't quite fear that made me hesitate. We'd long been inextricably bound by our costly and public rivalry, but however parallel our paths, I now realized we were very far apart. I had become, in every way but one, the man I sought—a man whose very existence was based solely on faith. All I had to do was lift the phone, call those on my list, and set a date and time, yet still I hesitated. I was scared. I wanted someone else to lead me up the mountain.

Rawlings didn't want a guide. He wanted someone to go with him.

I had to call Cory immediately, and not merely because a Rawlings solo run might affect the film's prospects. There was no one else to call. She stopped me the instant I uttered his name. "Alex, there's no such thing as coincidence. He and Rory have been fishing for info on the movie, and I'm not talking. What'd they want?" She remained silent after I told her.

"Cory, are you thinking what I am?"

"There's a lot to think about. You first."

"We're in a catch-22. I can't do the show, but if he goes on his own and breaks it, no matter how good our movie is, America's gonna be watching our boy from Texas instead."

"Relax," she said. "Rawlings doesn't *want* you to go with him. Rawlings *needs* you to go with him. He *can't* go without you."

America loved a winner. Rawlings needed a loser, and every red-blooded citizen would cheer the Texan's triumph over the fake German cop with a shaved head.

But not one of them grasped my true inner calculus. I wasn't interested solely in notoriety, as was everyone's first guess, nor in money. Breaking the record wasn't another checkpoint en route to my goal. In the absence of The Driver, it alone had become *the* goal. Rawlings would go even if it couldn't be broken. I'd only go if it could. Spike and Bullrun were willing to risk others' lives—and Rawlings even his own—for entertainment. I would not.

Rawlings had an excuse to go. I'd been waiting for one. And he'd just given it to me.

Although I couldn't go with him, he couldn't go without *me,* and the first public attempt to break 32:07 in twenty years would bring down a draconian curtain of civil and criminal charges on the participants. The final step on my path, so inconceivably dangerous that I had never considered the one option now forced upon me, now lay beyond a closing door.

I had to see. I had to know.

I had to go. Alone. Without a guide. As soon as possible. Before Rawlings.

"Alex, are you there?"

"Sorry, just thinking . . . Cory, if Rawlings *did* go, could he break it?"

"I'll send more on Diem and Turner, show you the rough cut, then *you* tell *me.*"

CHAPTER 26

"So whaddya think?" said Cory at the end of the world's first screening of *32 Hours, 7 Minutes.* She was sitting on my couch in between The Weis and Nine, Team Polizei consigliere Shawn Canter on my emergency movie-watching futon, Skylar in my lap on one recliner, Lelaine Lau—my Audrey Hepburn-esque business partner—on the other.

"Maaaaaaan," said Nine, "I can't believe these Diem/Turner guys had a spotter plane."

I turned to Cory. "Now we know where the spotter-plane legend came from."

"Cory, Alex," said The Weis, "if all these Express guys said they'd go again, how come no one has? Why haven't you?'"

Cory cracked a smile at him, then at me. "It *would* be great to shoot some B-roll in the M5."

"Aliray," said The Weis, "do you think 32:07 can be broken? Seriously."

Everyone's eyes darted between us.

"I don't know."

"So you," said The Weis, "supposedly one of the best in the world at this kind of thing, even with all your scanners and gear, say it can't be broken?"

"Of all the drivers I've ever met, Rawlings is the only one who thinks it's possible, but he's basing that on far less information than we have."

"Alex," said The Weis, "what does Yates say about the old records?"

"Remember, he only recognizes the 32:51 record from the '79 Cannon-ball. Once the movie comes out, the 32:07 time will be recognized."

"But what does he say is possible now?"

"Thirty-six hours."

"I'll quote Diem," said Cory. "Records are meant to be broken."

"Call it a recon run," said Canter. "Shoot your B-roll, drive safe, see what happens. Alex does some talking-head stuff, and there's your movie."

Cory nodded. "A peek over the edge."

Nine glared at me. "Moron . . . is this what you wanted?"

"Aliray," said The Weis, "you do it, I'll help you prep."

"Alex," said Canter, "what time are you going to shoot for?"

"It's just a recon," I said, looking Cory in the eye. "I'll do the math, let's say . . . 36 hours?"

"I say 37," said Nine.

"I say 34," said The Weis.

"Guys," I said, "if we don't do it by mid-December, we have to wait until April."

"Are you insane?" Cory shook her ahead at Nine, then turned to me. "I can't believe *you* of all people want to wait until April. Suppose we go and get some amazing time, and *then* you decide you want to give 32:07 a shot. The real deal. We'll have to wait until *after* next summer. We've got to do this *now,* just in case. *Just* in case."

The silence made it clear that everyone had greatly underestimated this young independent filmmaker from L.A. Everyone else went to Sundance and prayed. Cory didn't care. She would do anything for this movie, including a run. A big run. *The* run only Rawlings and I, whatever our motives, were willing to attempt. Everyone else, the rally people who didn't run, or come back, the muscle-car guys, the Ferrari guys, the Cipriani diners, the mattress-tamers, every sports-car-driving banker in New York except Maher—all of them were joking. Cory Welles was not joking.

"Cory, the M5 will be ready within four weeks. Whatever it takes."

"Christ," said Nine, "you're talking right before Christmas. The weather, man, it's suicide. This is like *badidea.com.*"

"I'll buy max-performance all-season tires. Everyone, even *I* don't know the legal ramifications of what we're going to do, so this conversation *cannot* leave this room."

"Always inventing drama," said The Weis. "I'm hungry and I miss my wife. I say we adjourn."

Everyone sighed with relief until I stood and said, "I think we should all sign nondisclosures. Cory?" She nodded. "Good, in that case, I love you all, thanks."

Cory cornered me immediately. "Alex, *you're* scared that if Rawlings finds out we're going, he'll go solo, no matter what."

"Precisely. If anything goes wrong, if he's caught, or kills someone, we're screwed. My name's on a movie called *32:07*. If some crazy prosecutor starts digging around and asks *anyone* who's the most likely to try to break it, I'm probably in the top three. Then we'll never go, ever."

"Done. I'll have my attorney prepare NDAs for everyone. We'll keep it secret until . . . I guess until we figure out what to do?"

"At least until we're back safe, or maybe until the movie comes out. The beauty of it is that no one who knows Team Polizei will *ever* believe that I could make a run and not go public the same day. Any leak will sound like a bullshit rumor. They know I can't keep my mouth shut. Enough talk; time for pizza, ice cream, and bed."

"Good boy," The Weis said on his way out. "You're gonna be fine. I'm proud of you."

"Enough man love," said Nine, behind him. "Aliray, do I have to ask who's copiloting?"

"No."

"I hate you."

"I hate you, too, but think of it! The first ones to try in twenty years! Nine, if we beat 36 hours then Yates is wrong, which means everyone is wrong."

"Man, you're gonna owe me a lot more than Taco Bell this time."

"I'll buy you In-N-Out Burger when we get to L.A. And I'll even split the driving with you."

"That sounds like a really good deal, Mr. Trump, now should I turn around and bend over, too? Try this one . . . I take the burger and you do all the driving."

"Cute. FYI, I can't drive in Arizona. If we're stopped for any reason, my '04 Bullrun arrest might come up on a police computer. We have to stop at one or both ends of Arizona so you can drive that leg."

"Wait a second, if you're driving and we're pulled over outside Arizona, how do you know all the police databases aren't connected?"

"I don't. In fact Homeland Security has been trying to connect them since 9/11."

"Thank God," said Nine, whose new IT consultancy lent him unique insight into such matters. "That'll take years. Anything else?"

"I need you here every day after work, six to ten, Monday through Thursday, until we go. Someone's got to double-check my nav and fuel tables."

"But I suck at math."

"Me, too. Get some sleep, Mr. Goodrich."

Everyone left but Skylar, with whom I watched TV in bed until she fell asleep without a word about the evening's events. Only now did I see how much I'd changed since we'd met a year earlier. I wondered if she loved me too much to try to deter me, or if she feared being sacrificed because nothing would.

At 2 A.M. I snuck out of bed, my vibrating phone noisily walking itself across my hardwood floor. "Aliray," Nine whispered, his words spoken from a tiled bathroom like that in which I, too, now hid, "have you thought about what happens if we break 36? I mean . . . in a big way?"

"Take a wild guess."

"Dammit, now I'm *definitely* not gonna get any sleep. Seriously, do you think we can?"

"Do *you*? Now I've got to go to bed before my girlfriend leaves me over this, and so should you." I hung up, but suspected he hung up on me first. I closed my eyes and tried in vain to sleep.

I stopped answering the phone roughly two weeks later, uncomfortable with having to lie even to close friends about why I'd stopped going out, and why my visit to the West Coast, purportedly to work on the film, might last as long as several months. I wondered how career criminals explained their periodic long absences to civilian friends, then quickly understood.

I needed eight weeks to complete work for which I had three. Our conversations, although held in English, became a hybridized jumble of military and mathematical terminology utterly impenetrable to all but Cory, The Weis, and Nine. Nine and I had each already spent at least 40 off-work hours preparing and test-driving the M5. I'd spent another 20 on police-radio-frequency research, barely a quarter of what I thought necessary. We spent painstaking hours of slowly scrolling, at maximum screen resolution, mile by mile through the Garmin's *Shortest Route* feature's best guess at the shortest route. The elimination of errant turns and gratuitous mileage was so important we began eyeballing the trip on-screen in near-real time, an ordeal made worse during our shift change, groans punctuating the hourly prying of a computer mouse from an atrophied claw that had once been a hand. Having cut the route down to 2,817 miles and revised the fuel/time tables, we attempted to correct the errors cascading down the spreadsheet with every mile and minute shaved.

We cursed Microsoft tech support's policy of hanging up on anyone using their software for what might be a criminal endeavor, then cursed each other for not suggesting we tell them it was a high school science project. Whatever errors remained on our increasingly complex driveplan, we settled on its projection of 36:27.

Between Nine's IT background and my love of the Military Channel, countless driveplan revisions led to nomenclature such as *Version .86Beta (Recon -12)*. Not only did this add gravitas to a document of such vast felonious import that we fought to conceal our giggles from The Weis (seated at my desk, hoping to save our lives through nightly analysis of National Weather Service forecasts), but the numerical suffix also counted down the days to departure, a constant reminder no fear-inspired levity could cloak.

On Friday, December 2, I began my survey of potential departure points as close as possible to one of Manhattan's three Hudson River crossings. The Garmin's mystical calculations suggested the Holland Tunnel was one mile closer to Los Angeles than the Lincoln, and nine miles closer than the George Washington Bridge. The Garmin also listed thirteen parking lots within one-quarter mile of our dream pick, which on a Friday night at midnight was only 10 minutes from my garage. I prayed, circling the tunnel entrance in increasing, stepladdered arcs around Tribeca's complex network of one-way streets, always returning to the center to gauge its distance from the few indoor, guarded lots I found suitably proximate. A cluster of Port Authority police officers awaited me on my sixth slow tunnel drive-by. One pointed at me, another raised his radio, and just when I thought another pass might get me arrested under suspicion of scoping out one of New York's most visible terror targets, I spotted a familiar but unexpectedly placed sign over their heads. The London-based Classic Car Club, a high-end sports-car time-share dealership, had just opened its gorgeous New York showroom 50 feet from the mouth of the tunnel. The patron saint of Nonviolent and Unprofitable Crimes must have been listening, because in a fortuitous coincidence I'd long ago met the CCC's owners, and they'd been more than familiar with both Gumball and Team Polizei.

Cory returned Sunday, December 11, with a mountain of large, hard plastic camera and DV deck cases. With the surprise addition of James Petersmeyer, a twentysomething assistant cameraman Cory deemed essential on the run, four of us would share a space smaller than allotted just one in supermax solitary confinement.

"Two best friends who've run out of good jokes," said Nine, "a hot, non-smoking, hippie black belt who's got us by the balls if we tell a bad joke on camera, and some surfer dude we don't know? It's the worst road trip of all time, only ten times longer."

WEDNESDAY, DECEMBER 14, 2005

AI DESIGN—TUCKAHOE, NEW YORK

58 HOURS TO DEPARTURE

"But how are you going to prove it?" said Matt Figliola, president of AI Design, the *Robb Report*'s pick for the country's best automotive customization specialists. Matt's six feet three inches barred him from sitting in clients' cars of Italian origin. Resembling Paul Sorvino, he alternated between the latter's on-screen grimace and his own young son's red-cheeked glee whenever I personally appeared to request installation of yet another illegal device. The Weis, Nine, and Cory approached as we stood by the M5, by far the dirtiest, most dented, highest-mileage car present, its $35,000 book value (not including thousands of dollars of modifications useless to anyone else) but a fraction of the next cheapest car in the garage. Charles Graeber, a six-five, thirty-two-year-old, Hunter Thompson-esque writer for *Wired,* the *New York Times,* and *National Geographic,* who spoke like he gargled with charcoal and gravel, and who, unarmed, had survived many unexpected meetings with Africa's surliest meat-loving predators, sat uncomfortably hunched forward in my driver's seat, already pushed back against its detent. Kenny Karasinski, AI's young, goateed, shaved-headed Master Electronics Specialist, a man as responsible for keeping me out of jail as Seth, sat beside Graeber, pointing out and explaining how much of my gear had been concealed from prying eyes—and what couldn't be.

"We wanted to bring *him,*" I whispered, looking down at Graeber, "but he wouldn't fit in the back that long without crying for mercy. We're doing witnesses at the start and finish, all the video, E-ZPass, gas and toll receipts."

"Why bother if you're not trying to break it?"

"Maybe something good will happen," Cory piped in, poking me in the arm.

"If Aliray had any balls," said The Weis, "he'd give it a shot."

I gave him a nasty glare. "You'd try to stop me if I really wanted to."

"What a coincidence." Cory chuckled. She gave me a furtive glance and silently mouthed the letters *N, D,* and *A.*

"Yes, Matt signed the nondisclosure. I gave him the whole story."

"Don't worry," he said, "we've got dirt on guys much more famous than this nutjob, but none of theirs is nearly as entertaining."

"Matt," she said, "do you think the record can be broken?"

"Everyone says it's impossible, but if anyone can, it's Alex Roy." He proudly pointed at my new pair of trunk-mounted scanner antennas. "No one on the planet preps as much as he does. He's crazy, but in a good way. Crazy, but smart."

"Tell 'em about the Enzo guy!" Kenny yelled from inside the M5.

"Oh yeah!" Matt smiled. "So you should see some clients' faces when they recognize Alex's BMW, even without the Police and Gumball stickers. One guy comes in with a Ferrari Enzo, and you know what he says? 'Do you think it's okay to sit in Alex Roy's car?'"

The Weis rolled his eyes. "Don't get too cocky. It's not you, it's the car."

"I'm telling you," said Matt, "this *has* to be the most famous BMW in the world."

The Weis nodded at me, his eyes devoid of humor, and pointed over his shoulder at Matt's empty office. I followed him like a truant child. He closed the door and turned to me with a dour expression I'd only last seen on my father's face, five and a half years earlier.

"Wait," I said, then hoped to lighten the mood by adding, "Bad news first?"

"No jokes, Aliray. You listen to me, because this is as serious as it gets. I'm proud of you for going all the way with this race business, but if you think you're special because a bunch of kids and some idiot with a Ferrari think you're cool, someone's gonna die. You do this for yourself, not to beat some record or those rally idiots, and you'll come home safe. You want to prove something? Tell Nine now before you kill Cory, too. Everyone else thinks you're some crazy genius who gets away with breaking the law because you're funny, but it's not funny anymore. I *know* you're scared. I'm scared for you. This is the most dangerous thing you've ever done. You'll be driving so fast so long, your fastest day on Gumball will look pathetic, and if you ever become famous for any of this, and I mean paid, not just pictures on a website, and you come back acting like some Hollywood prick, I'm going to smack you in the face the way I wouldn't my own son."

"The Weis . . . can I say something?"

"No, but are ready for the good news?"

"You hate me?"

"The weather looks good."

"So now that I might get killed, you don't hate me?"

"I'll hate you less if you break 35. Why are we talking? Let's go and make faces at Nine while he checks out Cory."

CHAPTER 27

The Worst Road Trip of All Time

I was wrong. Yates was wrong. Everyone was wrong.

It might have begun in Ohio, when my driveplan projection first went awry, or in Oklahoma, where my recalculations grew so inaccurate we began ignoring the plan altogether. Awash in white noise, we switched off the scanners in New Mexico, breaking such protocol for the first time. By Arizona, we stopped calling out police cars, so many having evaporated after we'd concurred on their positions, makes, models—even the height of their antennas. Nine and I exchanged harsh words for the first time. Cory began cutting off our increasingly incoherent remarks. It wasn't merely fatigue. Something was wrong. I wasn't scared when we crossed into California. I was terrified, but I could not stop.

I had 16,500 miles of experience doing precisely this. I could have written the book on high-speed, illegal endurance driving. Nine had ten years of semiprofessional racing behind him. Cory had spent three years studying the U.S. Express. No one was more knowledgeable, no team more capable.

But all our assumptions were wrong, and we couldn't know why or by how much until our wretched, tedious ordeal was over. I theorized we'd been hallucinating since our thirtieth hour. No one knew, because, in our penultimate breach of protocol, we'd stopped talking.

The V1's alerts no longer made sense. I turned it off, the first time in fourteen years I'd driven without it. Approximately 100 miles from L.A. we spotted dozens of patrol cars' lights flashing on a service road. The predawn convoy sped north toward the U-turn/overpass under which we'd just driven south. Our electronic countermeasures (ECM) and comms were useless, Petersmeyer asleep, Cory silent, Nine spent. All I could do was drive. Blinded by an eerily luminous fog bank through Lone Pine Canyon, I slowed to 40.

No one complained. In the left lane I saw what appeared to be an overturned yacht. "Guys," I rasped, slowing to fifteen, "is that—"

"Yes," Cory said flatly. Nine didn't answer. The fog cleared as we neared the I-15/I-10 interchange, our final turn, after which a mere 42 minutes remained. We caught up with a four-lane-wide rolling roadblock, their blue and red beacons flashing at the end of the traffic jam behind which we were trapped. We were still one exit from our turn. An otherworldly light suddenly flashed over the car. A helicopter flew past, its spotlight dancing among the cars ahead. Traffic stopped. The police ahead began funneling cars toward the shoulder.

There was only one possible explanation, but before I could suggest faking a breakdown, abandoning the car, and running, Cory had an idea.

Based on a 36:27 drivetime, our ETA in L.A. was 5:34 A.M. (PST). The witnesses were to stage at the Santa Monica Pier Finish Line at 5:30 A.M., just in case we were early. We missed them by more than an hour and a half.

Because Cory knew a service-road shortcut the Garmin didn't.

Because they were still asleep when she tried to call with our new ETA.

Because our speed had inverted the cascading projection errors.

Because everyone had been wrong.

Except for a Santa Monica police cruiser unwittingly parked 30 feet from the finish line, no one saw us pull up and stop on the pier. I took a picture of the Garmin screen. Our overall average read 80.5 mph, but I was unable to calculate its significance. The total elapsed time was clearly wrong. We sat silent, each reaching through our undead stupor for the correct answer. The pier's stilts creaked as the police car rolled toward us. I lowered the window and steadied my shaking hands on the wheel. It wasn't fear. I was too tired to laugh when the officer ordered us to move. I reluctantly said yes, unwilling to risk slurring my words through a temporary reprieve.

We couldn't have known how much we'd suffer. No one did. I thought we might have died, only to arrive in a city emptied of life. This was the punishment for what we'd done.

Cory tapped me on the shoulder and nodded. One minute had passed since arrival. It was 3:54 A.M. (PST). It was Sunday, December 18, 2005.

It was true—34:46

Thirty-four hours and 46 minutes.

One hour and eight minutes *faster* than Brock Yates and Dan Gurney—the Master and the Champion—when they won the 1971 Cannonball Run in 35:54.

One hour and five minutes shy of the legendary David Heinz and David Yarborough, who set the final 1979 Cannonball Run record of 32:51.

Two hours and 39 minutes short of David Diem and Doug Turner's 32:07.

We'd been wrong about almost everything, but we hadn't failed. We had just set the eleventh fastest cross-country time in history. By accident.

Cory lived four miles away. Half an hour, at an average of 9 miles per hour. No one spoke until we arrived.

"The proof," I whispered, "the tapes . . . do you have a safe?"

"I bought one. Just in case."

I was too tired to cry.

Just before dawn, standing over her dining table, with a large calendar and a laptop displaying historical weather patterns, we selected the next available target window.

Nothing could stop it.

CHAPTER 28

The Longest Tunnel in America

We had much to learn. We had to re-create the conditions of 3446's calamitous final leg. We had to see. We had to know. I bought another V1. Cory would shoot the entire practice drive, allowing me to correlate the V1's alerts down to the mile marker, waypoint them true or false in the Garmin, then study potential traps in Google Earth. I had to evaluate my new, professionally programmed scanner. We had to understand what happened in Lone Pine Canyon. I had to do this having not slept for the 41 and a half hours we'd been awake the last time we reached this point.

I glanced at the Garmin again.

Our driving average had been 86.1 mph. Overall, including fuel stops, was 83. Only the latter mattered, and it was an incredible figure given the conditions, 2.5 mph faster than our 80.5 on 3446. We wouldn't beat Diem/Turner's 89.4, but we didn't expect to. They only achieved 32:07 on their second run in 1983, incorporating the lessons from having come in third in '82.

I was elated.

Based on the 215 miles driven this test, I extrapolated a run of just under 34 hours. Without a CB radio or laser jammers. Without Nine operating the GPS, checking bridges and on-ramps for speed traps, or helping keep me alert. Without kill switches for the brake lights, or *all* the rear lights. Without the Kenyon power gyrostabilized Steiner 7X50 (military) binoculars for long-range, daytime spotting. Without our new Raytheon NightDriver thermal camera system or its twin seven-inch displays—one each for the driver and copilot—for medium range, nighttime spotting. Without a ground controller reporting traffic and weather in real time. Without a trunk-mounted fuel cell nearly doubling our capacity. Without an air-to-ground radio. Without a spotter plane.

All of which would be ready for our all-out assault on 3207. The target date was twenty-six days away—Saturday, April 1.

"I've had enough," my dad groaned. "I'm tired." It was one of my last visits before he died, but I couldn't remember exactly when. It had to have been before the talk that changed everything. Maybe.

"Your father is tough like a lion," Genia said when he was first diagnosed. "If he wants to live longer, he will."

But the corollary was also true.

"Dad, you can't say that, I . . . I don't know what I'm doing—"

"You'll figure it out. You've always been . . . a little lazy. Too much. So tired."

"Don't say you're"—my voice went up an octave—"tired! I *know* what that means! I need—"

"You . . . you were such a good boy . . . a beautiful pianist. But you didn't want to play. I stopped paying for lessons. You wanted to draw. Beautiful drawings. So fine. Always making big pieces. So much detail. Too much. Then . . . too big, not enough time. I don't know what to tell you."

"But what does this—"

"You gave me a birthday present. You were eleven. A model car you built. An Austin-Healey, like I had. I was so happy. You brought it to my office, but the wheel . . . one of the wheels broke in your pocket—"

I remembered.

"—and you took it back. You promised to fix it. You were very sorry. In tears. Becky thought I made you cry. But it was you."

That, I didn't remember.

"I never saw that car again. You made me very sad."

"Dad . . . I'm sorry. That was a long a time ago. I don't remember, but I *am* sorry."

"Not so long ago. You made me cry. You don't know. You don't know."

I *did* die on 3446. But I was also reborn. It wasn't clear to me at first, but it became so in the voice mails and e-mails left unreturned, curious friends asking my whereabouts on birthdays and dinner parties missed. On those few occasions I ventured out socially, I, the great rambler, could barely speak—let alone listen—to anyone I didn't already know. I hated myself for succumbing to invitations from old friends, even if only for an hour. Every minute unspent on reviewing *Driveplan .91Beta (Assault 22)*, or parsing www.speedtrap.org for new entries, or individual states' sites for road-construction schedule changes, or watching hundreds of hours of Cory's interviews with the U.S. Express drivers, or scrolling through the Garmin maps or Google Earth to find speed traps (actual or potential) I'd missed after watching the entire 3446 video in real time, was one that could put me in jail, or cost me my life.

Every Friday and Saturday remaining in March had to be spent testing the M5, the new night-vision system, and the power gyrostabilizers for the binoculars and camcorders. I had to test traffic levels, tollbooth wait times, and police-patrol frequencies and locations, from the CCC as far as the New Jersey–Pennsylvania border. I had to determine whether—since the M5 wore different size wheels/tires front and rear—we could or should carry two spares. I had to measure the range and refueling time of the M5's new 35-gallon double fuel tanks, which meant driving the car round-trip to Washington or Boston every week until departure, during which I had to test the fuel transfer speeds of the different pumps used by the major gas-station chains. I had to call every suitable station within our target refueling windows (+/- 50 miles, in case we missed our projected fuel consumption), confirm their pump types and hours of operation (since two-thirds of the run was at night), and only then could I waypoint them in both Garmins. I had to determine by how much the 19.9 MPG fuel economy achieved on 3446 would decline at speeds 12 to 20 percent higher. I had to determine whether we could lower our mandatory fuel stops from 3446's seven to Diem/Turner's five and a half (or better), then synchronize them with putting Nine at the wheel through Arizona.

I had to test our Travel John emergency urination bags—under race conditions. I had to rewrite my will, brief Alfred and Genia as to what might happen, and what to do if it did. I had to see my mother and brother, in private, separately, to do the same, then apologize at length for having to do so.

I had to test the air-to-ground radios, which required driving to upstate New York when The Weis could find time away from Astrid and their newborn son. I feared stepping inside their house and seeing her cradle six-month-old Owen, my godson whom I'd barely seen—for obvious reasons. That any young, successful father would leave, even for 72 hours, to fly a single-engined, Cessna rental cross-country on a dangerous and potentially criminal enterprise, out of loyalty, for free, merely because a childhood friend requested it, made no sense even to me. I wasn't sure I'd do the same, but I had the benefit of being last among my friends on the life-marriage-baby time line, nor did I have any friends crazy enough to make such a request, which saved me from wasting time pondering the hypocrisy of it all.

I had to find a backup pilot The Weis would both approve of and get along with, since I couldn't fathom why his slated copilot—Keith "The Captain" Baskett, part of our inner circle since becoming The Weis's flight instructor fifteen years earlier, who now piloted 747s weekly from New York to Shanghai—would possibly go through with it.

I was the worst among us, and running out of time, so I lied with increasing virtuosity to everyone I knew and met as I networked, trying to find friends—or friends of friends—who worked for major news organizations, would shoot our departure and/or arrival, *then* sit on the story until some undetermined later date, or, if I failed, a major law or accounting firm that would validate our time as if it were an Olympic event. I had to find out why Rawlings had been in New York at least twice since the prior September, and if he had paid a telltale visit to the Classic Car Club. If Rawlings and the CCC's helpful but unwitting manager, Zac Moseley, had spoken, or if I couldn't convince Moseley to stay open later than in December, I had to find a backup departure location. I had to find somewhere to hide the M5 once in L.A., a location close to the pier yet totally concealed, from which a shipper could retrieve it out of sight from passing traffic, just in case the authorities came looking. I had to rent another car, locate an airport with a regional carrier the police were unlikely to contact during a manhunt, book a flight with the fewest possible stops in states we'd driven through, then arrange for the car's return to L.A. by the fastest method, all at the lowest cost.

And I had to sleep, but what few hours I could were those of the undead.

I had to see my doctor again, so scared was I about my physical state that Dr. Shapiro, a family friend whom I'd known since childhood, to whom I confessed the reason for my visit, didn't believe me, then—based on my longtime hypochondria—rejected a request for my third visit in as many weeks. I sought out Dr. Manevitz—a fellow Moth board member and the only psychiatrist I knew—who specialized in celebrity, government, corporate, and high-stress cases, for my first-ever such visit. He suggested I reconsider my plans, and ordered me to eat better and get more sleep.

And then there was the big one. Nine and I could make it even if *Driveplan .91Beta (Assault -14)* was toilet paper, except for a strategic hinge of such magnitude our entire run would fail were it not properly oiled. The drive-plan dictated that PolizeiGround and the all-new PolizeiAir intersect for the first time in St. Louis just after dawn, no later than 10 and a half hours into the run, split up only for their respective refuels   to occur simultaneously, if possible—and stay in communication so as to shorten any gap to reinterception. But, outside of the Coast Guard and military, the only organizations with experience managing the cooperation of low-speed aircraft and ground traffic were the very enemies we desperately wanted to avoid: highway-patrol aviation units.

Calling them for advice was inconceivable, so I decided to call them for advice. I called those most feared along our planned route—the Ohio State Police—and inquired (as a writer) about the various distances, speeds, and altitudes at which patrol cars and spotter aircraft communicated. They told me little of use.

I had a lot of work to do.

And for all this I sacrificed my dear, uncomplaining, Grace Kelly reincarnate, Skylar. She'd seen me off on Gumball 2005. She'd seen the video of my bad passes in Italy. She knew about the Battle of Rome. She knew more about my world than many of the drivers, but while their girlfriends fretted about competition from Prague's best, Skylar knew I might not make it back. She hadn't just feared the recon itself. She'd had faith in me that I lacked. She'd feared what would happen if we made it. By the day I got back, it was too late. She knew I'd returned a different person, now responsible for volunteers willing to risk their lives solely for friendship, planning a mission whose potential lethality could be talked around but not laughed away, blindly committed to staking everything for reasons I could no longer clearly explain, even to myself. Not once did she try to stop me, but if I saw her face beside the car door on the night of April 1, I could promise nothing without lying. I couldn't forget her mournful expression the night of Friday, December 16, and I couldn't bear to see it again, which is why within a few days of coming home I closed off my heart to focus on the task at hand.

THURSDAY, MARCH 30, 2006
POLIZEI EXPRESS JOINT OPERATIONS CENTER
2030 HOURS
49 HOURS TO DEPARTURE

"If you think you can do 31," said The Weis, "why are you projecting 31:48?"

"Why not 31:30?" someone called out.

"Let's not get cocky," I said, looking at my copy of *Driveplan 1 Alpha (Assault -2)*, which I had just distributed to everyone in the room. "Recalculating the projections because we're feeling good is—"

"Why not 30?" came another voice.

"Aliray," said The Weis, "why don't you just duplicate the 3207 guys' plans?"

"I'd rather have goals we can surpass than miss targets and make decisions, in a moving car, based on desperation."

"Look, Aliray, we want you to go fast. We're not flying the plane so you can sit on the cruise control at 105. The only way to break this record is to go irresponsibly fast."

"Ladies, gentlemen, and The Weis," I said, "let's be serious. This is not a laughing matter."

"Then stop smiling," Nine called out. This was the first and last time PolizeiAir and PolizeiGround would meet before departure, assuming weather didn't push us to the April 8 rain date. Although we could drive through weather, all of us wanted to see the first illegal cross-country racing spotter plane in twenty-three years deployed to maximum effect. Diem/Turner's interviews suggested the plane hadn't been the decisive factor in setting 32:07, but their aircrew had been hired guns.

We had The Weis and the Captain.

"Aliray," The Weis said, "we were laughing because you were laughing. Now we can't laugh? Some of us have families, you know, wives and children waiting for us, and we're here listening to some bald guy who tricked us into flying a Cessna cross-country? Don't tell me to stop laughing, tough guy, because this *isn't* funny, it's sad."

"Actually," said Nine, "now that you mentioned Aliray being in charge of you guys with the wives and kids, it *is* pretty funny. You guys, man, you're crazy."

"No," said the Captain, "you guys stuck in that car are crazy."

Graeber sat and took notes. Lelaine, to whom I'd long bragged about my oldest friends' intellect and charisma, smoked a cigarette by the window. Cory's bespectacled business partner and cameraman, Robin Acutt—a six-five, thirty-four-year-old South African whose gentle demeanor belied strict adherence to protocol and procedure, and who, despite his height, was assigned to the plane—loomed over me, camera in hand.

"Guys, please," I said, "the cameras are rolling. Think of your children who may see this someday. If any of you have objections to the plan, please say your—"

"What?" said Nine. "Is someone getting married?"

"Some of us may be getting divorced," the Captain said with his usual calm.

"Let's proceed," I said. "Bad news first. Weather. The Weis, the Captain?"

The Captain unfolded an enormous aviation chart on the table. "It's going to rain," he said. "There's a storm likely in the St. Louis area, right around our intercept point. Could be heavy cloud cover, so we may have to fly over it while you drive under, both heading southwest until we can descend and locate you. Some rough patches for us, but it shouldn't be a problem."

"But we do have a problem," said The Weis. "Weight. We've got two guys over six-five coming in the Cessna, both weighing at least 220 each, plus myself and the Captain and all of Robin's camera gear. Depending on conditions, we might have a problem. Even in good conditions, all that weight's going to mean landing for another fuel stop."

I'd thought of everything—pertaining to ground operations. I hadn't considered the catastrophic ripple effect of adding Graeber, the only third-party journalist/witness on the actual journey, to the plane's manifest. An additional landing—and the subsequent delay in their catching up, slower once again because of the additional weight—would dramatically decrease our aerial recon time.

The Weis read my concern immediately. "Aliray, I promise you we'll catch up. We'll find you. The road curves, we fly straight. As long as you give us consistent location updates, we'll get there."

I trusted him. It was The Weis. Even if he was wrong—which he never was—the Captain would be with him, and the Captain really was never, ever wrong. If anything did go wrong, I'd have grist on The Weis forever, and I'd never fly the Captain's employer again.

Spirits were high when we adjourned. Only a freak line of tornadoes, or a sick child, or an Outside Context Problem could stop us.

FRIDAY, MARCH 31, 2006
AI DESIGN
0830 HOURS
37 HOURS TO DEPARTURE

"Well . . . you've got two problems," said Matt, rotating in his wheeled Recaro office chair, surrounded by half the AI staff, even those absent taking personal pride in the happiness of their most infamous customer. "One ehhhhh, and one bleeccchh."

"Bleeccchh news first."

"All right," said Kenny, whose clipped, lawyerly explanations would have made for movie dialogue, "you requested we install the thermal night vision out of sight in the front air dam. We concurred. You said your car's temperature gauge ran high last night. We think you're getting airflow reduction."

"How much airflow reduction?"

Matt rubbed his head. "I'd guess 25 percent."

"Solutions?"

"Number one," Kenny paused, "you . . . could take out the night vision."

"Let's be serious."

Kenny and Matt burst out laughing. Mark Palines, in charge of all things Polizei not within Kenny's realm, chimed in from his nearby desk.

"Just keep that car moving," he said with knowing grin. "Fast. If you need to average at least 89.4 mph to beat 32:07—"

"Just keep that car moving," said Matt. *"Do not stop."*

"That won't be a problem."

"Now," said Matt, "for the bad news."

This was Mark's realm. "You described some throttle hesitation around 4,000 rpm. It's most likely the mass air filters—"

"I'm embarrassed to say I don't know what those do."

"You want me to explain?"

"I'm out of time. How long to replace them?"

They offered to do it for free. A nearby BMW dealer had the parts. I napped until they were done just after lunch, called Cory to explain, then got in the car for a leisurely drive through Westchester. I pulled out of AI's driveway.

Then the engine died.

1930 HOURS (APPROX)
26 HOURS TO DEPARTURE

I feared lava would pour out of the phone when I told Cory. The plane was ready. The camera crews and witnesses were on one hour's notice. Only the car—*my* leg of the tripod—remained. AI and I had one hour to salvage three months of exhortations, labors, and pleas, because after this weekend we might never be able to reconstitute PolizeiAir again. The wives wouldn't have it.

I wasn't angry or disappointed, at least not yet, and I wouldn't feel shame until I knew whether it had been my negligence or Murphy's Law, although the latter would still be my fault. The greater the task, the greater the foresight necessary to anticipate and mitigate. I had a problem, and I was responsible for solving it.

Whatever it took.

"Just order the parts," she said with unexpected calm, "and come home. Then I'm ordering you to get some rest. You'll get the parts, but we'll all do better if we wait this out together. Now keep making those calls."

Matt was on the phone with an executive from BMW North America; Mark with a midlevel manager at BMW's East Coast parts depot; Chris Van Steen, AI's second in command, was on the phone with the manager of the West Coast depot; and Kenny was talking to the service manager of a New Jersey BMW dealership who'd been dining with his family when the phone rang.

I watched their body language, and saw our chances grow slim.

Which was why I was on the phone with a used BMW dealer in Northern California, negotiating for the purchase of the two parts that seven different BMW Master Service Technicians, including three M-Division specialists, had agreed were the problem. My friends on M5Board.com had also concurred, which was how I found the one dealer who was willing to strip the parts off of a used M5 sitting in his lot. With enormous shame yet no reluctance, I agreed to pay double the new retail price for both a used Camshaft Position Sensor and a Throttle Pedal Actuator and Potentiometer, on the condition that the seller get them to Federal Express no later than 5:45 P.M. (PST) and ship them overnight for Saturday delivery.

It was time go face Cory, and wait. I'd been waiting most of my life, and on September 20, 2005, when Rawlings showed up at my house, had vowed never to do so again. But now I had no choice. I was the prisoner of events I had set in motion.

Just under 26 hours remained.

The Saturday FedEx delivery window closed at noon.

Driveplan 1 Alpha (Assault Final) demanded a 9:30 P.M. departure.

No more than nine and a half hours for repairs, road testing, and final prep.

I knew the value of time. It was the only currency I counted anymore.

Then I saw the weather report.

CHAPTER 29

Driveplan 7 Alpha (Assault Final)

SATURDAY, APRIL 1, 2006
CLASSIC CAR CLUB—NEW YORK
ASSAULT RUN START LINE
2116 HR (EST)

One-hundred-and-fifty mile road test completed, I texted The Weis. *We are a go.*

The Weis, the Captain, Graeber, and Robin were already on a commercial flight to St. Louis, where they would spend the night with our old friend George ("The Bulgarian") Kruntschev—his wife displeased even by indirect involvement in our "totally irresponsible, dangerous, and possibly criminal" adventure—before rising at 0400 Sunday to confirm our ETA, proceed to the private airfield and Cessna awaiting them, and take off on standby orbit over the city.

But once again PolizeiGround was running late.

I stood beside Cory as she knelt to remount the front bumper camera, half our run's uninterrupted forward-facing video record now in jeopardy. I'd failed to warn Cory and Robin of the laser jammers now hidden in the grille, and allowed that morning's camera installation to proceed. We were all now paying the price.

I'd bought at least two of everything, but I couldn't buy time.

"I want a mountain of evidence," I'd said to Cory a month earlier, and thus our Time Validation Plan was born. The M5 would carry six video cameras, the plane two, the three chase cars one each, with two camera crews at both the start and finish lines. Both Garmins' CF cards would record latitude, longitude, bearing, speed, time, and elapsed distance, up to a limit of between six and eight hours, I estimated. Gas, toll receipts would be archived in the armrest. E-ZPass records were available online. Cell-phone providers stored data on handset locations. We would punch a time clock at the start, and the same time clock would be flown to the finish for punch-out.

We needed multiple third-party witnesses at both ends, but my efforts to convince ABC, CBS, CNN, FOX, NY1, the *Wall Street Journal,* or Slate.com to cover our journey had failed. None agreed to withhold the story for the 366 days until the applicable criminal statutes of limitations expired in half the states we'd cross. The Big Five accounting firms, the *Guinness Book of World Records,* and Seth all refused to cooperate in any potentially criminal venture.

Those more understanding, now present and nondisclosed, included Noah Robischon and Joel Johnson (editors of technology site Gizmodo.com), Mike Spinelli (editor of automotive site Jalopnik.com), our mutual friend Noah Shachtman (contributor to the *New York Times, Wired,* and *Popular Mechanics*), photographer Jeff Forney, and Erik Lopez—the backup pilot who had suggested carrying a spare tire in the plane, and dropping it beside the car if necessary—who was good friends with my platinum-haired pixie-cut, angelic good-luck charm Maggie Kaiser, whom I'd begun dating without truly conveying the danger of what might happen, and who had agreed to fly the time clock to the finish line. There we would meet automotive writer Gary Jarlson—friend of Diem and Turner, and witness to the 1982 and '83 U.S. Express finishes, the entire PolizeiAir crew, and possibly David Diem (who I thought might object to our effort to break his record) among others.

But this would all pale compared to 32 hours (or less) of nonstop front-bumper video. I asked Cory the dreaded question.

"To fix this . . . 5 minutes," she said, "then 10 more for final checks."

I rounded it up to 20. We'd depart at 9:36 P.M.

Six minutes behind *Driveplan 1 Alpha (Assault Final).*

I wasn't going to worry. Everything else *was* going according to plan.

I couldn't buy six minutes, but I could make them up.

All but two of the witnesses kept their distance, as if the car were a shrine or a holy artifact upon which even a hand might diminish its power. I was relieved for not having to ask, because I was most interested in the two who didn't.

I had contempt for most celebrities. I'd met some on Gumball, others merely by living in New York. Few had done anything of intellectual, cultural, or athletic significance. Idolatry sickened me, but when I recognized the two leaning in through the M5's windows, both looking exactly as I imagined, legends known only from pictures, transcripts, and video, I instantly snapped out of my robotic, preparatory daze. I was speechless. So was Nine.

"Now, *you* two," said the paternal Mike Digonis, 1982 U.S. Express winner and driver of the infamous 212 mph DeTomaso Pantera, with all the charisma of the handsome, mustached young tough who'd beaten Diem/Turner one year before they broke the record, "are some crazy sons of bitches."

"I wish I was going with you," said the gray-haired yet energetic Steve Stander, 1981 and '82 U.S. Express veteran, whose Auto Trix garage had been the official start line. "Good thing you're out of space, because I don't think my wife would approve. First guys giving it a go in twenty-three years, good stuff, really, good for you."

"Mr. Digonis," I said, "Mr. Stander . . . it's . . . it's really an honor to meet you—"

"Forget being nice," said Digonis, "you have no time." He and Stander hadn't seen each other since 1982, but they understood each other, and us, well enough to complete each other's thoughts. "Run us through your gear and plan," said Stander.

Nine laid *Driveplan 1 Alpha (Assault Final)* on the trunk. I unfolded our atlas beside it and began. No more than a dozen people in the entire world would have understood our exchange.

2124 hours

"Your equipment and prep work looks good," said Digonis.

"Good work, really good work," said Stander. "You've got a shot."

"The car sounds good. You're running for fuel economy, which is the right one for today. In '82 we ran for speed, you know, and I only got six miles per gallon in the Pantera, but of course we were cruising in the 170s. Even with extra gas stops, the fuel-economy guys couldn't catch up. But those days are over now. It's a real shame."

"Stealth," said Stander, "is your only shot. If anything happens, call me or Mike. I'll stay up. If nothing happens, just call me when you get there." He unfolded a wallet full of his grandchildren's pictures and pulled out a Patrolmen's Benevolent Association card—the first ever given me I knew would work.

"Listen, young man," said Digonis, "what you're doing is a beautiful thing. You'll be fine, your spirits are good. To spend this kind of time and money to go out and do this . . . it's crazy. We can never know why we do it, but any man willing to break his neck is all right, as long as he doesn't take anyone with him. It'd also be good to stay out of jail."

"Mike," said Stander, "how the hell *did* we stay out of jail?"

"That's hard to say. I got stopped seven times."

"And these two"—Stander flicked his thumb at us—"are hoping to get there without being stopped even once! I love it! And going out alone . . . I'm not sure if that makes it easier or harder. Maybe we should just get in the Caddy right now and show them."

"Steve," I said, "if you want to go, there have to be other guys who want to. How come no one's gone out in all this time? I mean, *has* anyone made a run?"

"Oh, that's a good one! If anyone had, I'd be the first out there!"

"I think," said Digonis, "this is the kind of thing we would have heard about. You can't organize something like this without word getting out to certain people."

"But someone's got to organize it," said Stander.

"One last question," I said, "is it true? What Yates said about 30 hours?"

"Absolutely," said Stander, "but everything has to go perfectly. *Everything.*"

"I would so say so"—Digonis paused—"back then. Now? Well . . . someone has to try it to find out."

"Like you two." Stander laughed. "Nobody knows. It's been twenty years."

"Hang on," said Nine. "So you guys think 32:07 can be broken no problem?"

"No, no no," said Stander, "32:07 is if everything goes perfectly, except maybe a little bit of weather, *and* you guys don't mess up. It's one or the other. Better than that, I'm talking about perfect. No weather, driving all out."

"You guys," said Digonis, "I really do admire you for doing this. Most men want to, and only a rare few get the chance."

"Just don't do anything crazy"—Stander grinned—"and I mean by *our* standards. Now go say good-bye to your friends and get in the car before we take your place."

Nine ran to the bathroom. I hoped one last splash of icy water on my face might exorcise the obsessive, unfunny stranger behind my eyes long enough to say good-bye to Maggie, Lelaine, and my mother, smoking in silence from the exit gate. Something had happened to the man they knew. I opened my vanity mirror and recognized the face, but not the cold, blank eyes and pursed lips. Nine was back before I realized I'd spent a full minute staring at my reflection.

"Digonis and Stander?" he said. "Jesus, to have those guys come see us, it's the coolest that could have happened. Digonis reminds me of your dad."

We both smiled.

We were now professionals, perhaps the last echo of a peculiar, dying-but-not-quite-dead subset of motor sport, and we'd just received the blessings of its elders. If at any moment my father had walked in and shaken hands with Digonis and Stander—if they had known one another their whole lives and never connected the dots back to me until meeting at the CCC—I wouldn't have been remotely surprised.

I checked my watch—*2131 hours.*

Inspired by my love of naval tradition, Ross's perennial calm, and Nine's (perhaps) involuntary adoption of a faux-English accent whenever speaking to Emma, I'd suggested we artificially raise our level of discourse until our new, far-stricter in-car safety and spotting protocols made it impossible, at least without laughter. There would be no laughing this time, because there was no fear to cover up.

"Aliray, you've gotta take a minute with Maggie. Here she comes. I'll check the tires one more time while you guys talk. Take the minute. You owe her that."

She was glowing with excitement, both for what she thought we might accomplish, and for her part in it. I could have burst into tears at the mere thought of disappointing her. She didn't know the truth. Since the day we'd met I'd been a machine, utterly focused, with barely a word about the danger, or what I was prepared to lose to see this through. We met *after* 3446, and all she heard or knew was *Alex Roy always makes it.* I had done her a potentially tragic disservice by allowing her into my life when I did, and now I *had* to make it, if only not to shatter the dream she earnestly clung to—that I would devote as much to her as I had to my task—and deserved to see fulfilled.

"Be safe," she said, and hugged me.

Nine closed his door, the tire checks complete.

"I will, Mags." I only called her that when I was serious.

She pulled her face from mine. I feared she sensed something was wrong, but then she placed her head on my chest and whispered, "Then squeeze me—"

Cory slammed the trunk. "We're ready!"

I squeezed her back, we both let go, and she backed away with a devilish grin. "I *better* see you in 31 hours!"

I wasn't *really* worried, so I smiled and got in the car. "And *you* better not check your bag with that time clock inside, just in case."

The portents were in our favor, great forces already on the move. We were going to make it. All our fortunes from the prior night's Chinese takeout said so. That day's *New York Post* horoscope said so. My car number was 144. The national map in our atlas was *on* page 144.

I closed my door. I was not here to drive. It was to deploy everything I knew, the sum total of my experience focused through a prism upon every second of every minute of every hour until the car stopped on the Santa Monica Pier.

The CCC gate began to rise.

"Time check, Mr. Goodrich. My watch reads nine thirty-five P.M. The BMW master clock reads same. Driver's GPS clock's the same. You?"

"Copilot GPS clock's still groovy, oooops . . . make that *same*."

"Thorough as always, Mr. Goodrich, start track logging on my mark . . . three, two, one, mark. Reset trip computers on my mark, mileage first, three, two, one—"

"Mark!" we said in unison.

I put the car in first gear. Nine unfolded *Driveplan 1 Alpha (Assault Final)*.

It was Saturday, April 1, 2006. Lelaine held the time clock up to my window. I punched our time card then slipped it into my visor. The local time was 9:36 P.M. (EST).

The Port Authority police waved as we passed. We drove into the tunnel, but this time it was just the Holland.

CHAPTER 30

Naked Daytime Running

SATURDAY, APRIL 1, 2006
HOLLAND TUNNEL WESTBOUND
MILEAGE 1.4
2141 HOURS EST

"Last chance," said Nine.

"To back out?"

"To confess."

"I wish we were running against Rawlings. Or Collins."

"Rawlings made his choice. Collins you can call anytime."

"You?"

"I've never done a bad thing in my life, until now. Too late anyway, tunnel exit's in sight. Mr. Roy, you know the way."

Nine and I had driven this and the upcoming stretch of road hundreds of times, but never as we were about to.

"Mr. Goodrich, stand by for this trip to become a lot less fun."

I never wanted to be a pioneer, but Digonis and Stander could tell us no more about evading modern law enforcement than we already knew. Times had changed.

My high-speed driving protocols had been tested on 3446 at an overall average of 80.5 mph. Our clock never stopped, and with a total of 28 minutes for fuel and bathroom stops, achieving 34:46 required cruising at 90 mph or more. Every minute below the target average required a proportional higher sprint above, once as high as 145 mph, somewhere in the California desert.

And not one police car noticed. Not one civilian called 911.

Now, these protocols had to function at cruising speeds of 95 to

100 mph—starting in 15 seconds and ending when we were jailed, killed, or had arrived in Los Angeles.

"Cory," I said, "you know the drill. If we miss one, call it out!"

Outbound from Manhattan, the Holland Tunnel would emerge onto Fourteenth Street in Jersey City, a four-block-long stretch of gas stations and warehouses at whose western end, four lights from the tunnel exit, lay the first of fewer than a dozen navigational decisions between New York and L.A. We had to earn time credit for trade against traffic and weather, which meant slicing across Fourteenth Street's six lanes to avoid locals who might block us behind one or more red lights, each representing a time loss of one to two minutes.

We were already six minutes behind schedule. I couldn't halve that in the next four blocks, but—if I chose my lane poorly—I might double it.

"All windows down!" I called out. "All eyes open!"

Street racing—i.e., one or more untrained drivers drag-racing over short lengths on city streets—is dangerous and irresponsible, but it is not as dangerous as "urban racing," a subset of the former I'd only ever seen on rallies, where one or more cars weave through traffic over various distances. I was totally opposed to street racing and urban racing, but having practiced the latter throughout Italy to great effect, and in light of a pressing engagement on the Santa Monica Pier, I would make the only exception on the entire run.

"I've got the right!" Nine yelled.

But there was an exception to the exception. Police officers are trained to spot erratic or dangerous behavior. Tailgating, multilane passes, shoulder passes, high beams, honking, and passing at a >2X speed differential would attract their attention, especially in urban areas. Stealth was key. Stealth was safe.

"I've got the left!" I yelled back.

Hence the hazy, nonelectronic half of our high-speed driving protocol: *Drive as fast as possible—without inciting a 911 call.*

We burst out of the tunnel entrance. "Ramp check right!" I yelled—the instruction to check any merge for police—but Nine's head had already snapped right as mine went left.

"Ramp's clear!" he yelled back.

"Street's clear!" I veered right and lunged through a gap in traffic that centered us down Fourteenth Street's six lanes—an urban-racing position as powerful (yet still vulnerable, due to its visibility to police hiding to either side of the perpendicular streets) as a cornered rook. We darted forward, passed the first intersection, then the second, accelerating past

60 mph—twice the local limit—toward the fork between Route 1/9 and the I-78 extension.

"Scanners up?"

"Scanners up!" Nine responded, turning both volume knobs to maximum, the car suddenly filled with metallic hash and terse chatter, both scanners picking up overlapping dispatchers' instructions, tense voices, and the sirens from two police chases currently in progress.

"We're here," I said, "and they're after some idiot with expired tags."

INTERSTATE 78 WESTBOUND
APPROACHING DELAWARE RIVER
MILEAGE 62
2230 HOURS EST (APPROX)

"Thermals clear!" Nine leaned forward, his face lit by the pale white light cast by the copilot's night-vision screen above the glove box. The rest of our cockpit glowed red, AI having replaced all of the white interior lights such that—like a submarine or flight crew—we could leave them on without affecting our outward visibility.

"Lean back, Mr. Goodrich. If the road's straight and flat and there's no median wall to hide behind, a police car's going to look like a big white blob."

"Sorry, I just can't believe this thing is legal."

"Ramp check!"

"Thermals clear."

"Now, Nine, aren't you glad we don't have to wear goggles the whole time?"

"I guess those are for the budget illegal cross-country guys."

"Nine, once we cross the Delaware, *after* the tollbooth, kill the rear brake lights."

"Got it . . . ramp check!" Nine had begun calling them out himself. "Ramp clear!"

I knew we were doing well, but we were too busy with our protocols for on-the-fly calculations. We'd know more when we hit the first waypoint in Columbus, Ohio, over 460 miles away.

"Mr. Goodrich, please activate Scanner Bank number two, Pennsylvania."

"Bank two Pennsylvania active; bank one, New Jersey, locked out."

We crossed the Delaware River at approximately 10:35 P.M. (EST).

We were consistently cruising at 95 mph or more.

And no one noticed.

The Weis called 30 minutes later. Nine listened intently, silently performing one thermal and one ramp check while I awaited what could only be the weather update I feared. "Ten-four, The Weis, I'll inform Aliray. Out."

"Before the bad news, did he ask about our average? It's way up, right?"

"He doesn't want numbers until we hit Diem/Turner's figures. The bad news is the weather's getting worse. They're grounded, but he thinks they can take off and meet us somewhere southwest of St. Louis. But the storm's headed our way. It's starting to rain in Indy."

Indianapolis was 650 miles away. Every mile the storm advanced eastward was one less mile of dry road we desperately needed to cross as quickly as possible before dawn. The M5 could easily cruise at 150 mph in the wet, but not in the United States, at night, for four hours.

We were meeting or slightly exceeding the driveplan, but that would soon end. Running at eight-tenths my skill and six-tenths the car's capabilities, we were now in a race against that storm. We needed to cover maximum ground on dry road surface. We needed to increase our average and build time credits before it was too late. We needed to meet the storm head-on as far west as possible. We needed to cross Ohio—and meet the most feared highway patrol in the country—before the storm hit the state's western border. If we failed, the run was finished.

"Nine, fire up the Garmin's XM NavTraffic."

The M5's engine, previously a low throb, rose in pitch.

"Frequency of reporting, Mr. Roy?"

"Every 10 minutes, and kill all the rear lights."

"Not just the brakes?"

"Pennsylvania's dead tonight. Why advertise? Let's go dark."

Our overall average was in the upper eighties, and rising. Our running projection was below 33 hours, and still dropping.

INTERSTATE 81 SOUTH

APPROACHING HARRISBURG, PENNSYLVANIA

MILEAGE 163

2340 HOURS EST (APPROX)

BEAR LEFT AHEAD ONE-QUARTER MILE.

"Easy," said Nine, "this is your exit."

"Are you sure? I don't think so."

"You programmed this thing."

TAKE RAMP LEFT.

"Check it now, Nine, before it's too late."

"What? You don't trust your own programming? Just take the turn."

Fifty feet down the ramp to I-83/I-283S, we knew it was wrong.

"Sorry," he said sheepishly.

"There's cars all over this road! Hit the brake lights! We've got to get out and turn around!" I downshifted for the first time since the start line and accelerated toward the next exit, its ramp just visible approximately one mile away.

"Aliray, easy into the turn, easy, easy!"

"Prepare for heroics." I stopped at the bottom of the ramp, poised to run the red, make a left, and double back, but a police car stopped perpendicular to watch the strange blue car with the three antennas and glowing red interior. "If only he knew. I love you, man, but seriously, if we miss the record by five minutes, we'll know why."

"Sorry."

"I was kidding. It was at least half my fault." We were back en route in four minutes. Stander said a time of 32 could tolerate one mistake. We'd just made ours—less than 5 percent into the run.

The storm's eastward march accelerated.

I held the car steady at 120 mph, west toward the Ohio border.

SUNDAY, APRIL 2, 2006
INTERSTATE 70/76 WEST
VICINITY OF SOMERSET, PENNSYLVANIA
MILEAGE 306
AFTER MIDNIGHT

Nine and Cory were silent as the M5 snaked through the low hills of western Pennsylvania at 105 mph, the absolute safe limit given the dark road's increasingly damp surface. Ramp checks were infrequent, the exits too far apart. Our Xenon lights reflected a ghostly blue-white against the mist. Nine peered at the thermals for stray deer that could kill us all. The V1, Blinder, CB, and scanner volumes were all at maximum. We hoped to hear signals blocked by the terrain, or at least verify that all our gear hadn't broken at once. We'd seen only a handful of cars, almost all in the opposite direction, and I exploited this by running the world's longest racing line on a public road, surpassing 85 miles. We tried to stay calm after our overall average rose to 90.3 mph, but its significance made our optimistic, gloating smiles hard to conceal.

Our running projection was now 31:38—*if* the Garmins could be trusted. At this pace we would gather enough time credit to defeat the storm.

The silence was suddenly pierced by the primary scanner: PASP D2 159.075: *"Dark-colored BMW, late model, high rate of speed, no taillights, approaching the 106, 107—"*

"All lights back on *now!*" I yelled, letting off the gas until the car slowed to 79 mph, then set the cruise control. This wasn't Gumball. There were no exits, no parallel roads, no other cars to claim we'd been mistaken for, and no time-killing hideouts with newspapers and table service. "Nine, distance to the West Virginia border?"

"Too far to make a run for it. Next turn is ... the I-76/70 split, in 28 miles."

PASP D2 159.075: *". . . he's gonna call back with a better description—"*

I shook my head. "*Who* the hell could *that* be? We haven't seen anyone. It can't be a local running behind us, not in these conditions."

"In this weather no police car can overtake us. They have to deploy ahead and wait until we pass, or set up a roadblock, but they don't know enough about us at this point. On this road at this speed, we're sitting ducks for the next half an hour. Nine, we have to make a unanimous decision. You know the options."

Nine zoomed out on his Garmin. "The next town big enough for a police department that's gonna care is ... Donegal, about 15 miles."

"That's it. We roll at 79 to Donegal, then go all out to the West Virginia border. We need to get some distance from our mysterious caller."

"I concur."

"Cory, you're entitled to a vote."

"You might not want to hear this, guys, but I say you drive all out *right now.*"

"Do it," said Nine. In the rearview mirror I saw Cory smile.

Donegal and the rest of Pennsylvania were eerily quiet. We entered West Virginia with the Garmins optimistically displaying an overall average of 91.4 mph, our running projection now 31:15, We didn't get excited, for not only was the storm ahead of us, we were about to enter Ohio, the most feared state in the nation for speeders, highway scofflaws, Cannonball Run and U.S. Express drivers. The Ohio State Police massacred them year after year, such that drivers planned longer routes that avoided the state altogether. Zanesville, Ohio, was where Diem/Turner received the only speeding ticket of their record-setting run. Had it not been for a mandatory visit to night court, they might have achieved 31:45 or better. Cory had actually interviewed the ticketing officer, now retired, and confirmed that Interstate 70 remained a heavily patrolled corridor. The rain over Indiana had worsened. The 227 miles across Ohio represented our last chance for big speeds before sunrise.

We approached the border on cruise control at 79 mph—14 mph over the limit—but the speed trap I'd anticipated (and even waypointed in the Garmin) was unmanned. The brisk night air and long straightaways gave us our first demonstration of the thermal camera's true power, allowing for hill-to-hill sprints at 140 or more, sometimes increasing our average by as much as one decimal point. The fuel gauge was low. I had made my final contribution to our precious time credit before our first driver swap. I had been driving for just over five hours. I'd probably lost five pounds.

"Nine, prepare for the world's fastest fuel stop. I'll pump. You clean the thermal cam and laser jammers. Break out the Casios." Cory handed each of us one of the twenty-dollar Casio G-Shocks bought specifically for its large display and piercing alarm.

Each was set for a five-minute countdown.

"Remember," I said as we pulled into a gas station just past Zanesville, "when the alarm goes off, you have 30 seconds to get back in the car. Countdown begins when the car stops rolling."

"Just don't kill the car power," said Cory, "we need it to keep the cams up."

"Good point. Nine, you think we should leave the car running?"

"I think it's against the law."

The driveplan called for five full and one half-refuel stops—the former no more than 5 minutes, 30 seconds each—for a total of 30 minutes stopped time.

"Nine, Cory, the countdown begins . . . now."

We were approaching the Indiana border. We'd passed seven Ohio State Police cars—more than New Jersey and Pennsylvania combined—not one of which noticed our passage.

"Nine, I'm not spotting for a sec. I want to check our progress."

"I'll take it down to a hundred."

I lit the driveplan with my red-bulbed headset. "The bad news is our fuel economy is way below projections. We're getting 15.5 MPG, so we're looking at six stops instead of five."

"Hey, guys," Cory called out, "why don't you just shut up and drive? You're going to miss a cop if you're not careful."

"Aliray, what's the good news?"

"We're about to hit Indiana."

"Aw yeah." Nine giggled. "Flat, straight, good. I'll pick up the pace."

"Not yet, I've got two speed traps waypointed up ahead, I'll let you know when to open it up. Stand by . . . for one on the right before border exit into Richmond, and another at the on-ramp right after the interchange."

WESTERN INDIANA

"That looks bad," said Nine.

The sun had begun to rise. A thick gray line appeared on the western horizon.

"That is bad," I said. "Just drive all out until the last possible second."

The thermal camera, our greatest ally, would soon be useless. I unpacked our daytime equivalent, a set of Steiner 7×50 (military) binoculars for which I should have begun weight training before selecting them for this critical task. Designed for tank commanders for use in spotting enemy vehicles up to several miles away, each lens had individual focus/distance controls. I set them to one mile and raised the hard green rubber eyecups to my face.

"Aliray, I can't say I'm looking forward to holding those things to my face for five hours."

"Cory," I said, "can I get some of that Dramamine?"

APPROACHING THE ILLINOIS BORDER

"We're ahead of schedule!" I yelled into my headset. "The Weis? The Weis?"

"Can . . . speak up . . . or . . . slow down . . . buy a new phone?"

"I think we're gonna hit St. Louis a little early!"

"Earl . . . how . . . uch early . . . about . . . weather?"

"We're in it now! But Nine's accelerating!"

"Is . . . at rain . . . noise . . . hear? On . . . th . . . car?"

"Yes! Rain and wind! Nine's got us pegged at 110, in the rain!"

"Oh . . . God . . . will ca . . . u back—"

I texted him our averages and ETA. He responded 30 seconds later.

storm intensifying make best possible spd good job be careful call 100 miles out

The copilot's Garmin said 93.4, which seemed high. I swiveled the driver's Garmin toward me, which read the same, 93.4 mph. That was impossible.

"Cory," I said, "look at the screen." She leaned forward, saw the number, then looked at me. "Cory, the time-projection sheet says that's 30:36." We wondered if they were right.

"We have a big problem," said Nine. "The gas gauge, it's near zero."

"Strange . . . we've only gone about 300 miles since the refuel. The fuel cell is supposed to dump into the main tank."

"Well, clearly it isn't, or it is and the gauge is broken. I don't know which is worse. You want to take a chance?"

"Just pull over when our range hits 30 miles. Worst-case scenario, the cell's not dumping, which means we're at eight stops instead of five and change. At these speeds, we can still make it."

I turned around to give Cory an encouraging smile, but then I saw the rear window, the view totally obscured by the two enormous rooster tails we were trailing. I hoped police weren't trained to calculate speeds based on their height.

"The good news is," said Nine, "this car couldn't run any better if it tried."

We switched seats at the gas station. No one needed to say it. Both of us preferred that I take the necessary risks in the rain, but even I held back as the clouds blocked out the rising sun, making the thermals useful once again, albeit for safety rather than police evasion. Between the fuel stop and thickening traffic, our average had fallen to 92.1, still an incredible figure, but with both The Weis and the XM NavTraffic reporting worsening conditions, one guaranteed to fall.

"It's getting really dark," said Nine, "where are we?"

"You tell me. That was the sign for Effingham. Where's that?"

"About . . . a hundred miles from St. Louis."

"I have to slow down, but it terrifies me to see the needle go below 95."

If the storm kept growing, PolizeiAir wouldn't take off. Once PolizeiGround passed St. Louis, every mile we drove west while they remained on the ground reduced the likelihood of *any* intercept. It was simple math, but math no one had suggested anyone ever calculate, let alone add to the driveplan just in case. If they hadn't taken off by the time we hit clear weather, the Polizei Aerial Recon plan was finished, and with it any chance of breaking 32:07. We had a thousand miles to cover in broad daylight, from St. Louis to somewhere in New Mexico, and the plane was our insurance policy.

The weather grew worse. We missed them.

INTERSTATE 44 WEST
APPROACHING SPRINGFIELD, MISSOURI
210 MILES SOUTHWEST OF ST. LOUIS
MILEAGE 1160

"Naked daytime running," I said, "this is exactly what I was afraid of. We're at 105 mph in the open with civilians around. I don't like it."

"At least no one's called us in. We would have heard it on the scanner."

"It's amazing what you can get away with if you're polite. I always signal, never tailgate, and look, our mileage has improved since I've been drafting, and—"

"Thanks, Mr. Nader. I'll keep trying to reach them."

"It's probably a waste. I need you spotting. If I can keep us above a hundred in this traffic without the SWAT teams showing up."

"Cowbell Air, Cowbell Air," Nine said into the Vertex handheld, "this is Cowbell Ground, over."

"Nine, there's no way they can hear us. Forget catching up."

"At least the weather got nice. And everyone in Missouri thinks we're a police car, even without the stickers."

"That's *not* a good thing."

Nine played with the radio settings. It hissed and howled.

"Nine, just stay on those bear checks. The truckers have already saved us about twenty times. Forget the plane. If they can catch up, they'll let us know. And keep those Steiners up!"

"Cory," said Nine, "do you have any more of that Dramamine?"

"Cowbell Ground, Cowbell Ground, this is Cowbell Air . . . what is your position?"

The voice of the Captain. "There is a God," I said.

"Cowbell Ground, Cowbell Ground, this is Cowbell Air . . . currently approaching Springfield . . . what is your position?"

"We're almost in Springfield!" Nine yelled. "They've gotta be right behind us!"

"Then radio them back and look out the window!"

"Cowbell Ground, we can hear you keying the radio, but your signal is garbled, please text your position."

"You know what?" Nine said as he typed. "If we ever do this again, we have to find a better way of meeting the plane."

"We had considered putting an aircraft transponder in the car, but there was no room, and The Weis said it wouldn't work from the ground. That's why we decided to put white stripes on the roof. Nine!"

Our average had fallen to 92—a running projection of 31:03—but was sure to enter free fall for the next 10 hours, or 11, or 13, or as long as it took to cover the day stage before realizing we'd never make 32:07, in which case—

"Cowbell Ground, Cowbell Ground, this is Cowbell Air, received your message, checking the maps."

The voice of The Weis. My heart began racing.

"Cowbell Ground, this is Cowbell Air, you guys must have been really booting, we have passed Lebanon, approaching Springfield at maximum speed, please send updates, including your speed."

"Nine, we just passed Lebanon! Tell them! Text them! Oh . . . my . . . God, do you think—"

Cory flipped rearward and held her camcorder to the window.

"Cowbell Ground, we are descending for a closer look, stand by, passing on your right."

"Aliray, if these guys actually find us, I mean, if this actually works, forget the criminal part, this is absolutely the—"

"I see them!" Cory screamed. "On the right! Ahead on the right!"

Nine and I leaned forward. Of all the impossible events of the prior 13 hours, the sight of our lone, white, single-engined Cessna aerial recon unit made everything I'd ever seen or done in a car seem humorously insignificant.

"Cowbell Ground, we have you in sight, do you copy?"

Nine lifted the Vertex to his mouth with a wide grin. "Cowbell Air, this is Juan Nueve, aka Jon Nine, do you copy?"

"Cowbell Ground, we're gonna switch up the code names in case anyone's listening, you are hereby designated Ozzel Ground, we are Ozzel Air."

"Copy that, Ozzel Air, are you referring to Admiral Ozzel, the guy Darth Vader kills?"

"Ten-four, Nueve Actual, you guys are kicking ass. Keep it up, Aliray."

"Ozzel Air, how far can you see out?"

"If you knew math we'd tell you, Ozzel Ground. We'll only report if we see something. Right now . . . no cops, median clear up to this overpass, ramps clear, all clear all the way to second overpass."

"Nine, Steiners up for plain brown wrappers." Except for unmarked police cars, we were safe.

Missouri law enforcement—long considered by Cannonball and Express veterans the second most fearsome after Ohio—was clearly not equipped to stop integrated air/ground operations by a citizen intent on crossing this great nation in 32 hours and 7 minutes or less. Still, it was with great relief that we crossed into Oklahoma, with its light traffic and flat terrain perfect for long-distance spotting from a low-flying plane.

Our overall average hit an inconceivable—and I was sure this would give Yates a seizure—95.7 mph, for a running projection of 29:45, *if* the Garmins were accurate, *if* we maintained our speed, *if* the fuel cell stopped hiccuping, *if* the weather remained clear. But no one in the car was capable of talking, or laughing, or gloating—we were now upended, inverted versions of the trio that, at this very point some four months earlier, had started to lose any sense of reality, our situational awareness that of a blind soldier stumbling down a muddy trench. Now, as we approached the halfway point of our journey, 31 was in our grasp.

Thirty—the Lost Chord of Cannonball—was possible.

And 29:30—the inconceivable—was just over the horizon.

We approached the Will Rogers Turnpike Mainline Plaza—the first of only two tollbooths remaining before L.A., still approximately 1,500 miles and half the country away—westbound on Interstate 44, in the vicinity of Vinita, Oklahoma. I handed the attendant $3.50, she confirmed that the road ahead was clear of police on Sundays at lunchtime, and I put the car into first gear for a gentle, fuel-preserving, slow-acceleration run back up to a conservative 95 mph cruising speed. Our lane discipline and overwhelmingly good road manners hadn't incited a single 911 call. That was quite a surprise, but not as surprising as when the car started to violently buck back and forth—Nine poised to ask how and why I'd missed the clutch—and the engine died.

"PolizeiGround, PolizeiGround, we see you stopped after the tollbooth, please advise sitrep. Orbiting toll plaza, Polizei Ground, do you copy?"

We'd made it the 50-odd feet to the right shoulder.

"PolizeiGround, PolizeiGround, do you copy?" I turned down the Vertex volume.

"Listen to me very clearly. We have a 2-hour-and-10-minute lead over the record. Every second we're stopped will be spent diagnosing and fixing this problem. I intend to get this car moving, and keep rolling west until that 2-hour-and-10-minute credit runs out. The countdown begins *now*. Do you understand?"

"I'm in," said Nine.

I already knew Cory's answer.

CHAPTER 31

Time Is the Devil

Breakdown. The Omigod of Outside Context Problems.

I restarted the car. We broke down three miles later. No one spoke. I restarted it again, exited I-44, and broke down four more times in the half mile to the Shell station in Big Cabin, Oklahoma. We refueled and called AI—who agreed it was likely an electronic problem. I disconnected the battery and reset the engine computer. I theorized the car would keep running if only I kept it above 3,500 rpms, below which the problems began. In sixth gear, this was 95 mph—the perfect cruising speed, ironically, if only we didn't hit traffic or have to slow for a cop. We restarted and made it another 60 miles before hitting Tulsa city traffic, and stalling once again.

We restarted for the seventh time. I set the cruise control at 95 mph.

Nine optimistically lifted the Steiners to his face.

"Ozzel Air to Ozzel Ground, keep it up, Aliray, we're gonna scout ahead."

We were approaching Bristow, nearly 80 miles since the initial breakdown.

"Cory," I said, "we're not stopping until *if* and when the overall average falls below 90."

"Ozzel Ground! Full-grown eastbound! Eyes open!"

"Nine! You see any marked police cars?"

"Not yet! You sure you want to maintain this speed?"

Speed meant capture. Slowing meant breakdown. Traffic was flowing at 80 to 85 mph. I moved to the right lane to increase the parallax angle to the oncoming trooper—decreasing his radar gun's accuracy—and held at 91 mph. We were rapidly approaching a truck, forcing a choice between passing in full view of the trooper or slowing to below 80. The left lane was suddenly blocked. I braked to avoid hitting the truck, downshifted to fifth to maintain the rpms, then, in the instant I depressed the clutch once again to enter fourth, the rpms fell below 3,000 before I could reengage—

"I see him!" Nine yelled.

—and the engine died.

I pulled over on the right shoulder. Nine held the Steiners on the trooper until he passed in the other direction, 84 miles since the first breakdown, 1,372 miles from New York.

"Nine, did he see us slow down and stop?"

"I'd pay a million dollars to know for sure. My heart's about to explode."

OKHP Mobile 154.9050: *". . . vehicle stopped at the 198 westbound—"*

"There's our answer." I grabbed the Steiners from Nine's lap. The exit ramp for Bristow, Oklahoma, was in sight. "I don't care if this car catches fire while we push it up the ramp. We cannot let him get a look inside this car."

"Code red! PolizeiGround, full-grown making a U-turn on your six! Good cover at the exit ramp ahead! Get that car moving, PolizeiGround, you can make it."

I restarted the car, but it died instantly. Ready to give the order to push, I turned to Nine, then in my rearview mirror spotted the Oklahoma State Police car approaching on the shoulder. I hit the hazards. I couldn't remember whether our rear license plate—INPOL 144—still wore its anticamera/antilaser cover.

"He's not getting out," said Nine.

"Do you want me to pick the excuse, or do you want to vote?"

I silently ran through all those I could remember.

"Man," said Nine, "what if we just tell the truth?"

"The truth?"

"Sorry, Aliray, I just hate lying."

"Cowbell Ground, Aliray, now would be the time to get out and act innocent. Cowbell Ground, do you copy?"

Nine keyed the Vertex. "Copy that, Cowbell Air."

"Nine, I *will* tell him the truth, just give me the teriyaki bag. I'll look more innocent carrying it."

"I ate it all after the first breakdown."

"Then give me the empty bag and a piece of anything stinky," I said, opening my door. "Now everyone stay calm. Cory, don't raise that camera. He might think it's a gun. Nine, leave the scanners up so you know what's happening. Kill and hide them if he cuffs me, or follows me back."

"Alex," said Cory, "*you* relax. Just do your thing."

"Trust me. I impersonate German cops for a living."

I got out of the car and waved to the trooper. With an expression of sincere but good-natured exasperation—to which I added a mouthful of jerky and a conspicuously empty bag—I walked over to his open window. The officer, sitting uncomfortably upright in his thick bulletproof vest, was already writing up a report.

"Hey, Officer!" I exhaled deeply into his passenger compartment. "Boy, are we glad to see you!"

"New York—" he said, his pencil momentarily stopping as he learned the flavor of what Nine had handed me, "you've come a long way."

"Just a little drive cross-country."

He closed his logbook and looked up. "What's the problem?"

"A little engine situation, but I think we're good."

"No need for a tow, then?"

"Nah, I think we just need some coolant, and some more jerky."

"You want me to wait?"

"I think we got it. There's got to be a gas station at the next exit, right?"

"Bristow," he said with finality. "You'll find everything you need. Good luck." He opened his logbook once again, then waited until I returned to the M5 before moving off the shoulder. He didn't wave back.

The car died again 17 miles later, at I-44's Turner Turnpike toll plaza.

"Nine, we've averaged mid-eighties in the hundred miles since the first breakdown. Tell me the credit's run out and I'll call it, but I'm still not stopping until we're in a major city. If we stop, we need to hide this car immediately, after what we've done."

"*Cowbell Ground, Cowbell Ground, approaching Oklahoma City airspace, will be peeling off for refuel, please maintain location updates every 10 minutes for reintercept west of the city. Cowbell Ground, do you copy?*"

"Copy that," Nine responded, but his tone expressed what I had come to understand since the second breakdown. No one, including The Weis and the Captain, was going to give up until I made *the* decision. We were 15 miles from Interstate 40, the second-to-last turn before Los Angeles.

"*Cowbell Ground, you are clear of bears for about two miles, all the way to the I-44/I-35 interchange. We are peeling off for refuel. Good luck through the city, see you on the I-40. Cowbell Air out.*"

We could go it alone, but I suddenly realized how lonely we would be. Only a handful of people in the world knew there were three people in a blue sedan on a mission, not interested in bothering anyone, just trying to cross the country in one day and two nights. The plane disappeared. I couldn't wait to see them again. In person.

"Nice work, Aliray, I can't believe we've picked up the pace."

"I just hope we can maintain this through the city."

Team Polizei's heretofore-indomitable E39 BMW M5, universally considered one of the finest cars ever made, respected veteran of three Gumballs and 3446, its glass and metal eyes witness to nearly 15,000 high-speed miles across thirteen countries, having performed flawlessly under conditions unseen outside of the Paris-Dakar and the 24 Hours of Le Mans, died in the center of Oklahoma City, on the right shoulder 500 feet north of the I-44/I-40 interchange, 1,451 miles from New York, 1,342 miles from the Santa Monica Pier.

Cory burst into tears.

"The car," Nine said quietly, "it's impossible."

"Jon," I said firmly, lowering all four windows for our first fresh air in three hours. I shuddered against the cool wind flowing up my sleeves, then down my neck, then pooling around my ankles. I leaned forward to pull up my socks. My clothes were completely drenched. My pants had slipped six inches below my waist.

"A twenty-dollar part . . ." he muttered. "Has to be . . . has to be."

"Jon, we're going again. I don't care how many times it takes."

"I dunno, man . . . I dunno."

"We'll make it next time."

"Aliray, man—"

"Don't explain. I understand. I have my reasons. You have yours. Cory?" I looked over my shoulder. Cory stared out her window, west, past the last, low buildings on the city's outskirts, her eyes repeatedly following I-44's gray path leading off to the horizon.

"Cory?"

"Hells, yeah," she whispered. She'd go alone if she had to.

Then I remembered. *Alex Roy always makes it.* Maggie. Time clock. Already in the air. Too late to stop her. I started typing. "Jon, you tell the boys overhead. I'll call for a flatbed. We have to move before the police show up. Cory, can you—"

"—reserve a hotel with a garage hidden from the street?"

I caught her eyes in the rearview mirror. Even in disaster, we could smile—

"Oh . . . my . . . God," said Nine. "Don't stop, don't stop, no!"

My eyes shot past Cory's reflection to a dark narrow shape approaching. Motorcycle. Oklahoma City police. I hit the ECM master power kill.

The officer rolled up to Nine's open window, lowered his bike onto its kickstand, and leaned inside—his helmet and mirrored glasses slowly turning to scan each of our faces.

"Wow!" he exclaimed, revealing a delighted grin as wide as any Gumball fan's. "Now, *this* is the most amazing car I have *ever* seen! When I saw all those antennas on the back, I just *knew* . . . I *just* knew! Hey, what agency you guys with?"

"Well, Officer," I said, "that's a long story."

"Whoa!" His head turned to the dashboard, then to the fixed camera over my shoulder, then the handheld in Cory's lap. "Oh! *I* get it! You're making a movie! Cool! But I guess you've got some car trouble, huh? I better get you a tow right away so you can get back out there. But where to? BMW's not going to be open on Sunday. You know, I've got a friend . . ."

If the Missouri State Police were hunting for a blue BMW with antennas, then *every* minute spent in the state of Oklahoma was one fraught with danger. Especially if the officer knew where the car was being towed.

But we couldn't leave the city until the car was hidden, stripped of camera gear, and secured for immediate shipping home.

Our new friend was eager to stay and chat after arranging a tow to a nearby garage—conveniently owned by an ex-cop he was sure would give us a discount—but a sudden and fortuitous radio dispatch sent him off with enthusiastic waves all around. He was still in sight when I called *another* tow truck to take us to the nearby Waterford Marriott and its concealed parking lot, to which we rode in silence. The aircrew was already on its way to meet us before flying back to New York. I informed my mother; Cory, the other witnesses. Maggie would find out when she landed in L.A. I booked a ticket to meet her the next day. Nine booked one to Miami. Cory booked one to Hawaii, then began removing the camera equipment. I leaned back and closed my eyes for the first time in 33 hours.

I already knew when the next departure window opened.

I would need PolizeiAir to deploy one more time.

I couldn't ask Nine to go again. Gumball 2005, 34:46, 14:51 to Oklahoma. Nearly 7,500 miles in the face of incarceration and death. With me. I'd wait him out until final preparations for the next run, just in case he changed his mind.

Replacing him would be a formidable task.

But the countdown wasn't over.

Now that I'd paid the price for my hubris, I knew exactly what improvements would be necessary for next time. I'd already e-mailed AI asking for the third-through-tenth diagnoses overlooked three days earlier. The most likely—a fuel-pump filter—was one I'd naively omitted from my preventative maintenance list. Failure is the great teacher, if one allows it to be. I'd failed, but even in failure everything was going according to plan.

And then came the phone call from Oklahoma City BMW—the police were there. I thought my life was over.

"Bad news first," I said to Seth from a secluded bench in LAX's arrival terminal.

"Before I tell you, is there anything you want to tell me first?"

"You know what I did."

"I can't represent you unless I know the truth. Are there any weapons or contraband in that car? Anything besides the usual gizmos?"

"Seth, you *know* me. C'mon. How bad is it?"

"They want to get inside that car, but they don't have probable cause. Not yet."

"But *nothing* happened other than the breakdown, I swear. No tickets, no accidents, no calls, nothing."

"Well, smart-ass, apparently you made a phone call while standing in line at the Oklahoma City airport. Someone nearby overheard snippets of your conversation. You were describing . . . shall we say . . . some very interesting activities. That person works for the governor of Oklahoma. It didn't take long for the state police to open an investigation into the identity of the owner of one particular and very special BMW."

"But I only called my mother, and my girlfriend, and—" AI, to whom I'd given a brief but potentially *very* incriminating summary, if any bystander could possibly have pieced together the totally unbelievable facts of our story.

"Seth, what exactly did they overhear?"

"They overheard *BMW, breakdown, night vision, escape, cops, spotter plane, Pennsylvania,* and *150 miles an hour.*"

"So . . . what constitutes probable cause? What can they charge me with?"

"Right now they have no idea what you were doing, in Oklahoma or anywhere else, but the BMW guys had your Team Polizei Web page up when the investigator arrived. I'm sure *that* was an amusing scene. Absolutely hilarious. You weren't wearing police outfits this time, were you? Using the lights and sirens?"

"Please, Seth, never in the United States."

"Good, but the investigator is now well aware of your reputation from Gumball, and he is *most* curious as to what you were doing in *that* car in *his* city, fully equipped with everything you talk about on your website. They know Gumball isn't in America this year, *and* that there aren't any other events going on right now, *and* that your car isn't wearing any stickers anyway. So they're quite curious about that phone call from the airport."

"What did you tell them?"

"I told them the truth . . . that you were driving cross-country, that you're an animated speaker, and that you were probably trying to impress some girl with your amazing driving adventures."

"That *is* a plausible explanation, and ninety-nine percent true. How did they take it?"

"They want to know what happened in Pennsylvania. He's sending an investigatory request to the Pennsylvania State Police, asking whether a blue BMW was reported involved in any accidents or crimes in the last three days. If they don't check your credit cards and the toll records, we can always suggest that no car could possibly have traveled from Pennsylvania to Oklahoma in such a short span of time. Don't even tell me how long it took you. I might have to fire you as a client. Just tell me . . . did you have any run-ins in Pennsylvania?"

"Yes. A scanner report. Someone called in a blue BMW at a high rate of speed, heading west . . . without taillights."

"And that was you."

"Yes, it was."

"That *might* be enough to get a warrant to open the car. Alex, think. Is there anything inside that would suggest what you were doing?"

"I . . . I . . . yes."

"Precisely what?"

Lacking any luggage and assuming we were free and clear, I'd left behind . . . everything. The Steiners and Kenyon gyrostabilizer would appear odd, but innocent. The Raytheon Thermal Imaging System was an unknown. The rest read like KITT's technical specs from *Knight Rider,* crossed with Jackie Chan's Subaru from the original *Cannonball Run,* only far worse. Both scanners—set to the Oklahoma State Police frequency bank—and the instructions given me by the radio expert I'd hired to program them, including his name and number. Both Garmins, one displaying our route, the other our elapsed time and distance. If connected to a PC running Garmin's (conveniently expensive) MapSource application, our precise tracks—including time, speed, bearing, latitude and longitude—could be downloaded and viewed. The Blinder laser jammers. *Driveplan 1 Alpha (Assault Final),* and a card from Maggie wishing us luck.

Seth, audibly scribbling notes, took a deep, long breath. "Alex, does the driveplan actually *say* 'Assault Final' on it?"

"No."

"It's still bad, but not as bad. What does Maggie's card say?"

"I can't remember verbatim, but something to the effect of 'Don't kill anyone,' 'Break the record!,' 'See you in L.A.!,' and 'Love, Maggie.'"

"That, too, is going to be a problem."

"What if I fly back to Oklahoma City *right* now, walk in there, and remove all that stuff? Or steal my own car and hide it somewhere else?"

"Alex, *do not*, under any circumstances, set foot in the state of Oklahoma."

"The BMW guys love Gumball. Can I just ask them to pull those items and ship them to me?"

"That might have worked before the police showed up, but now they've put a hold on your car. No one can touch it, not even open it. If you're charged, it would be considered tampering with evidence."

"So there's nothing I can do?"

"Alex, you're a schmuck for putting either of us in this situation, but here's the good news. What do they have on you? You have a spotless record. You're a successful young businessman. You pay your taxes on time. You're involved in your local community. You volunteer for charitable works. Maggie loves you. Besides having a fetish for dressing like a cop once a year while on vacation, you're a model citizen. So here's the deal. They're going to hold your car for three days. If nothing comes back from Pennsylvania within that time, BMW will ship your car back to New York."

"That's it? I'm free?"

"That's it. Wherever you are, just stay there. And do us both a favor. Don't drive. Anywhere. Until further notice. Take a cab. Since I'm a nice guy, give me the receipts and I'll take it off your bill."

"And if they open that car, what can they charge me with?"

"That's a tough one. Maybe nothing. Maybe speeding, reckless endangerment, road racing . . . there's no precedent for what they could do. You did say you're the first, or at least you think you're the first, to try this in what? Twenty-five years?"

"Something like that. Seth, I should have asked you this before I left, but I was afraid you'd ask why, and then you'd have refused . . . and maybe even turned me in."

"I'm sure I would have. What is it?"

"I want a complete list of all the applicable criminal statutes in every state I passed through, on this and the recon run. Statues of limitations, tolling laws, everything."

"We've already started. Just in case. It'll be ready by the time you get back. But, Alex, I want you to think about something. I never knew your father, but it seems from everything I've heard that he was quite a man. Once this is over, I want you to ask yourself . . . is this what he would have wanted?"

Seth couldn't have known the terrifying depth of his question, nor could I have answered it just then, or for the three days I intended to hide—speechless, shell-shocked, and terrified—with Maggie in my hotel room in L.A. I had always been ready to pay the price for my actions. To do so victorious was noble, but to do so in defeat made the risks taken and sacrifices made appear those of a madman, or an idiot.

I was going again. But my clock couldn't start until this one stopped. In motion or at rest, plaguing me at all turns, was time.

Time was the Devil.

But on Thursday, April 6, the Devil's clock ran out.

I reset mine.

The M5 returned to AI yet again for refitting and upgrades—among them a second Vertex radio, and *two* more Garmins and roof-mounted antennas.

The target date was Saturday, October 7, 2006. Columbus Day weekend. Twenty-six weeks and two days away.

CHAPTER 32

The Patron Saint of Nonviolent and Unprofitable Crimes

I became blind to everything beyond what was necessary to reach the summit. Nothing and no one was spared. Although she would say the opposite, Maggie left me, and understandably so. She had suffered for my arrogance, and continued to suffer as I committed every waking hour—often nightly, until 3 A.M.—to research that made the prior drives look childish. She asked whether I was capable of balancing my task with a life that included her or anyone else. She deserved to be happy. I deserved to be alone, and had to be until someone—aware of the potential, terrible cost to both of us—could understand and forgive me for what I intended to do. I was incapable of lying about who I'd become, and who I yearned to be by the second week of October. She gave me an ultimatum. A wiser, more grateful man would have tossed everything else aside and said yes.

I said no.

Ross had called. He needed a copilot for Gumball. If Nine didn't change his mind soon, that October so would I. Briefing, orientation, and practice would take his replacement months. Ross was first on the list.

The 2006 Gumball would have three legs—London to Belgrade, Phuket to Bangkok, and Salt Lake City to Los Angeles the latter the perfect method of auditioning the world's most veteran Gumballer for the task at hand. I sent Ross, with whom I hadn't spoken in ten months, an NDA, which he signed and returned without question. Our relationship existed in a peculiar netherworld in which there was only one reason to send such a document. On Sunday, April 30, precisely four weeks after the Oklahoma breakdown, Ross—hereby designated Team Polizei's new Master Pilot—and I left London in his temporary contribution to Team Polizei's 2006 garage, a jet-black *Commonwealth of the Bahamas Nassau Tax Evasion Intercept* liveried Bentley GT.

"Now, Mr. Roy, tell me more about this little drive you have planned."

Ross and I—with a combined eight Gumballs, three Bullruns, and one and a half cross-country runs between us—ripped across France and Belgium so rapidly that fans watching the ALK.com tracks thought we'd placed our CoPilot transponder on a train, or possibly a plane. The fearsome Morley—"I'll *get* you!" he'd threatened the night before the start. "You'll see!"—somehow caught up despite crossing the Channel one train behind us, Ross having wisely purchased a VIP Eurotunnel ticket without which even we'd have had no chance against him. Luckily, the police stopped both of us in tandem two miles shy of the first checkpoint at Belgium's Château Beloeil, and we—an overstuffed manila envelope of euros at the ready—had the exact change to pay our fine and were released while Morley's SLR was seized for improper documentation—a shockingly inconvenient oversight for a veteran of his stature.

This, and our commanding lead over the third- and lower-placed cars—blindly cruising into an ambush whose manpower grew by the minute—gave us sufficient time to visit the château's stunning orchid gardens before heading toward Vienna. Five hundred and seventy-four dark, silent miles later, punctuated only by the occasional flash of halogen bulbs overhead—each triggered by sensors embedded in the Autobahn asphalt, and irrelevant thanks to our Euro-spec anticamera plate covers—we arrived to a heroes' welcome at the Austrian border control. We signed autographs and met the local police chief before another first-place finish in Vienna, where we sipped tea in Kursalon Park while awaiting Muss and Seamus for the final leg to Budapest. They, having remembered our prior year's magnanimity, led us all the way into the city before pulling aside to gift us first place. Ant and Pete might have beaten us, had they not broken down one block short of the flag.

I wasn't upset upon discovering that our car had been sabotaged overnight. I was fascinated. Having determined that the saboteur's placement of a rotting trout in the Bentley's air dam had loosened several screws vital to its stability at high speed, Ross immediately fashioned new locking brackets out of three wire hangers and a handful of cable ties. I didn't care about having to forfeit that day's leg through Serbia to Belgrade. We already had a commanding lead in the overall stage rankings. All I could think about was what might have happened had Ross been in the M5, stopped in Oklahoma just one month earlier.

SUNDAY, MAY 7, 2006
HARD ROCK CAFE HOTEL AND CASINO
LAS VEGAS, NEVADA
FINAL MORNING OF GUMBALL

"Sabotage again?" said Ross, putting a good face on his worsening flu as he knelt beside me behind the GT. "Who was it this time, Mr. Roy?"

I snipped off the last long strip of cellophane that had only five minutes earlier wrapped the entire car. "Well, since the key to sabotage is for the maximum possible inconvenience to be wrought upon the target by a proportionally lesser act, I'd say this was the work of—"

"A lesser intellect?"

"Yes, I'd attribute this, the London salmon, the London license plate theft, the Budapest trout, the Salt Lake stink bomb, and the Budapest dog shit on the door handles . . . all of it to Ed Leigh." Leigh, perennial host of the Gumball TV show, had been tasked with annoying us—for the viewers' entertainment, theoretically—which, given our resilience and his failure to impede our progress, had led to increasingly juvenile and dangerous pranks.

"Mr. Ross, we need to make a strong showing."

"A *statement.*"

"We need to be first, and not by a little bit. It can't be close."

"Agreed."

"I'm talking about a huge margin, Master Pilot Ross."

"But of course, Mr. Roy."

"*No* mercy."

One critical problem remained. I'd failed to repair or replace the external Garmin antennas essential to navigating the 381 miles of the final stage through Death Valley to the finish line in Beverly Hills. The Bentley's insulated glass blocked the built-in antennas' reception, and the factory system—like the ALK CoPilot—wasn't designed to replot routes or render and update maps at speeds in excess of 100 mph.

We needed help.

ROUTE 190 WEST
DEATH VALLEY NATIONAL PARK
235 MILES FROM RODEO DRIVE FINISH LINE

"It means they're tracking us!" I yelled over the 120 mph wind roaring in through Ross's open window. "Some of them! Maybe *all* of them!"

"How do you mean?" he yelled back.

"*Look* at the CoPilot! It's suggesting taking *this* to U.S. 395, then following *that* all the way to L.A. Just keep holding the Garmin out the window until it gets the plot—"

"How much longer do you suppose? It's getting rather sandy in here—ah! There it is!" He raised his window before placing the sandblasted Garmin back in its dash-top mount. "I hope this was worth it. I also hope your unit wasn't destroyed."

I wiped the display with my thumb. "Yes! You see? The Gumball-recommended CoPilot route is 250 miles, but my gut tells me that one of these tiny roads off to our left can shave at least 20 or 30 off that."

"If we don't get lost or run out of gas."

"Better yet, Mr. Ross, if one or more of our pursuers really is tracking us, I mean calling their girlfriends back home to check the ALK site to find out where *we're* going, that is *precisely* what I hope will happen, but not to us!"

"Mr. Roy . . . you truly are a bad man."

"That's not all. Our little Porsche friends are somewhere in that row of red cars following us. I have something very special in mind." I grabbed the CB handset to address the car directly behind us, a black Ford GT with white stripes, the only Gumball car ever equipped as well as the Polizei M5, a car copiloted by one Dr. Gruene (aka Eric Ward), a first-timer whose psychotic professionalism matched my own, and the driver, a former enemy whom we alone—despite his history—had chosen not to underestimate. Gumball had forbidden him from participating as aggressively as in the past, but nothing prevented him from convoying in relative and cooperative safety with Team Polizei, even if we were in the lead.

"Dr. Greune, this is the Polizei, do you copy?"

"Gruene's busy on the Garmin, Polizei, this is Jerry, over."

"Our Garmins are out. Can you take the lead and plot a shortcut off one of these side roads?"

"Copy that, Polizei . . . Dr. Gruene projects . . . next left in two miles . . . Wildrose Road. Will save at least 25 miles. Aren't you worried about all these guys following us?"

"Let's make the turn. I've got an idea. Stand by."

We made the turn. A line of red and black dots followed in the mirror.

"What next, Mr. Roy?"

"We turn off the CoPilot so no one can track us or follow us. This route is definitely *not* in their CoPilots."

"Mr. Roy, you really are far worse than I thought."

"Oh, there's more. We refueled in Las Vegas and our fuel is *already* low, which means every car following us that didn't fill up is even lower. And if any of them can hear their radar detectors, when they light up they're gonna brake hard. *And* we can assume that if they see us accelerating, they're going to think it's safe, and punch it to catch up, and if *that* happens a couple of times, they're going to run out of gas on *this* road, and   "

"Mr. Roy"—Ross smiled, taking the CB from my hand—"you drive. Please allow me . . . Hello? This is Mr. Ross from Team Polizei, do you copy?"

"Ten-four, Mr. Ross, this is Jerry."

"Why, hello there. Mr. Roy has two requests . . . first is that you turn off your ALK unit, over."

"That's a Ten-four."

"Mr. Roy would also like permission to pass. I do believe you know why."

"Dr. Gruene is already laughing, over."

"Thank you so very much. Now, if you would be so kind . . . Torquenstein, please deploy the radar drone."

Torquenstein's Ford GT was equipped with the one item I'd long considered unethical, yet now essential given our foes' lack of spirit—a rearward-facing police radar gun. As expected, multiple blasts emitted minutes apart elicited enormous clouds of sand and dust to our rear, our pursuers responding as I predicted.

I hoped no one we liked was back there. I rationalized this as a civic duty ensuring everyone—except us and our coconspirators, of course—a slower, safer drive. By the third blast, our pursuers were but red and black dots in the mirror. Through his tears Ross handed me a second handkerchief. I made a mental note to procure—if I ever rallied again—a boxful. Laughing blindness was extraordinarily dangerous at any speed, but more so at 140 mph.

"I've been thinking," said Ross as I turned onto Wilshire Boulevard, 250 miles and two and a half hours later. "Torquenstein and Gruene . . ."

"I know exactly what you're thinking. It's the right thing to do."

"How far are we from Rodeo Drive?"

"With lights and sirens, less than five minutes."

With legitimate first-place finishes into four out of nine checkpoints so far, we already had an insurmountable lead. There was only one thing left to do for our friends in the black Ford GT in our mirror.

"Torquenstein, this is Mr. Ross, do you copy?"

"Ten-four, this is Torquenstein."

"Mr. Roy and I propose we pull into the finish line side by side."

"Copy that, Polizei. FYI, people tracking us are saying we've been fighting it out all afternoon."

"Now, that is a good one."

Ross and I were minutes away from our first unequivocal Gumball victory—for time—verified and validated by our on-board cameras, fans, witnesses, and the ALK CoPilot tracks.

But the celebration wasn't ours alone.

"Mr. Ross, please tell them drinks are on me until midnight."

We made the final turn. The LAPD moved the barriers and waved us through. Rodeo Drive was devoid of cars except for those that had skipped the Death Valley checkpoint. They beckoned us forward, toward the end of the street, where Grimaldi had held them open—just for us.

Of the thousand-odd people watching as we shook hands with Team Torquenstein, there was but one I noticed as she approached from across the street—a slim young woman with short platinum hair, dressed all in white, pulling a wheeled suitcase. She'd come to surprise me. We both smiled, and for a moment I saw another, happier life in which the only wheeled transportation I used was a bicycle. It might not have been too late, but then Maggie saw beside me the Englishman she'd heard so much about, and I saw in her eyes recognition of terrible plans still in motion.

"The bunnies are waiting for you," said the Gumball TV show's producer. "Michael, Alex . . . what are you doing? We've got to get a shot of the winners with the bunnies!"

"Just *one* moment," said Ross, the two of us standing at the edge of the Playboy Mansion's outdoor pool, just a few feet away from a pair of rouge-cheeked, fuchsia-clad, round-bottomed, fishnet-legged, high-heeled, bunny-eared cougars seated upon a large rock, their mottled skin aglow under the TV lights. Dozens of Gumballers lurked around them in a tightening semicircle, pondering when and how best to proceed. "Alex and I need just one moment of privacy."

"Good thinking," I said semisarcastically, "a thousand people crowded around us, and not one of them will pay attention to us as long as those bunnies are sitting there."

"An incredible run, Alex, the most exhausting Gumball yet. We should be proud of ourselves. Really, first has a quality all its own."

"Just *tell* me."

"The truth is, if you and I, who have nothing in common besides Gumball, who travel in vastly disparate social circles, are now among the two most veteran drivers in our little circle, and if neither of us has found the slightest shred of evidence of any such secret races among like-minded gentlemen, then—"

"You'll do it?"

"If no one else is taking the leap, it would seem all the more reason."

"Mr. Ross, is that a commitment?"

Ross, the only five-time veteran I know of—who, despite his flu, had ridden 3,000 and flown 14,000 miles in eight days, driven up to six hours per day, slept no more than five each night, fixed the car twice, and retained his composure and humor throughout—looked tired. If he had twenty-four hours to recover, I knew he'd get back in the GT and drive me the 2,794 miles home to New York. If he had five months to prepare, I knew he could—and would—take Nine's place.

But, for the first time since we met, Ross didn't have a ready answer.

"Michael, I'm serious. I need to know. If you need more time, or if you want to see all my research—"

"Alex, does anyone other than yourself think 32:07 can be broken?"

"Only Rawlings."

"Perhaps someone who's done some research? To the degree you have?"

"No. Not that I know of."

"And your driving protocols . . . you know we only used them perhaps fifty percent of the time, and only on the American leg. On my behalf, I wouldn't quite call that an audition, or even slightly adequate practice. I want you to be perfectly honest. How much more difficult is the full cross-country? Surely—"

"Bad." I paused to avoid giving the impression I was joking, or exaggerating.

"I'm sure." He nodded. "I see it in your face. You never laugh when discussing it."

"One Express driver said it made anything on a track look pathetic. Anything."

"Is that all?"

"Another guy said Paris-Dakar was the only thing worse."

"On that basis alone"—Ross chuckled—"I'll do it. But there is another matter. Jon has a lot invested in this, and in you. I can't go until he's fully withdrawn, out of respect for him and, I think, sensitivity to your friendship. I think Mr. Goodrich will need a little more time than you've given him. A lot, perhaps."

"If it makes you feel any better, I told him I'd ask you. He said you were the only one he felt comfortable with taking his seat."

"Too kind, but I say you give him until July or August. But, Alex . . . *you* have a decision to make. I want to do it, but you *need* to do it. The logistics, the film crew, the spotter plane, it doesn't seem likely you'll pull them together again. This Cory woman, and Weismann and Baskett . . . you have to make it *this* time. You need her, and no pilot-for-hire can be trusted, or remotely as committed as your current air support. So, the odds of success decrease with every naked run thereafter. The question for this next one is . . . if you're stopped by the police even once, what would be the effect, positive or negative, of a foreign national at the helm?"

I wanted to lie, to him and myself, but it was too late for such machinations.

"I don't know, Ross."

"Then you best find out, and since this is so important, please allow me to take care of the bunnies while you call your attorney. And I'll find out whether any possible criminal charges may hinder future visits to your fine country. It would be highly unfortunate were I unable to visit my American girlfriend."

"Ross . . . you have an American girlfriend?"

"By then, I may. Now go pay attention to your little Maggie before she gets upset. She's more popular here than the bunnies, and she came a long way to surprise you. Wait . . . you *have* told her you're going again, haven't you?"

"We haven't discussed it since—"

"Alex, you must tell her immediately. You musn't drag it out even for a second. To lose her slowly, to hurt her slowly, it's far worse than any crime you may commit come October. She's quite lovely, by the way. If I didn't know what you had in mind, I'd say you were a fool."

"Are you in jail?" said Seth, the waves crashing against the sand in front of his New Jersey beach house. This was always his first question when I called on weekend nights. "Because if you're not, I'm hanging up right now. It's Sunday."

"I'm free, I'm in L.A., and I'm safe."

"What's all that noise in the background?"

"I'm standing in front of the Playboy Mansion."

"(A) The last good party there was when I was your age. (B) You're a jerk. (C) You have 30 seconds."

He cut me off at precisely 30. "Check your e-mail, smart-ass. You and your buddies aren't going to like the spreadsheet of applicable laws I sent you."

"But what if I bring a foreigner?"

"(A) Don't do this. (B) How the hell should *I* know? There's probably fifty thousand cops employed by all the departments in all the jurisdictions you're going through. One guy may hate Italians, another guy Germans. Where's your friend from?"

"England."

"At least he speaks English. That might help if you're stopped. My advice is to take a long hard look at the spreadsheet. Even if you make it safely, there are places you may never be able to go again. Think about whether you want to risk everything your parents gave you. Think about the fantastic girlfriends you turned your back on for this. Think about the business."

"Look, if you're not going to turn me in, do you have any useful advice?"

"Go fall in love. Be happy, have kids . . . and don't call me again until you've changed your mind, or it's over."

"I'm sorry, Seth."

"Don't be sorry. Be safe. I care about you. I'm going back to my kids now. Good-bye."

I went back inside and found Maggie talking to Seamus and Muss, who had flown in from Budapest for Gumball's finale party. Other than Ross, they were the only two I trusted to keep her—the only female present not employed by Playboy—unmolested while I was gone. I apologized to her for running off.

"Must have been really important!" Seamus bellowed. "Good God, man! First you bring a fine young lady to this den of filth, then you leave her to make a phone call?"

"Wasn't she safe with you?"

"I," he said, beating his chest, "would never leave my date with any ex–British army officer who wears a kilt to the Playboy Mansion!"

"Sorry, guys, I had to call my attorney."

Maggie took both my hands in hers and looked into my eyes. "Did you really just call him?"

We returned home the next day. The countdown continued, but for us, it was too late.

Cory and I spoke for an hour virtually every morning and night. She, too, existed in a tunnel whose only exit was some four-odd months away. We discussed Ross's keen remark. Cory and I *would* go as often as necessary, but the next run was likely the last time PolizeiAir would deploy with The Weis and the Captain at the controls. It was our last chance to deploy multiple film crews within the film's budget and timetable. If another assault was required in early 2007, the cost of hiring private pilots and camera crews—essential for documenting our effort for posterity—would force a decision. If I truly believed what I'd told myself for nearly six years, personal bankruptcy would be a small price to pay compared to the alternative. If I had to raise money, that would betray everything I held dear. The canon of modern automotive entertainment—the street-racing videos on YouTube, and films like *The Fast and the Furious*—made that clear; *32 Hours, 7 Minutes* would probably be the first and last effort to respectfully document an epic, untold chapter in American history.

The Driver. Secret races. The Wall. Perhaps those days *were* over.

I no longer cared. One thing remained.

I was going to drive coast-to-coast as fast as possible—over and over, crushing the beehive, if necessary—until I got there. Fast. Just once.

I had to do it *this* time.

"Wasssuuuup? Miss me, Mr. Pol-*eez*-eye?"

"*Rowwwww*-lingsz!" I yelled back across the Soho House's sixth-floor lounge. I hadn't been there in months, but the 2006 Bullrun's impending departure from New York demanded that I leave the house. I took malicious glee in booking their most prominent table for dinner with five of the world's most infamous road-going outlaws. The 9:30 crowd still contained the more conservative post-work drink holdovers, but somehow I knew Rawlings and his entourage wouldn't need cars to scatter these pigeons. "*Wilkommen!*" I called out. "*Wilkommen im der Soho Haus!*"

Rawlings stomped toward me with a broad grin sharp enough to hack bark off a tree. He stopped halfway between the crowded bar and a neighboring table, his cowboy boots clattered as he performed a five-second jig of greeting, then he froze, slapped his hands together, and began the world's loudest one-man game of patty-cake. Once sure of the room's attention, he doffed his enormous cowboy hat and dropped it on the much smaller head of a woman, who—in an attempt to ignore people she obviously preferred not to see at the vaunted Soho House—had foolishly turned her back on a man toward whom one should never turn one's back. She spun to face him, then, upon seeing the theatrically angry cowboy face he reserved for the weak-minded, she recoiled as if a snake might bolt out of his mouth if she dared speak without permission. He retrieved his hat, curtsied, then strutted toward me and offered his hand.

If he only knew how much respect I had for him. If he only knew how closely I paid attention. If he only knew the terrible guilt I felt lying to him.

He saved me in 2003, fought me in 2004, fell behind me in 2005, yet I would always place him on a pedestal. He and I were trapped, two men with no one else to fight. There was no one else. Dennis Collins was his The Weis—men with a surfeit of skill, yet nothing to prove.

I stood up and reached out to shake his hand, but his arm suddenly darted forward and with a loud slap his palm fell beside my (luckily) empty plate.

"Howdja like that??!?!?" He nodded toward where he'd just placed a large skull-and-crossboned Gasmonkey Garage sticker on the Soho House's white plastic retro-mod table.

"Nice, Richard. Let me guess. *Not* removable."

"Not unless your buddies here've got a blowtorch! I want you to meet my new copilot!" A bushy-blond-haired, short, generously gold-necklaced, nose-, ear-, and pinkie-ringed, and very white Texan dressed like circa-1992 Axl Rose stepped forward holding up his driver's license. "Meet Michael Jackson! It's true! That's his name!" Rawlings howled as he and Jackson dropped into seats across from mine, "Now ain't that somethin'?"

"Where're the Collins brothers?"

"Riiiiiiiggght here!" Dennis called out from across the lounge, his brother Michael—perhaps the best rally navigator alive other than myself—in tow. "Nice to see ya!"

The quartet, now lined up in one row, began slapping their hands on the table, first in a flurry of overlapping stickers, then in impromptu drumming that would have cost me my membership had yet another long-lost voice not pierced the din.

"I have *never*" said Frankl, his reedy tone reserved only for the most con- temptible, "seen a larger assortment of criminals, charlatans, and sycophants, not one of whom is qualified to drive. I didn't see your strollers parked downstairs. Are you actually here for the Bullrun? I didn't know the Soho House offered toilet-training classes!"

"Goddammit!" said Rawlings. "Alex, can we get the check?! This is the kinda place that charges just for sitting right?"

"Don't worry," I said. "I'm seating him on the far end, where every girl's spoken for. It'll drive him nuts. He likes you, by the way . . . okay, I'm lying. He respects you."

"Whatever, man, gotta say it sure is a shame you're not doing Bullrun this time. New York to L.A. should be real scenic!"

I shrugged. "Politics, money, car trouble . . . it's a long list. Besides, six days cross-country? C'mon. No rally should do New York–L.A. It's an insult to our Cannonball forefathers!"

"What about that *32:07* movie? Is it ever coming out?"

"Soon . . . very soon. A year, maybe. You know these low-budget indie movies. How about this idea? I'll bet you one dollar I can beat you from New York to Miami."

Dennis burst out laughing. Rawlings backhanded him in the stomach.

"How about this one, Mr. Polizei? Me and Dennis . . . 29:15."

"What?" I said, then they, too, froze, the three of us rapidly exchanging glances, the crowd around us dissolving into hazy shapes buzzing against a wall before a broken reel projector. I paused for several epochal seconds before saying, "Twenty-nine fifteen?"

"Yup," said Collins, "29:15."

"Twenty-nine fifteen what?"

"Cross-country!" said Rawlings.

"You know it!" Dennis giggled and raised his glass.

"Told you I could do it, Alex."

"But what did he say next?"

"Just kidding!"

"Alex," said Cory, seated at her desk 3,000 miles away, "are you in the Soho House bathroom right now?"

"Yeah, I couldn't wait to tell you."

"Just keep your voice down in case one of them walks in, just in case it's true. Did he really say 'just kidding'?"

"Yeah, but it could've meant anything."

"Alex, maybe he just wanted to intimidate you, or they don't want you to know they went . . . for the same reasons we don't. Or maybe he still wants to, and is trying to bait you into telling him what he needs to know, so he *can* try."

"I think . . . I think we ignore them and—"

"Stay on plan. Now go back there and act normal."

I smiled through the rest of dinner, then wished Rawlings, Jackson, the Collinses, and Frankl the best of luck on a safe Bullrun. They headed across the street to the Gansevoort Hotel for Bullrun's official prestart party. I went home and began building a new driveplan from scratch.

Driveplan .5C (Merciless Assault Reprisal -79).

Seventy-nine days; 1,890 hours. It might not be enough time. Unless I had help. Even if I had help.

But once again the Patron Saint of Nonviolent and Unprofitable Crimes shone his disco ball upon me, because he called me back within 10 minutes.

CHAPTER 33

The Driver

SATURDAY, SEPTEMBER 9, 2006
HOLLAND TUNNEL WESTBOUND
NEW JERSEY SPEED-TRAP MAPPING
VERIFICATION DRIVE NO.5
2141 HOURS (EST)
27 DAYS, 23 HOURS, 55 MINUTES TO DEPARTURE

"I can't believe you're asking me this," said twenty-one-year-old engineering student Jean-Francis (aka J.F.) Musial, who in the three months since I'd NDA'd him had proven himself a better friend than people I'd known as long as he'd been alive. A Gumball fan who'd taken my picture at the New York Auto Show in 2005, J.F. had subsequently offered to update the Gumball144.com blog during Gumball 2006, but I quickly recognized how much more he had to offer. I taught him everything I knew about Gumball, 3446, and the Oklahoma incident, and he took over nearly half the necessary research for the upcoming October 7 run, dissected and corrected the old driveplans, and became an indispensable weapon in our impending and final assault.

We were now on our fifth New York–to–Pennsylvania border recon and ambush-point verification drive, a leg for which J.F. had mapped out every potential speed trap, which I had then programmed into the Garmins—now numbering four, each with its own dedicated roof-mounted antennas—precisely as instructed. If I had a J.F. in every state, 29 hours might be possible.

He would drive his black Polizei ECM–modified Audi A4—the first of three *UnderkoverPolizeiRekonVideoKinoEskort* chase cars for the run—out of the CCC 15 minutes ahead of us, cameraman beside him, and send back data on traffic and police locations until we caught up and passed. He would then log all communications, track our progress on the master map, send us real-time NOAA weather and traffic reports, coordinate with PolizeiAir, and inform all parents, spouses, boyfriends, girlfriends, and next of kin of our status.

"With the time you've put in," I said from the M5's passenger seat, "you deserve a say. Cory and I respect your opinion."

"But . . . I'm just a fan who's helping out, I can't help you pick a copilot."

"Don't underestimate what you've learned. Before my father died, I asked him how I was going to go on. He said someday I'd wake up and wouldn't be able to remember what life was like when he was alive."

"But you remember him, right? You always talk about him."

"I remember everything that happened before, and everything about him, but I can't remember . . . what it felt like to know I could call him. Now all I know is that I can't. It's the same with what I'm doing now. I can't remember who I was before this started. Before Gumball 2003. Before Rome. Before Rawlings made me the bet, then after Oklahoma. Someday you'll wake up and nothing will be the same. I think everyone feels it, but not everybody follows it to the end. I used to be the laziest person in the world. My dad even told me. Look at me now."

We drove in silence for the next few minutes.

"J.F., you know I'd take you . . . if I could."

"Me? Are you insane? I don't have enough experience."

"Not yet. But you have enough to drive the first chase car out of New York. I guarantee you half of The Drivers from Gumball would say no if I asked, which I can't. No one knows anyone until they've seen what they do against the Wall."

J.F. was silent.

"So, let's go down the list of potentials. Start obvious, then go crazy."

"Jon Goodrich."

"No. Worried charges will screw his business. He travels a lot. The good news is he's flying in the spotter plane."

"All right . . . what about Michael Ross?"

"Amazing guy, my number one pick, but he's concerned over work/travel issues if we're caught. Homeland Security watch list. Also, he was arrested in California on the '03 Gumball. Red flag if we're caught on the last leg. If we go down because of it, he'll never forgive himself. Can't say how well he'll spot American undercovers. On the flip side, he loves adventure. If I ask, he'll go."

"Remy? Or Kalbas?"

"J.F., those guys are so good and so cool, they'd either laugh at the suggestion, or they've already done it and didn't feel the need to tell anyone."

"Nicholas Frankl?"

"One of the best. Perfect, and he's hilarious. But very close with a lot of people I don't want finding out. We may have to keep it secret for months, maybe years. Next."

"Jodie Kidd? She drives for the Maserati factory team."

"I like her, but I don't think she'll spend 30 hours in a car with a guy like me."

"Dennis Collins?"

"In my top three, but too close to Rawlings."

"Rawlings?" J.F. chuckled.

"Don't laugh. I actually thought about asking him."

"Alex, man, you two together . . . the earth would explode, you'd break 29 hours, man . . . it'd be—"

"Nuts, but there's no way we could keep a Roy/Rawlings team-up quiet. And if we're caught or something bad happens, we'll blame each other until we're dead. They'd have to put us in separate cells."

"Joe Macari?"

"Respect him, but don't know him well enough."

"Alison Cornea?"

"Same."

"Peter Malmstrom."

"Love that guy, but he doesn't know the undercover cars."

"Spencer?"

"Don't know him that well, and he's English. Heard he was a good guy."

"Ant or Pete?"

"Huge respect for those guys, but we're not close, and they're English."

"Charles Morgan?"

"It would make history, but he has kids, and the same issues as other foreigners."

"Oliver Morley?"

"We'd shatter it, but he'd smack my face the first time I said 'ramp check.'"

"The Dust to Glory Baja 1000 winner?"

"Kevin Ward. We'd also shatter it, but no way to bring him and keep it quiet. Married with kids, and he and Bret Haller are organizing the Unlimited Class for the Carrera Panamericana."

"You doing that one?"

"Fight battles you can win, tough guy. People get killed on that. I'm not ready."

"We're running out of people."

"We already did. No one thinks it can be broken except Rawlings and Collins, and they don't know what we know."

"Alex, man, are you *sure* it can be?"

"If I didn't think so, I wouldn't go. All that matters is that we try."

"You really won't try again if you don't make it?"

"After Oklahoma I said I'd go as many times as it took, but that's not very realistic. Look at what it took to do *that* one, and I still blew it."

"I know, man, this is like a full military operation. It really is crazy."

"Like going to Mars, only privately funded. It'll be nearly impossible to set this up, this way . . . the plane, the people . . . ever again. At least for me."

"But don't you *want* to break it?"

"It doesn't matter," I said. "It's the journey. Maybe that's the lesson in all this."

"C'mon, how will you live with yourself if you give up?"

"J.F., I lied to you. Of course I want to break it, but I have to prepare myself for failure, or I'll literally lose it if we get a flat. The journey excuse is the only way. It's the mature way. Now you know why the copilot choice is so important. It's the biggest unknown in the largest gamble I'll ever take. It'll determine whether I live with regret for the rest my life."

"Did you ever consider Cory?"

"Ahhhh, well . . . if balls were skill, she could drive the whole thing alone. But she needs more high-speed training, and she wants to shoot a movie more than she wants to drive—that is, until the movie's done. She'll do her own run one of these days. It's inevitable."

"Torquenstein?"

"Technically he's as good as us, but I don't know him well enough . . . hang on, the CoPilot Garmin Primary says . . . approaching first speed trap . . . Ambush Waypoint, two miles, log says three potentials. Exit-ramp median right, right shoulder on overpass, left shoulder negative."

"Alex, I'm telling you from experience, tag this one yellow. I live around here."

"Only forty or fifty more to go. If the Jersey yellow count ends up forty and red is only ten, we'll cross the whole state in—"

"Under an hour, in traffic, on a Saturday night. *That'll* be something to see."

"Which you will, if you can keep that Audi A4 moving without hitting us.

Next Ambush Waypoint in four miles . . . Exit 33, three potentials, first is center median, no barrier, before overpass, second is center median, after overpass, behind support pillar, third is right merge after overpass, behind trees."

"Correct . . . but, Alex, there is one person you never talk about."

"Don't say it. I've been thinking about him the whole time, but it's complicated."

"Sorry. I'll drop it."

"Let's have some fun, college boy. Instead of reading these off the Garmin, how about I test *your* memory for the next few miles?"

It was a shame he wasn't coming, because he remembered every single one.

Ross had been right.

I needed to. Everyone else merely wanted to.

Except one.

We hadn't exchanged more than a few words in three years. We were very different people, in different circles, but if my perception of him was correct, he'd commit without hesitation. He was the perfect choice in every way but one—he wouldn't follow orders if he thought he knew better. I was the same way.

He was a better driver. I was better at everything else.

For six years I'd put down my cards one by one, my bets and wins ever-increasing, but now total commitment was required. If I won, what I considered his weakness might become a strength that—interlocked with mine—drove us to the summit.

I would entrust him with far more than my life—*if* he could answer the most difficult question in the world.

MONDAY, SEPTEMBER 11, 2006
POLIZEI 3207 (MERCILESS ASSAULT REPRISAL) HQ
26 DAYS, 7 HOURS, 14 MINUTES TO DEPARTURE

I finished watching the raw 3446 footage. In real time. Again.

I had to accept who I was. I was a full-time Endurance-Rally Driver—one of the best in a small, peculiar, somewhat invisible subset of motor sport—but that didn't make me a world-class race-car driver. In my sphere, I could beat better drivers through discipline, minor art, and heavy science. In theirs I ranked dead center.

But mine was an Outside Context Mission, straddling both worlds.

My heart pled to have Nine beside me, but now I needed him in the plane.

"Alex Roy," he said with faux nonchalance, "calling me at work, after all these years. Must be important."

"Don't take it personally. This is the call you want. We need to talk. What are you doing the next five weekends?"

"Wrong time of year for Gumball. La Carrera?"

"No."

"What should I pack?"

"Nothing. No room."

"Why five?"

"Rain dates."

He didn't answer. He'd seen the *32:07* trailer. He knew me.

"I have one question," I said, having been through this with him once before, "but I need the answer in person."

"What's the question?"

"Why?"

"Okay, Alex . . . but you go first this time."

SATURDAY, OCTOBER 7, 2006
CLASSIC CAR CLUB—NEW YORK
2124 HOURS (EST)

My phone vibrated. "Message from The Weis," I said, "on behalf of the Captain, Nine and Robin."

Ur going to smash it we love aliray.

I held the screen up for him to see, and in his eyes caught my first-ever glimpse of youth—possibly even fear—then it was gone, and the fearsome driver in which all had so much faith squinted and said, "Let's do this."

Fear of a bad weather report would have been a good thing—an absurd but comforting reminder of why I'd picked him—but fear over our task wasn't in the driveplan. I already bore enough of it for all in the car.

The gate began to rise.

"You ready?"

"Alex," he said with a dark grin, "I am *so* ready."

Lelaine approached with the time clock.

"Then," I said, my confidence strangely boosted by the briefest exposure to his heart, "hand me the card."

I looked forward to demonstrating how much I had learned since the last time he'd sat beside me. The first and last legs were mine.

I punched the time clock. It was Saturday, October 7, 2006, 9:26 P.M. (EST).

CHAPTER 34

The Storm Chasers

Cory, Nine, The Weis, and I had long debated the moral and legal implications of our plans, especially the differences between our runs and the original Cannonball and U.S. Express. I suggested that the 77-mile discrepancy between our driveplan's 2794 and Diem/Turner's 2871 posed a legitimacy problem. Cory suggested we make our target 31:07, since the mileage differential could be covered at 90 mph—the average required to break the record—in 51 minutes.

Nine suggested our lack of competition made it easier. The Weis thought it made us slower. Cory agreed. I suggested it made it harder. We weren't merely alone out on the road—a recurring and terrifying thought whenever I saw our plane overhead, and imagined how we appeared to them—we were alone in our psychological makeup. If just one other like-minded person would run against us, our absolute times would be irrelevant and we could take solace in knowing we weren't—literally—crazy. But, once having decided to go alone, we were left only with a time to beat, and time had no mercy.

The individual motivation required made us even lonelier. The danger was high. There was no prize money. The more we learned, especially after one and a half runs, and especially given my (and Nine's) experience from Gumball and Bullrun, the longer our communal list of reasons *not* to go.

After Oklahoma, we stopped laughing them away.

Cory and I never fully explained our motives to each other. We couldn't. We tried, but the conversations took too long, so we gave up.

I needed to go, and Nine wanted to help. But Nine wanted to help *me* more than *he* needed to go. After Oklahoma, Nine understood what I'd left unsaid. Another breakdown wasn't the issue. We had been at the limit of our capabilities. We had taken enormous risks, yet even greater risks would be necessary. What would be required was greater than his motivation. I thanked God his loyalty remained even higher, because his presence on PolizeiAir—waiting to take off just a few hours and several hundred miles away—calmed my anxiety over the struggle on the ground.

INTERSTATE 70 WEST
APPROACHING ZANESVILLE, OHIO

"Drive faster," said Maher.

"I'm doing 110, *and* we're in Ohio. Ramp check."

"Ramp's clear. Dude, there's *no one* out here."

"Zanesville, Maher, bad karma. Diem/Turner went down here."

"But Roy/Goodrich didn't, twice. Stay in the triple digits."

"Relax, Maher. You just said our overall average is 91 and change. Last time we came through here . . . I think it was just over 90."

"But you hadn't lost time for the first fuel stop yet, and you didn't know as much as you do now. Your overall should be 92. The projections are too conservative. We need to build credit wherever we can."

"Then give me a thermal check."

"Thermal's clear. You gonna pass this truck on the right?"

The Polizei *never* passed trucks on the right. "Maher, what do you see ahead of him?"

"I see 125 mph."

What could be known of our task, I knew, and I knew what couldn't be known—new speed traps, police aviation and unmarked-car patrol routes and schedules, road closures due to accidents, emergency construction and traffic—and I erected a virtual fortress against capture and/or delay.

I saw success in the protocols I'd honed over 25,000 miles of high-speed driving. Maher saw failure in what I might have overlooked. Where there was doubt, I chose caution. Maher did not. He was of the Kenworthy school. I'd cofounded the Polizei/Rawlings academy. The former's students dominated Europe, the latter's the United States.

But Maher and I shared something unique, for we shared a common *why*. His answer was so concise, so elegant, so subtle, so *obvious*, I was embarrassed to answer in kind. His answer was mine, distilled down to six words.

I want something money can't buy.

I'd had a guess, but only then could I clearly picture him on the end of the line, in a suit and tie, seated at one desk among many, his and other phones ringing incessantly, countless men's voices overlapping in a large room in a tall building owned by the Bank of America.

Something money can't buy.

Within one minute of my asking, when he—having not yet seen a single planning document—turned to me and said yes, I knew I'd been right in my choice. Whatever his goal, he needed to go across. Without me, he couldn't go. Without him, I couldn't succeed. I never imagined I could be so right about one of whom I knew so little, or so wrong about the consequences.

I sensed we were ahead of schedule, and sought confidence in knowing by precisely how much, but Maher wasn't interested in checking our progress against *Driveplan 2 (Assault Reprisal),* or in communicating with Polizei HQ.

"If you think too much about your credit," he said, "you'll get lazy. Hammer down. Every chance you can get. *You* talk about assault, then do it. Attack. Show me."

He didn't want to try again, and neither did I. If only I drove a *little* faster—ironic given that I'd probably just set the unofficial land-speed record between New York and Zanesville, Ohio—and if only *he* followed our oft-tested protocols, we'd be the perfect team. The first overnight was the fastest and easiest stage. We wouldn't be tested, as drivers or teammates, until St. Louis, by which time we'd each occupy the seats best suited to our strengths.

I was suddenly very, very motivated. I couldn't get to the first refuel fast enough.

INTERSTATE 70 WEST
SOMEWHERE IN CENTRAL OHIO

I pulled into the first refuel and driver swap—my first legacy a historic overall prestop average of 91.7 mph. Cory and Maher sprinted inside. I stood alone between the car and the pump, gripping the nozzle in my left hand while unzipping my fly with my right. I surveyed the houses nearby, their occupants unaware of the criminal mischief taking a break in their midst for what I hoped was no more than 6 minutes and 15 seconds. I listened to the twenty-sixth gallon of premium flow. The pump clicked. The hose thumped. Steam rose from the asphalt before me. All *was* going according to plan. I zipped up. J.F.'s disembodied voice bleated in the headset I'd forgotten I was wearing.

"Can you hear me, Alex? Alex? You're flying! On or slightly ahead of projections . . . I project low thirty-ones, and dropping consistently. Just get out of that gas station within the next 60 seconds."

"Okay," I said, checking the Casio, "we'll make it."

"And don't forget to send latitude and longitude every 15 minutes. Maher didn't send me any."

"I'm copilot next. I guarantee you'll get them." I looked up at the stars. "You know . . . when I saw the city glowing in the mirror way back . . . it was like I'd never see it again."

"What are you talking about?"

"It's okay. If I don't see it, I mean. I chose. This is what I want to be doing, no matter what happens."

"Just take a deep breath, Alex, keep this up, and you'll break it—"

My Casio beeped again, then I heard two more beeps distant, one behind me and the other by the gas-mart entrance. Cory's hair whipped like a weather vane in a high wind as she sprinted toward me. Maher closed the driver's door.

I couldn't wait to share the news of our projection.

"Alex, don't forget the air intercept has to move up if you get much faster. The St. Louis chase-car intercept, too. I'll notify them, but you've *got* to keep those updates coming."

"Will do—"

Engine. Movement. Peripheral vision. Black. White. Cory saw it, too, her imminent return delayed by a less conspicuous, slow, yet still awkwardly stilted gait, during which she repeatedly turned her head to determine our new visitor's intent.

"J.F.!" I whispered. "Police car!"

"What? They're after you already?"

"Strange . . . we've been really stealthy." I turned to the M5. Maher impatiently pointed at the pump. I nodded in agreement. The pump bell rang. I jammed the nozzle into its bracket, slid into the passenger seat, and fought the urge to turn and peer through the gap between the pumps, lost, and stared at the officer inaudibly talking into his handset. Cory closed her door just as the local town's sparsely equipped Ford Crown Victoria patrol car's door opened. I recognized the entry-level Gall's private-label lighting and siren array on the dash. Team Polizei was a good customer.

"Let's go!" said Cory. "Alex! Fuel receipt?"

"Goddammit . . . I forgot it when the cop pulled up! Wait!"

The officer's left boot touched the ground.

"Can we go now?" blurted Maher.

"Order copies from Amex!" Cory yelled. "Dave, just go!" Maher rolled out of the station with unexpected control.

"Scanners up," I said, "CB up, ECM green, thermals green, GPS, power, all green."

"Mr. Roy," said Maher, suddenly accelerating harder than I liked up the merge ramp, "everything works on my side, but I've gotta tell you, man—"

"Watch the rpms, Dave. You're in third. Fuel economy, and that cop might be watching. Do you *know* what this car sounds like from outside under acceleration?"

"Relax, here, *there's* fifth. Alex, I'm really worried about our time."

"Are you insane? J.F.'s projecting 31 hours and change, and we're only halfway into the first night. My Garmin says my driving average was . . . just above 92."

"Too slow, Alex. Trust me."

"Dave, I know how good you are. Just don't get a ticket trying to prove it."

"I'm telling you . . . triple digits the whole way or we're not going to make it." He merged onto the barren interstate at 120.

"Then, Mr. Maher, I invite you to open it up. Do your best, please." He immediately surged to 130.

"I was kidding, Dave."

"I wasn't."

SUNDAY, OCTOBER 8, 2006
INTERSTATE 70 WEST
SOMEWHERE IN WESTERN INDIANA
0530 HOURS EST (APPROX)

"Maher, you've got to slow down for a minute. I can't call The Weis, *and* J.F. *and* spot at 135 mph."

"Are you actually asking me to slow down? I mean, really slow down?"

"Would you rather we miss the intercept with the spotter plane *and* the St. Louis chase car?"

"Fine. One-fifteen. You call, I'll do double duty."

"Holy shit!" said The Weis over the crackling cell connection. "No wonder I can barely hear you! Wait . . . you guys are something like . . . 30 or 40 minutes ahead of projections?! And *you* drove the first leg?"

Maher, spotting a semi in the left at 80, drifted right.

"That's right," I said nervously. "Yeah, The Weis, that was me."

"Good boy. Proud of you. My God . . . and Maher's picked it up even more? I've got to wake the Bulgarian—" Maher accelerated to 120. The M5 shuddered as we passed the truck at a 40 mph differential. "Jesus, what was that?"

I shook my head. "A bad pass." Maher snickered.

"Relax," said The Weis, "if we're still talking, he knows what he's doing. Call me when you're 100 miles out. Good luck! Don't get caught . . . this is incredible—"

The connection cut out.

"I'm back-spotting, Dave, and that was *not* a good move."

"There's no one for him to call out here. Burns more gas to slow and speed up again."

"Ramp check . . . and it's clear. I hope you're right. Pass on the left, Dave. You want to pass a truck? One hundred max. Twice across and I've never had a trucker call me in."

"Okay, sorry. Who's the Bulgarian?"

"George Kruntschev, but we just call him the Bulgarian. Paul met him at Columbia Business School. Very connected in St. Louis, in case we're caught. I think he's friends with the mayor. Ramp check . . . ramp clear."

"Thanks. What's he driving?"

"Audi S4."

"I hope he's as good as J.F."

"I hope his wife doesn't stop him at the last second."

"Alex, can I pick it up now?"

"Ramp clear. Thermals clear."

"One twenty-five it is."

The CB crackled. I adjusted the squelch. *"—little blue car damn near blew my doors off!"*

"Nice one, Dave. That must be our friend in the truck back there. What's your plan now? Go faster?"

"Of course. What do you think?"

"They're behind us, it's all clear ahead. Let's get some distance."

"I like it when you talk like that. One-thirty it is."

"Thermals clear. Flat out."

"I can't believe you said that. It's like not even the real Alex."

"Dave . . . everything has its time and place, like this turn coming up in the thermal, I'd take it slow, just in case there's a cop on the right . . . just beyond *that* tree there."

The engine's growl rose in pitch.

"And," said Maher, *"I'm* saying it's Sunday before dawn."

———

J.F. sent a new projection: 30:49, and dropping.

Despite everything I'd learned in three years, Maher was still 5 percent faster. As long as his aggression was confined to the flat, open, night stages, I had no objection. The near invulnerability granted by the thermal camera made high-speed night driving far safer than daytime. Over the 1,405 miles composing his portion of the driveplan, a 5 percent increase in driving speed meant a 20- to 30-minute time gain. Ego-driven tradition—largely based on car ownership, and whether any women awaited us at the next checkpoint—would have made my next suggestion inconceivable at any other time or place.

"Maher, can you handle two legs back-to-back?"

"What's that . . . 1,300 miles nonstop?"

"One fuel stop. The way you're driving, it'll be 1,100, maybe."

"Are you serious?"

"I drove two in a row last time. It's tough. It'll screw up the driveplan. I can't drive in Oklahoma, obviously, so it'll mean one *more* additional stop."

"I'll do it, but are you sure we can afford the extra stop?"

"If you draft every truck, run a racing line—"

"—and never downshift?" He chuckled.

"Yeah, smart guy, you'll squeeze a little more fuel economy out. Maher, it is *absolutely* essential that this car not stop anywhere in Oklahoma. Even for gas. Do you understand?"

"Yes."

I didn't tell him about J.F.'s last message. There was a storm system forming in New Mexico. Once Maher found out, he'd do exactly as I did in April, but he'd be accelerating into thickening daytime traffic. I began texting J.F. our position for forwarding to The Weis.

"Alex, stop that. I need you spotting."

"Take it to one-ten and do double duty. They need to know."

"I need to drive fast. You need to spot."

"Dave, do you really want to miss that plane?"

"I don't want to miss that record."

Besides the absolute necessity of the aerial footage for validation, I knew that plane would cut an hour off our time. If only I could get Maher to believe it.

I didn't need J.F.'s calculations to figure it out. We were between 30 and 45 minutes ahead of projections. Not only was our overall average climbing, so was the rate of its ascent. Although The Weis's twin-engine Baron was twice as fast as the prior run's Cessna rental, its fuel consumption at the speeds required to catch up, circle, and find us would be proportionally higher.

If PolizeiAir was late, we'd miss them.

I couldn't slow Maher down even if I wanted to, and, strangely, I wasn't sure I wanted to. Although everything I'd learned remained true, none of it had made a difference in getting us this far, this fast. I was but a passenger, albeit a moderately useful one, unless and until he made a mistake.

I had to alert The Weis. I had to keep spotting.

INTERSTATE 70 WEST
N39 02.188 W88 46.402
0645 HOURS EST (APPROX)

"Are you sure?" yelled The Weis. "Aliray, those coordinates . . . you passed Effingham? So you're . . . 85 miles from St. Louis? We need to get to the airport *now*! Nine! Robin! They're less than an hour out! *Move! Move—*"

"Damn, Maher, I lost him again. I told you I can't spot *or* use the phone at these speeds. You know anything about cell-phone towers?"

"Not really."

"I'm not asking you to go 60, and this is totally coming out of my ass, but I think 135 is about the speed at which we move faster than rural towers can hand off the signal to the next one. Our phones were never this bad before."

"I'll take that as a compliment."

"The Weis had some good news . . . the weather's clear all the way through Texas."

"What's the bad news?"

"None so far," I lied. "Now, can you take it down to 120 so I can make sure the Bulgarian knows when and where to meet us? I want to hit up J.F. as well."

"One-twenty feels like a crawl. It's still dark enough for bigger speeds. I'll try to hold it down."

Maher remained silent as I texted J.F. His analysis came back 60 seconds later.

"What does J.F. say?"

"Still worried about our time? I thought you didn't want to know."

"Okay, I'm *not* worried."

"Maher, if I tell you it's good, will you get, I don't know, maybe . . . a little complacent?"

"Sorry, my bad."

"Mr. Maher, the projection is 30:49."

The engine's growl rose. Again.

"Don't say it, Alex. We can do better. A lot better."

I was starting to believe him.

INTERSTATE 55 WEST

CENTRAL ST. LOUIS

EARLY MORNING

"Where are you guys?" the Bulgarian yelled into his phone, the wind whipping through his open car window somewhere within three miles of us. "I just pulled out! Can you give me a road sign or marker?"

"We passed the arches!" I yelled. "Crossed the river, now turning, Interstate 44!"

"What? You're west of the river? What's that horrible high-pitched noise?"

"The gyrostabilizers! For the binoculars! And yes, we're west! Of the river!"

"Know something? My wife was right! You are crazy!"

"What?"

"You missed me! Or I missed you! How fast are you going?"

"Um . . . looks like 101! Now 105, 106!"

"You're going 106? On I-44? In the city? Where are you now?"

"Lafayette? Tower Grove?"

He closed his window. "My God, Alex, that's the center of town. Guys, good luck. I can't help you if you get caught, not for that. You guys are crazy. Be safe. I'm sorry . . . I just, I still can't believe how fast you got to St. Louis. Where were you when you called before? Effingham?"

"Cowbell Ground, Cowbell Ground, this is Cowbell Air, enroute to new intercept. Please increase frequency of updates, do you copy?"

"Sorry, the Bulgarian, gotta go!"

"We copy," I said into our untested Vertex headset. *"Cowbell Air, next update in one minute. Stand by."*

"Where's the Bulgarian?" said Maher, eyes straight ahead. "Running these speeds through a major city in the daytime, man, we're gonna need his help big-time if we're caught—"

"Better slow down, tough guy, because we missed him."

"How the hell did that happen? That would have been amazing footage."

"Well, Dave, maybe because I can only handle seven things at once, and we're so far ahead of the driveplan I can't project—"

"Dude, just throw that thing away. What if the cops see it?"

"I'll eat it, and they won't if you dial it back one percent. You said so yourself . . . we're in a major city."

"Alex, keep the driveplan. I want to see you eat that thing. Actually, I didn't mean that. What flavors of Vitamin Water do we have left?"

"Just Revive."

"Keep that as a chaser. Any Red Bull?"

"Nice and warm, just for you. One sip, and one sip only. No bathroom stops."

INTERSTATE 44 WEST
VICINITY OF ROLLA, MISSOURI

My phone rang. It was Nine.

"Aliray! Can you hear me? Aliray? Are you getting our radio signals?"

"Loud and clear! Why? Where are you?"

"Approaching Rolla, Missouri? Where are you?"

"Also approaching Rolla, Missouri!"

"We'll find you but we can't hear your radio! We're only getting clicking when you key the—"

DEEDEET!

K-Band. Police radar.

My foot instinctively went for the brake pedal—absent on the passenger side. My eyes darted to the V1's concealed display, just below the speedometer. A bright red arrow flashed, pointing straight ahead. Maher was accelerating.

"Nine! Hang on! Maher! *Why* are you accelerating *toward* the signal?"

"I think it's a false alarm. We're only doing 95. Don't know the speed limit . . . but we're only 10 to 15 above the flow of traffic."

"Are you nuts? We have a huge time advantage you're gonna blow if we get caught!"

"Alex, how do you think we got it? You've got to exploit every chance you've got."

"Aliray! We need your location, can you hear me?"

"Nine!" I yelled into the phone. "Negative on the radio! We'll pull over for an antenna swap! Stand by!"

"Antenna swap?" said Maher. "You surprise me, Mr. Roy."

"Thanks, now get off here. You can drive 140 all day once Nine has his eyes on the road from up top."

"This swap better work, dude. We're trading back some hard-earned time credit."

"Maher, if we get to L.A. *without* plane communications *and* with no tickets, I'll never question you again."

"If we get there under 31:07, I'll never question *you* again. Hang on . . . looks like we're low on gas."

"Which means . . . we're gonna have to stop in Oklahoma."

Up until that moment I had been searching for reasons as to why *my* strategy might ultimately prevail, why Maher needed to only do his best within the framework of *my* driveplan, and why we would both regret his naked aggression, however masterful.

But Maher, who had met and exceeded all expectations, had earned the arrogance to which he felt entitled. Ignoring my complaints had led to a per-stage time-credit buildup even higher than mine, itself higher than any of the historical run data I'd seen. Barring weather, we would shatter the record *and* exceed our margin of legitimacy. No matter how much I complained, he knew I would keep spotting, and we both knew success grew more likely every minute we remained in our respective seats. My defensive strategy—whether in range or accuracy—was now irrelevant.

Maher's strategy made perfect sense. Unless I or PolizeiAir specifically said *"Cop,"* he would drive flat out.

Until he couldn't.

I understood him completely. The faster he drove, the smoother his command of the car, the greater our credit, the lower our overall time, the shorter my stages, and the less they, slightly slower than his, would bring down the overall average he'd fought so hard to earn.

But, suddenly, the impending debacle in Oklahoma highlighted the potential disaster inherent in the plan he'd unilaterally foisted upon us. Victims of his incredible success, we were now faced with the consequences of his high-speed stages' fuel economy. I hadn't factored for this. He assumed I had. If either of us had perceived the slightest possibility of having to stop in Oklahoma, he would have insisted I drive the prior stage through Missouri, even if at the speed limit. But we didn't, and driving a third consecutive stage, for a total of 15 hours at or above 95 mph, would be physically impossible. Even for Maher.

INTERSTATE 40 WEST
60 MILES TO THE OKLAHOMA BORDER
1005 HOURS EST (APPROX)

"Alex, what does the driveplan say?"

"I ate it. Seriously, anything I tell you becomes an excuse to speed up."

"It'll make me feel better to know how well we did, just in case this whole thing ends in the next hour."

"Cowbell Ground," said the Captain, *"confirming ramp ahead is clear, we're scouting ahead." PolizeiAir descended to 1,000 feet, crisscrossed the road in front of us, then disappeared.*

"Maher, just get us as far across Oklahoma as you can."

"If I could drive three in a row, I would, man. Am I eight hours in? Nine?"

"I don't know. How do you feel?"

"Tired, but committed."

"Me, too."

"Is it clear to pass this truck on the right?"

I leaned right. "It's clear . . . with aggression."

It made perfect sense that Oklahoma should be the cauldron of all our efforts. It was precisely halfway across the country. Diem/Turner had broken down there in 1983, at the very same tollbooth haunting my dreams for the past six months. Interstate 40—the lone east–west artery suitable for 100 mph cruising speeds—offered the least cover from police cars and aircraft of any leg in the Driveplan. Although I had changed license plates since April—useful only in escaping a cursory glance, assuming our antennas didn't give us away— my name was almost certainly logged with the state highway patrol and one or more staffers in Governor Brad Henry's office.

"Cowbell Ground, this is Nueve Actual, you are across the border. All clear until further notice. Hammer down."

My brain, once a highly efficient machine, once capable of weighing the interrelated risk/reward ratios that made every minute of a high-speed solo cross-country run so intellectually fascinating, began to melt.

There were only two choices. Only one retained a piton in the Wall or beyond.

"Cowbell Ground, this is The Weis, all clear until the tollbooths."

I couldn't ask Maher to slow down. *If* we made it through Oklahoma safely, *if* we were to succeed *this* time, we needed that time credit to trade against the storm in New Mexico.

If anything went wrong in Oklahoma, the run was doomed.

Maher was already at ten-tenths.

He didn't need to know. Yet.

It didn't seem right that my efforts should end in the ignominious abandonment of all I'd learned. Nine and I had crushed Yates and Gurney's 35:54 by what I considered the only possible method, and now Maher was smashing the prism through which I'd seen, planned, and accomplished . . . everything, for three years.

"Cowbell Ground, the tollbooths are clear, hammer in, hammer out."

I wanted to get there, but not this way. I could no longer unravel the overlapping webs in which my life, this drive, and my purpose were suspended. The answer had to be on the pier. My father would know. His ghost would be there, behind Turner's and Yarborough's. Beside Sascha. Diem would be waiting. And Yates. Heinz. Maybe even Kenworthy and Rawlings. They were waiting for us, and they didn't care about times. There were no trophies. One only had to get there. No one else could understand. I had to make it . . . just this once. How much time I had spent . . . my life, Skyler, Maggie, sacrificed . . . so I could be here, now, in a car at 131 mph, for nothing other than an idea I could no longer explain. To anyone. I'd lost control, of events, even of my own car—

"Alex," said Maher, fatigue now in his voice, "how far from Oklahoma City to the pier?"

"Why do you ask?"

"Because we're gonna hit Oklahoma City in a bit."

"About 1,400 miles."

"What about these tolls coming up? Are these the tolls where you broke down?"

"Cowbell Ground, this is The Weis, you guys consider just making a run for it?"

"Alex?" said Maher. "Alex? I need you."

"Cowbell Ground, this is Nueve, you really should consider rolling through."

I pulled out my wallet. Maher slowed and veered toward an empty lane. I handed him $3.50 and held my breath. If there was even one undercover waiting, if the M5 failed—

My eyes fell upon the lower Garmin, the 2650, the copilot's primary. Our overall average was 93.7 mph. It had to be wrong. I checked the upper Garmin, the 2730, my backup. Our running projection was now 30:30.

We were almost halfway. Approximately 1,500 miles remained. Despite Maher's extraordinarily provocative driving, we hadn't been stopped. His second stage was almost over, after which he had one. I had two. We had an enormous time credit—a precious treasure soon to be mine to expend as necessary. I'd have 900 miles on which to exercise *my* judgment, the final 300 known to me virtually by heart. Then Maher would see.

Maher pulled out of the toll. "Looks like the car's going to make it."

So could we, if only for the storm.

"Cowbell Ground, Code Orange, Cop in the median. Take it easy for next mile."

"Alex, what's wrong? You're quiet."

"Sorry, Dave. Just thinking about that storm."

"We see you slow, Cowbell Ground, no need to copy."

"What storm?"

"J.F. says there's a storm in New Mexico."

"Wait . . . how bad is it?"

"It's still 450 miles away. Too soon to tell."

"Dude, it's over. We're not going to break it."

I couldn't believe his logic. We'd *already* made history. Nine and I had achieved—from New York to the first breakdown at the Will Rogers Toll Plaza—an overall average of 89.4 mph, or 31:56. Impressive, but insufficient for a legitimate claim on the record, even had we finished. Maher and I had averaged 93.7 mph over the same distance.

"You guys are all clear, Cowbell Ground, put the hammer down!"

"Dave. I think you're wrong. I'll call J.F. for closer tracking of it."

He glanced at his Garmin, then mine. "Do you really trust these things?"

"Totally."

"Alex, if we're in the high 93, then . . ."

"Yes, the midthirties. We can still make it."

"Are you sure?"

I couldn't imagine Maher slowing down under *any* circumstances. Except in the face of futility. He had to keep believing it.

"Yes, Maher, just don't push here. Too dangerous. Let's not blow it."

"Alex, the only danger is in *not* pushing it."

"We're going to make it. We're doing well."

"That's what I'm afraid of. Doing well."

The pier was 1,500 miles away. Texas was only 312. I raised the Steiners.

CHAPTER 35

The Omigod of Wrong

"The irony, Mr. Maher, would be if we get stopped right after I took over, and *I* got charged for all the crap *you* pulled."

"Won't be long now."

"*Cowbell Ground, I'm going 125 knots and you are outrunning me.*"

"Alex, if it makes you feel any better, I'll be ready to turn over the reins when this tank is empty."

"*Sweet Jesus,*" said a voice on the CB, "*these boys are trying to break the sound barrier!*"

"Not the sound barrier!" Maher laughed.

"*Cowbell Ground, you've got heavy traffic coming up, stand by.*"

Maher saw one last opportunity to accelerate and advance within the thickening rows of trucks slowing just ahead, and took it. I cringed.

"*Nice move, Cowbell Ground. Keep it up.*"

I shook my head. "So *that's* how you make friends?"

"Paul liked it."

"Of course The Weis liked it. He wishes he was in the car. By the way, we just passed where the cop stopped to help the last time."

"Now, *that* is ironic."

"Almost as ironic as how few gaps in the concrete median there are for them to turn around, and how fast the first cop we'd seen in 20 miles turned around and found us. FYI, we're coming up on the second and last toll in the state, pretty soon."

I spotted the booths rapidly approaching in the distance. I pulled out $3.50 and held it right by the shift knob for easy access.

"Cowbell Ground, you are all clear after the tolls."

"Alex! What's that?" The car shuddered, Maher's foot visibly on the brake pedal as we slowed into the clearest of the toll lanes.

"What is it?" I yelled as we stopped beside the toll collector. "How does the car feel?"

"I repeat, all clear after the tolls."

I turned down the volume so as not to attract the collector's attention. Maher handed over the money and slowly pulled out.

"Brakes," he said nervously, "but only under slight braking."

"We're about halfway, you're the car guy." My heart pounded. "Will something break loose and kill us?"

"I say no. Maybe warped discs? We can make it."

"We have brand-new discs, rotors, and pads. You have braking power?"

He braked again. The car shuddered. Again. "I think we'll make it," he said.

"I concur. Now hand me the toll receipt for the evidence bag."

"Here. I don't know how much more irony I can take," said Maher, accelerating through 100, "breaking down at the second toll would have been . . . man, whew."

"How about *this* one? Looks like we're refueling just west of Oklahoma City, *right* past my final breakdown in April."

"Oh, great—"

"Hey, westbounders!" said the CB. *"You got a bear coming up in the hammer lane!"*

"Bear?" said Maher. "Where? Not behind us. How come the plane didn't tell us?"

I raised the Steiners and frantically scanned the horizon. "I dunno."

"Here he comes," said another trucker, *"westbound at the 179."*

"Alex! Didn't we just pass the 179?!"

I put down the Steiners. "Yeah. They're talking about us."

"Damn, don't know if I've ever seen a BMW with that many antennas on it!"

Maher frowned. "Is that a good thing?"

"Was there some other car you would have preferred we take? Your Porsche?"

"Uh, no."

"Cowbell Ground, Cowbell Air, you're looking real fast from up here. Let's keep this up as far as we can, will warn on Oklahoma City approach."

Our most entertaining conversation since New York came to a dead stop.

Both my Garmins concurred. We were just over 50 miles from Governor Henry's office. Then we were 40. Then 30.

"Maher, I don't care if you have to coast this car past the city. Just do it."

Fifteen miles.

The I-44/I-35 interchange—northeast corner of the city's ring road and de facto border—was in sight. Although my speed-trap research indicated a northern route around the city (via the John Kilpatrick Turnpike) would have been safer, fuel economy and time dictated we take I-44—shorter and vastly more dangerous

Directly through the city's heart.

"Cowbell Ground, we are peeling off, will reintercept on far side, good luck."

"Cowbell Ground, Nueve calling. In case you go to the big house, recommend teriyaki fast-chew strategy . . . very stinky . . . ward off new friends on the inside."

I was too focused to think of a comeback. The Steiners hadn't left my eyes for 10 minutes. My shoulders were on fire. "Maher—"

"What?!" he snapped. I was strangely glad to see him so tense. It meant I wasn't alone. It meant he was aware his 10 hours of Herculean driving would be for naught if we were stopped beyond the approaching interchange.

We entered the city limits.

EL RENO, OKLAHOMA

FASTBREAK EXPRESS GAS STATION

25 MILES PAST OLD CITY HALL, OKLAHOMA CITY

1319 HOURS EST

"Cowbell Ground, we are orbiting north of you, standing by."

"Maher, I don't know how you got this car here."

"To be honest," Maher called out from the passenger seat, "me neither. Now which one of the Garmins are you using to calculate our ETA?"

"Ten hours ago you didn't want to talk projections." I stood beside the car, my eyes darting between my Casio and the pump's display. "Now that we *might* make it—"

"I know, I know." He fiddled with the 2730, which I'd kept on latitude/

longitude display for the updates required by PolizeiAir—*and* J.F.'s calcula-tion of our closure with the storm. "Ooops, guess it's not—wait, a minute ago this thing said our overall average was 93.6 mph, but now it's falling."

"Maher, a little ways back, before the traffic, it was above 95."

"What's that, timewise?"

I didn't want to tell him, then or now, because I'd been so amazed that I almost wanted him to keep going. My BlackBerry rang from within the pile of half-full Vitamin Waters, empty Red Bulls, and poorly sealed bags of jerky reeking even by the windy pump. Maher picked it up. His jaw dropped.

"J.F. says here . . . we're looking at under 30 hours, at least we were."

"And you said it's over. It's a miracle nobody called 911 about the blue BMW."

I spotted Cory running back from the station store. My Casio beeped. The pump clicked. I remembered to take the receipt this time.

"Make me proud," said Maher as I pulled out.

"Notify Cowbell Air we are back in action."

"Already did. I just saw them overhead."

I gently accelerated up the ramp toward I-40.

The scanner lit up:

OK DPS MISC B: *"—Alan just called, he wants you to be advised that there's an R2 flying north of town . . . just wanted to let you know he's flying pretty low."*

"Maher! They've *got* to be talking about our boys!"

"Should we warn them?"

"Hang on—" I tried to merge left onto the interstate, but two large trucks and a minivan passed without opening a gap. I dropped into third and made my first aggressive acceleratory move of the run, passing the min-ivan on its right, then veering left in front of it, then left again in front of a semi whose horn immediately signaled the driver's displeasure.

"Whoa, Alex. You can *so* not talk to me about bad moves after *that* one."

"I'm sorry. At least I wasn't speeding."

"You better be soon. Don't be sorry. Sometimes you just have to do it."

"Cowbell Ground, that was a nice one. Ramp one mile ahead is . . . clear."

"Let's see what you got, Mr. Roy."

"Maher, after what you did, I think it's best if I don't pull any more—"

OK HP DSPTCH B: *"I have a report of a blue BMW speeding, weaving in and out of traffic and driving recklessly, be advised, unable to get tags."*

———

Terrified by what I believed was my lack of raw driving skill, I had hidden behind technology and models since beginning my journey years earlier.

But Maher, the first master of the opposing camp to tackle this particular task in twenty-three years, had wiped my illusions away. I slowed for forward radar warnings until their origin could be identified. He used gut instinct to filter out false alarms. I slowed for scanner reports. He turned the volume down. I wanted to ask truckers for permission to pass. He didn't want to alert them in advance. My plan set a pace that could weather one catastrophe—and still succeed, maybe. Maher had no plan other than relentless attack, but his best-case scenario far outclassed mine. I knew we needed each other, but it was clear I had lot more to learn from him than he did from me.

Or so I thought, until the scanner report about a blue BMW, and everything I feared about his approach came true.

"They're talking about us," said Maher, Steiners to his face.

We both scanned the road ahead, then our respective mirrors. Traffic was thickening, and slowing. Oklahoma was flat. There was nowhere to hide unless we got out. We passed the exit at Marker 119. The vast fields north of I-44 offered no cover. A high-speed run toward one of the distant farmhouses would be visible from the interstate. The road gently banked left, then continued straight for several miles. Both predator and prey had long sight lines. We were naked.

"Well," Maher said nervously, "looks like we're stuck."

Racing *is* chess, the players evenly matched in forces, but not necessarily in experience. *I* had the experiential advantage, but nothing else. Trapped in the devil's endgame, our M5 was but a king attempting to cross the board—comprising just this one small stretch of Oklahoma—against one or more queens.

This was my domain.

DEEDEET. V1 radar warning.

The first queen. Directly ahead. Four miles or less. The next exit was approximately 3.75 miles.

DEEDEET. A second queen. Behind us. Four miles or less. The next exit was now approximately 3.5 miles.

Traffic prohibited the latter from catching up. The escape option remained open. Exit at Marker 115, hope our pursuer was too far behind to spot us, and run north for the first farmhouse. Await Cowbell Air's notification of all clear, resume our westbound course, and hope for the best.

But what of the queen ahead?

If a police car awaited us in the wide-open median *before* Marker 115, we needed to (1) move to the right lane, align ourselves with one of the semis to our left, adjust our speed to block the officer's sight line to the most infamous NY-plated BMW in Oklahoma, and proceed to the Texas border, or (2) in the absence of a semi, move to the right lane, listen to the scanner, and make a snap decision over whether exiting the interstate might constitute probable cause.

There were no further permutations to consider without more information.

We were already in the right lane. I was poised to commit.

"Maher! Police car behind us! Black-and-white! Ten car lengths!?"

His eyes flicked to the right mirror. "Copy. He's not moving up."

There was nothing else to say until we reached Marker 115, two and a half miles away.

One column. One row. One choice. Cars and trucks. Front and rear. At or below the speed limit. We were trapped, but only for the next two minutes.

"Code Red! Cowbell Ground, Code Red! Police car ahead! One mile!"

Median or oncoming, they didn't specify. We couldn't transmit, and I couldn't ask Maher to type or call back. There was no time. All eyes ahead. As if it would make a difference, we instinctively leaned forward. I scanned the gaps between passing cars, ten o'clock to eleven, Maher eleven to one.

If the cruiser lay in the grassy median's depression, police training dictated a position set *in defilade,* parked just off the westbound lanes, on the reverse slope, concealing the lower half of the cruiser, retaining clear sight lines of oncoming traffic, engine running, radar gun on standby.

We had a better chance of escaping an eastbound cruiser, the lone officer having to spot us across the widening median, *in* the gaps between the westbound left-lane traffic behind which we were hidden. If he spotted us, the median's width would add 15 to 30 seconds to his U-turn—and inevitable pursuit.

Marker 115. Less than two minutes.

"Don't see him," said Maher.

"Where *is* this guy . . . there! Eastbound!" My head tracked left at increasing speed until we passed him in the opposite direction, my eyes searching for brake lights and the telltale cloud of dirt signifying his crossing the median. "He's braking! Making the turn!"

Marker 115. One and a half miles.

My eyes darted to the left mirror. Dirt in the air, center median. Late-model American four-door, in profile. Moving across the grass.

"Crossing the median! Maher, we *have* to get to the next exit and hide."

The police car stopped on the westbound's left shoulder, perpendicular to the interstate, waiting for a gap in traffic behind us.

"Alex, man, I don't know if you're going to have a lot of room to hide out here."

Marker 115. One mile.

Our second pursuer pulled in somewhere behind us, and disappeared.

"It's only hearsay unless they catch you doing it, so don't speed and don't weave. You haven't broken any laws in Oklahoma in at least six months. He'll follow you—"

"*Should* we get off? *Right* now?"

Exit ramp. Marker 115. Visible in the distance.

Forty-five seconds.

"I'd keep going." Maher's eyes switched back and forth from the right mirror to the road ahead. "I'd just go."

Chess. Two queens. Behind us.

Thirty seconds.

King. Mobility. Limited.

Fifteen seconds.

Queen. Mobility. Infinite.

The column was suicide, but that *one* row—

OK HP MOB C: "*—blue BMW on up ahead of me—*"

"Maher, that's it."

OK HP MOB E: "*—confirm dark blue BMW . . . tinted windows looks like it has some antennas on it.*"

I gently veered right onto the exit ramp. It gently banked right, then left, then ended with a stop sign. We sat at what appeared the highest point in miles, vast green fields extending out 360 degrees. Local Route 270 was completely devoid of traffic. I turned right and accelerated firmly yet—without other cars for reference—innocently up to the local speed limit, which I presumed to be 55. A cluster of farm buildings lay just ahead on the left, a few hundred feet north of the interstate.

Too obvious, and too close, should one or both of our pursuers exit at 115 and actually *pursue*. If either pursuer made the turn, we would see them within 60 seconds. I would neither run nor lie. I had absolute and total respect for the law. I would plead guilty . . . to conspicuous (and uncomfortably forced) public urination, which was what I had planned upon arrival at the nearest suitable hiding position for the M5, behind the tall bushes conveniently located at the southeast corner of the intersection of East 1020 Road and Route 270, precisely one-half mile north of the interstate. This was the first-available, last-feasible, and therefore the final bastion of my hopes and dreams—and our run.

"We're stopping right . . . *here*! Maher, if anyone comes, tell them I had to piss."

I opened my door, hoping the residents of the farm across the street wouldn't call 911 over an act they'd consider natural if committed by one of the many animals nearby—or currently flying overhead, as the M5's roof clearly showed.

The scanner lit up.

OK HP MOB C: *"—confirm, they're ahead of me."*

"Alex! He thinks we're still going!"

Unless the first queen had gotten off.

I ran the ten steps to Route 270, ready to peer the half mile toward the exit ramp, give the all clear, and tout my superhuman tactical genius—

Then I spotted the black-and-white car approaching. It was the *first* car we'd spotted to our rear, before the second made the U-turn.

He was no more than 30 seconds away.

"Here he comes!" I yelled, running back to the car.

"What?" Dave yelled back. "Should we power everything down??!?"

"No! Don't—" Cory blurted, the first direct order she'd issued since camera prep in the CCC, but it was too late for her to protect the myriad electronics requiring uninterrupted power, for I had already hit the M5's master power kill switch.

"Alex!"

"Cory! They'll be here any second!"

She scrambled among her equipment, activating the backup power for what would be an entertaining but unfortunate discussion I'd rather she didn't record. I ran around the car, faced the bushes, and assumed a faux urination stance.

I heard the car approaching, mere seconds away.

"Maher!"

"I can't hear you!"

"Standby for the Storm Chasers!"

Storm Chasers. It was wrong. It was the Omigod of Wrong. It wasn't a good idea, it was a *great* idea. Charles Graeber had the answer. He'd written a *Wired* story about the world's most advanced storm-chaser car, and suggested that other than the lack of an anti-tornado body kit, the M5's ECM voluminous gear made it closely resemble an actual storm chaser. Better yet, most storm chasers were courageous hobbyists, volunteering to do a public service in loose cooperation with various state and federal agencies, not one of which was related to law enforcement. They wore a variety of colorful and heavily branded, official-looking jackets and hats, spoke in terminology impenetrable to anyone lacking a degree in meteorology, were highly respected by residents of the oft-stricken states in Tornado Alley (which included Oklahoma), and, Graeber assured us, any officer who pulled over a speeding car with out-of-state plates, four antennas, and a bumper sticker saying *Storm Chaser*—*especially* in Oklahoma—would have one question:

"Where's the storm at?"

Where one found storm chasers, one found storms, and Oklahomans—especially law-enforcement officials—needed to know when and where fellow Oklahomans might need help. Knowing whether one's family and home were safe was an added bonus of meeting any storm chaser, especially one in a hurry.

I had the answers, not because we were carrying Storm Chaser–labeled hats, T-shirts, notepads, pens, and one throw pillow (for Cory's comfort, of course), or because the four Garmins were labeled *Skywarn 1, Skywarn 2, Skywarn Backup,* and *Groundspeed Backup,* or even because I'd given myself a one-hour online crash course in storm speak. I would actually be able to help an officer as would the world's best storm chaser, because J.F. had printed out, spiral-bound, and given us a beautiful color-laser booklet of sixteen-hour-old weather data, which now sat in my door pocket.

I prayed the officer didn't ask to see it, because although there *were* storms on it, none of them were in Oklahoma. The good news was that, if asked, I could say with all sincerity that we *were* chasing a storm, just barely hinted at as of our departure from New York the prior night.

The bad news was that it was in New Mexico.

If he asked why, I could always say we were good guessers.

Black-and-white. Car. Beyond the bushes.

Two seconds.

One.

A white VW Beetle, its doors, fenders, hood, and trunk painted black. "Alex?" Maher exclaimed. "Wha—" The Beetle continued north on 270. I knew the orange-and-black oval logo on its doors, all too well.

"Goddammit!" I yelled, and sprinted back around the car. "Power up! All systems! CB and scanners to max!"

"Alex, what the hell *was* that?!"

"Buy a PC, break it, call the *Geek Squad!*"

"What a dirty trick." Maher shook his head. "Fake police cars, man . . . it should be illegal."

I pointlessly burned three miles of gas in the half mile back to the interstate, then merged back into heavy traffic.

"Maher, estimated timeloss?"

"One or two minutes? It sucks. Now we're definitely not going to make it."

"I would have said four. And you're wrong. Staying on would have done us in."

"You're right."

"Don't tell me our average. I don't want to know."

"Me neither."

"Cory," I said, "I'm sorry about the power."

"Cowbell Ground, Cowbell Ground, nice one back there. Scouting ahead."

"It's okay . . . I got most of it."

I flashed her a proud grin in the mirror. "I can't wait to see that on the big screen. Let's hope that was all of it. That other cop was the real deal, and now he's just ahead of us."

"Well," said Maher, "there's nowhere to go anyway."

"Cowbell Ground! Code Red! Cops in the median! About . . . "

My head snapped up. The Steiners were already against Maher's eyes. The median, having narrowed again, was clear as far as the overpass one-half mile ahead.

Twenty seconds away.

"—a half mile past the overpass! Repeat—"

Ten seconds to the overpass. Thirty seconds from the cops' location. I pressed the driver's Garmin map key. The next exit was six miles.

Five seconds to the overpass—and exposure.

We were in the right lane. Behind one truck. In front of another.

Now we really *were* trapped.

I could see the median widen beyond the overpass, the grass gently sloping up toward a copse of trees splitting the east- and westbound lanes. My eyes flickered as we emerged from the overpass's shadow.

"Cowbell Ground! Two in the middle looking at you! Half a mile!"

Although I didn't yet see them, it was clear that good deeds were repaid in unforeseen ways, because at that exact instant a tractor trailer slowly began to pass on our left. I matched speeds, keeping the truck in the *Cross-Country Racer's Ideal Police Line-of-Sight Blocking Position.*

The cops had to be positioned *before* the trees.

Fifteen seconds away.

Had to be. All I had to do was stay alongside the truck.

Ten seconds.

The distance to the truck in *our* lane began to close. I'd have to brake, any second.

"Maher! Look left! Under the truck!"

There they were, two police cars idling on the slope, their bumpers and headlights barely visible in the three-foot-tall gap between the interstate and the bottom of the trailer covering our escape. Maher grabbed the spare camcorder, leaned left, and thrust it past my chest.

Then they were gone, and so were we.

FIFTEEN MINUTES LATER

OK HP DSPTCH: "—confirm he lost his subject . . . now with Ford Aerostar van."

"Dude, at first I disagreed with you about getting off the freeway, but that was a *great* move. We'd have been toast."

OK HP MOB MISC: "—where the hell did that guy go?"

"Maher, I might not beat you on the track, but I know how to do this."

"Yeah, you do."

We shook hands.

"Cowbell Ground, The Weis here. Juan Nueve, the Captain, and Robin have all voted. Four out of four cross-country-race air-recon crew guys agree . . . that shouldn't have worked."

"Dave, how come you can drive like that for seven hours and no one calls, and I do it for three minutes and—"

"Because I'm Irish."

"If we make it, I'll buy you a lifetime supply of Lucky Charms, and"—I cycled through the driver's Garmin screens—"you were right. We only lost two minutes back there."

"I'll make it up."

"Good. Save your energy. That storm means we're going to have a blistering run at the end. I'll take it up a level in a minute, make a run for Texas, and then really pick up the pace. Get on the horn with J.F. and let's get the storm update."

OK HP DSPTCH: "—can you confirm not same blue BMW with antennas as last—"

I tried not to laugh. It was surreal. PolizeiAir zigzagging over the interstate. The scanner. Maher not spotting, but typing.

"You know, Alex, we still have a pretty decent credit. It would suck to lose it all in New Mexico and come in at 32:08. Screw it: 32:06. Even 31:08. Nobody would believe us. Not even with the movie."

"Thirty-one-oh-seven. Or it doesn't count. Thirty-one-oh-seven."

"Or better!" Cory called out from the back.

"Alex, where do you think we are timewise? How much credit do you think we have?"

"Before, you thought checking the projections was a bad idea. You said it was best to just drive flat out at every opportunity. Even if we knew for sure, if we were really running out of time, I'd be really surprised if you could drive any faster."

"You're right, but if the average is falling, that would be some incentive to hammer down. I'll text J.F. and see what he says."

"Well, we've got three GPS's up here, and all three estimates are slightly different." I tapped the driver's Garmin. "This one says 30:30. Factor in the storm, call it 31:30. All we need is 31:07."

"I want 31." Maher lifted the buzzing phone and stared at the display. "J.F. says heavy rains New Mexico, storm intensifying. We're gonna have to—"

"Attack the storm."

CHAPTER 36

Countdown

We missed the last fuel stop. The final driver swap. The stage I'd trained for far beyond Maher's ability to master it on his first attempt.

The trip computer estimated our range at 151 miles, then 93, then 104.

According to the Garmin, the next station, in Barstow, California, was 145.

Neither of us spoke. We'd trusted the BMW trip computer before, and we'd run out of gas. Together. In this car. But this time there was no one to call.

We no longer knew if any of it mattered, because we could no longer do the math.

Although it appeared to be Maher's fault, I was quite sure it was mine. I couldn't be sure, because although I was not yet hallucinating, Maher had just asked if I, too, saw stars ahead. I did, and said so, and thanked God it was true, because it was the third time he'd asked.

We'd been driving for 28 hours. I still thought we could make it. Maher did not. But we couldn't prove or even debate it, because the inter-Garmin discrepancy was too great, and our multiple watches and clocks were set to different time zones. I remained optimistic for the strangest reason, however. I *had* been through this before, with Nine, and achieved an incredible 34:46 without any psychological conditioning, or even expectations. The lessons of 3446 were many, among them that we had begun slurring our words somewhere in Arizona.

Maher and I were far better prepared *and* motivated, and we had only just begun drawing out our words, and the gaps between them, *and* we were 11 miles past the California border.

Two hundred seventy treacherous miles remained.

We'd all but given up trying to spot, because the thermals no longer worked.

If only we didn't run out of gas—

APPROXIMATELY 10 HOURS EARLIER
CENTRAL TEXAS

I'd kept it secret from him, but in the immediate wake of our Oklahoma escape, I gloated. Had he been driving, had I followed his advice, the run would have ended. But Maher hadn't seen it is a sign. His praise had been merely that, for J.F.'s increasingly frantic storm warnings only elevated Maher's determination. When spotting, my remarks were confined to "cop," but Maher became my first-ever copilot to call me *slow*.

I had the eleventh fastest time cross-country. I'd set the world record for crossing nearly half the country—NYC to Oklahoma's Will Rogers Turnpike Toll Plaza—1,287 miles in 14 hours and 23 minutes, broken only when Maher and I crushed it in 13:48 earlier that day. I had exceeded every projection on the driveplan, beaten Yates/Gurney, Heinz/Yarborough, and Diem/Turner, and yet, as the skies turned gray over Texas, I realized Maher was right. My record-setting first stage had been too slow. I'd been complacent. The drive-plan targets were too low. I'd only factored for one moderate storm, one Oklahoma-level crisis, and moderate traffic.

If anything went wrong, I was the one with no plan.

So I did as told, freed of a plan that was once a ceiling, yet now a floor. The memory of endless calculations and logic and choices faded as quickly as the indistinguishable terrain blurring on both sides. I accelerated into the gray cloud obscuring the plain ahead, thundering rain suddenly spattering our roof like marbles on tin. I double-flashed cars in the passing lane a half mile ahead, passing at a differential of 30, then 40 mph, until even Maher, audibly cursing the storm's diminution of our average, nearly choked upon having to tell me to slow down. By the time we approached New Mexico, despite all my efforts, our average fell to 88 mph.

Maher placed no blame. He'd feared this all along. It's what drove him. It was why he drove as he did.

Finally, after 1,776 miles, we understood each other. I prayed it wasn't too late.

He became fixated on the two Garmins beside his left knee. Their projections were close, but with every power interruption or satellite-obscuring storm, they grew more disparate. Were this Gumball, I would have suggested calling technical support.

I didn't want to know. I had already leaped beyond what I thought myself capable of. I was terrified of what I might do out of desperation.

"Alex, all these times and averages you've been throwing out, how sure are you?"

"J.F. and I made a spreadsheet. He's got one, and I know it pretty well."

"What do we need to break 32:07?"

"With 30 minutes of stops . . . 88 and change?"

"And 31:07?"

"Ninety-one point five? I think."

The storm worsened. Our overall average fell to 87.9—32 hours, 21 minutes.

PolizeiAir did their best to encourage the rare 130 mph sprint, but heavy cloud cover forced them off our path with increasing frequency. I got our average back up to 89, then 90, then 91, where it stayed until nightfall and our friends' inevitable departure.

"Cowbell Ground, Cowbell Ground, we're all real proud of you boys and girls. We're out of time, and we're outta light. Good hunting, drive safe, and we'll see you in L.A. Don't be late."

It was just light enough to make out the purple-gray clouds through which the plane threaded, diminishing in size with every glimpse I could spare between the sky and road, until they were gone.

I struggled through rain, traffic, and construction—often at 70 mph or less—to keep our overall average above 91. The slightest hesitation in passing, or 30-second entrapment behind clustered semis, cost as much as a decimal point.

My hands, now claws, pled to be stretched, massaged, and released from the wheel as frequently as possible, but I didn't want Maher or Cory to observe the first sign of the one enemy, immune to speed or logic, whose encroachment was inevitable.

I didn't want them to see my hands shake.

"Alex. It feels like you've been driving forever. How could you stand me taking two legs back-to-back?"

"Because, Dave . . . I feel strange telling you. I had a revelation."

"What's up?"

"I want this more than I need to be the hero."

"What do you mean?"

"I've been team captain, head of Polizei . . . the main driver, ever since we met. I'd take all the wheel time on this run if I could. On every run . . . but that's amateur talk. Safety called for splitting our Driveplan mileage fifty-fifty, and tradition calls for me to take the first and last stages, but if giving you even one more hour means we'll make it, I mean break it by that much more, that's what we need to do. That's what I want to do."

"Alex, at this point I don't think we're gonna break it at all."

"All the more reason, then."

"If you want me to take more, I'll do it, but I don't think I'll do much better than you are, not in this mess."

"Maher, I'm asking you, and I'm telling you, when I take the wheel at the Cali border, I intend to make a grand gesture."

"I sure hope so, because this storm's throwing our credit out the window."

"It's going to be close, Maher, but I think we'll make it. Maybe not 31:07, but definitely under 32."

"It's over." He tapped at the Garmins. "Wake me when we get there."

"*There* is in about five minutes. Gas stop, you're up." The phone buzzed. "J.F.?"

"Who else? More weather ahead. Worse than predicted. Worse than this."

We pulled over just south of Grants, New Mexico. I refueled while Maher cleaned the laser jammers and thermal camera, then inspected the tires. He was done two minutes before I would be, and took a well-deserved break to walk out to the edge of the station's brightly lit pump area. He looked out into the darkness, then turned back to the car, the tension in his eyes and mouth released, his face strangely sad. The pump clicked. I turned to replace the nozzle, but by the time I opened my door he was already in the car, his brow furrowed in deep concentration, hands wrapped around the wheel as if he might break it off its column. In that instant I knew that if ever another cross-country race were held, I would never run against him. Not because he—given a copilot of my expertise—would probably beat me, but because I might beat him. I couldn't bear it. I was the luckiest man in the world. For the last 21 hours my oldest friends had risked their lives to support my quest. However little they believed in it, they believed in *me,* and would forgive any failure out of love, but Maher was here to win, and he wouldn't have come without the same faith in me that I had in him. Of all the reasons I wanted not only to finish, but to break 31:07, I added one more. It was the only way I could repay his trust.

I wanted to share with him just one moment on the pier, time card in hand, with four digits that would mark us forever.

We left the station, driving in silence until Maher blurted, "Are you insane? Now we're never gonna make it!" I swallowed the half banana I'd bitten off, and offered him the other half. "Duuuuude! Bananas are bad luck!"

"Sorry. I promise you, we'll still make it. We won't fail. We can't fail."

"Alex, just promise me there aren't any more bananas in the car."

"I promise." That momentarily calmed him down.

"Thermal check."

"Thermals . . . no cop . . . but not clear. They're dirty, or wet."

Maher pursed his lips.

"Dave, pull over. Give me 90 seconds to clean them. Two-minute net loss."

"Two minutes we can't afford."

"Two minutes that may buy us 20. Without night vision, we're done."

We stopped. I cleaned them. It made no difference. We lost two more minutes. The weather got worse.

There was nothing Maher could do. His hands gripped the wheel ever more tightly, his knuckles ghastly white in the glow of the useless thermal display. He let go his right hand, poised to downshift, and I saw his hand shake against the vibrating shift knob. It wasn't the engine. His shoulders were frozen. He was hunched slightly forward. His face was taut.

But his driving was flawless. Aggressive, but flawless.

The weather began to clear in Arizona.

I informed J.F. of our now 89.2 mph overall average. He must have had the spreadsheet open and waiting, because he responded immediately.

31:52.

Traffic thinned out. The desert night's stars rose, first over the distant mountains, then in a vast twinkling curtain of welcome, whatever our speed, whatever our time.

After 10 hours, the storms were over.

Maher's face hardened, and for the next three hours I watched the Garmins' satellite-signal reception screens dance, their projections synchronize, and our average climb.

INTERSTATE 40 WESTBOUND
APPROACHING NEEDLES, CALIFORNIA
275 MILES TO SANTA MONICA PIER

"Final refuel, Dave, first station you see. Closest one."

Maher's final, superhuman stage was over. His terrifying example would be nearly impossible to match, even at my full ability. Whatever happened, I had to know and understand precisely what he had done.

I already knew how.

I feared distracting him by cycling through the Garmins' colorful displays, so with jittery fingers I texted J.F., who responded ever more promptly as we approached the finish line: *Miles since update 256/Time Elapsed/2:40, AvgSpd 96.*

Ninety-six mph over 256 miles.

It was inconceivable, and yet halfway across country, somewhere before the Oklahoma incident, we'd both seen the Garmin display a 95.9 mph overall.

That Maher had accomplished a 96 mph driving average, on the final night, given his dwindling energy, was . . . shocking.

He'd paid a price. He had summoned deep forces to combat the weight of 40 or more waking hours, more than half in a fast-moving car, every second—and even Maher couldn't conceal his awareness—increasingly fraught with mortal danger. He now spoke in clipped phrases. His eyes blinked.

But he'd brought our overall overage up, as J.F. pointed out, to 90.1 mph.

I began counting backward. We'd left New York at 9:26 A.M. (EST). A 31-hour-7-minute Drivetime meant arriving on the Santa Monica Pier at 1:33 A.M (PST). Our ETA was 30 minutes later.

Raising our average even one mile per hour would require 220 miles of cruising at 110 or more, past Barstow as far as L.A.'s I-10/I-15 interchange. By then it would be too late, for the final 58 miles west across the L.A. basin were among the most heavily patrolled in the nation. CHiPs country . . .

"Dave, you just missed the first exit . . . tons of stations."

"Sorry."

I was starting to worry. Twenty minutes earlier he'd made a pass bad enough to bump even my danger threshold.

He missed the second exit. *I* wondered what he was thinking. I glanced at my Garmins. He missed the third exit. They had stopped syncing, again. But then I knew exactly what he was thinking. And I was willing to bet on it.

"How do you feel, Dave?"

"Okay."

"If you want to go a little farther, I'm okay with that."

"I don't know. I kinda don't wanna to press my luck."

"But you *do* also want to press your luck."

"I feel capable . . . and confident, but you know when your body says—"

We passed another exit, and before we could decide, Needles was behind us.

"Alex . . . I am, actually. Tired. How far? To the next one?"

I cycled down the list. There were none within 20 miles. "Maher. Range?"

"Just tell me. How far."

"One hundred forty-five miles or so. Barstow."

What energy he had left, bled out.

Maher hadn't wanted to stop, and I hadn't wanted to stop him.

There were no more decisions to make, and nothing to do but count down the miles and minutes until we ran out of gas, for posterity.

Two hundred seventy miles from the Santa Monica Pier.

CHEVRON FOOD MART

BARSTOW, CALIFORNIA
34°53'14.86" N, 117°01'20.85" W
131 MILES TO SANTA MONICA PIER
1205 A.M. (PST) (APPROX)

By the time we coasted in, fuel wasn't our biggest problem. Maher was spent. What he earned in Arizona we lost to fatigue, and fatigue-compounding, single-lane construction zones. J.F. texted the Needles–Barstow figures: *Miles since update 155, Time Elapsed 1:47, AvgSpd 87.*

The pump clicked. It was too late for the important numbers. I closed my door, Cory hers, Maher his. We no longer slammed them.

"Alex," he said as I pulled out. "I've done everything I can. It's in your hands. We need to break it by one hour or none of it matters. I don't even know if we can. It's up to you. You need to drive like you've never driven."

I had to win this battle, tonight. I had volunteers I could never again ask to risk so much, nor would they for so futile a cause.

It was I who had chosen to fight, selected the field, and marked the target. No one else was here. No one was waiting for me. No one was coming.

I was at war with myself, and always had been. I, the weaker, would never win until I defeated, consumed, and became the stronger, and I had delayed the end through rationalization. *I will try again tomorrow.* But now I knew. I didn't want to come back.

There was only one way to avoid the compulsive regret of *what if.*

Distance, time, traffic, fatigue—nothing was in my favor except a gift I had received over and over, yet had never opened until Maher handed it to me at the Chevron.

I was responsible. For myself, and those who'd come with me.

I already had everything in the world money couldn't buy, except the dignity of having earned it.

I was at the wheel, but no longer knew who was driving. I wasn't the man who had left New York some twenty-nine and a half hours earlier. He was a stranger, and so was his mirror on the pier.

I had 131 miles to cover, and just under 90 minutes to beat 31:07.

I merged onto Interstate 15 and headed south.

"Maher! How far to the I-10/I-15 interchange??"

"Two miles! Maybe three! Didn't you hear that radar warning?"

"Yes!"

"Then why didn't you slow down?"

"False alarm! Just trust me!"

"Alex!" Cory yelled. "How long to the interchange? I've gotta call Josh in the chase car!" Josh Wexler was a film producer and college buddy of Cory's and was driving our third and final chase car.

"One minute?!" I yelled back. "Dave! Eyes open for a black Porsche Cayenne!"

"It better be a Turbo," he said with a grin. Cory yelled incomprehensibly into her phone. I spotted the interchange 45 seconds later. I nearly suggested standing by for heroics, but was too busy threshold-braking from 118 to 90, bearing right toward the I-10 ramp, apexing through the ninety-degree right at 80 mph, and accelerating at maximum power west on I-10.

"Dude!" Maher spun around in his seat. "Was *that* the chase car? If it's a Turbo, *that* was it!"

"Wait!" Cory screamed. "Wait!"

"Cory! We can't wait! It's a Turbo! Josh'll catch up!"

It was 1:02 A.M. PST—*51.9 Miles to Destination.* I had 31 minutes.

I couldn't focus on mileage or projections. I was driving 116 mph through traffic, and the figures probably weren't reliable anyway. I didn't care. It didn't matter. I was driving as fast as I thought I could, until—

"The HOV lane!" Cory shouted. "Go left! Left!"

"Gas warning light!" I called out. "Maher! Did you—"

"Yes, I tightened the gas cap! Don't worry, it's just a BMW thing. Alex, this shitcan up ahead is breaking the law. One guy solo in the HOV lane? That's so selfish."

"What do you want me to do?"

"Pass him."

"Maher, those are double-yellow HOV lane-divider stripes."

"Now I *know* I'm hallucinating," he said, grasping his door handle for the first time.

I passed him. At 117.

I-10/I-5 INTERCHANGE

18.5 MILES FROM SANTA MONICA PIER

1:17 A.M. (PST) (APPROX)

"I can't believe there're no cops out here."

"There never are," said Cory, "that's why everyone's going a hundred."

"Look at it this way," said Maher, "you're only 10 to 20 over the flow of traffic."

I gritted my teeth. "As Nine always says, 'I'm a law and order guy.' My feeling is, for every mile we drive without being stopped, a cop is saving someone who *really* needs help."

"Do me a favor, tough guy, stop talking and focus on driving. You're making me nervous."

"About the time?"

"About your driving!"

"Are you really nervous, Maher?"

"Just keep going! You're making me proud!"

"Alex! Wait!"

"Wait?" Maher and I said in unison.

"That chase car! Behind us! You just drove right past him!"

"Was I supposed to stop?"

"Dude, I think your front right headlight just went out!"

"Should I stop for that, too? How we doing on time?"

"I don't know, but I'm sure it's not good! Just keep going!"

A bright pair of blue-tinted headlights approached in the mirror. Cory needed the videographer in the chase car to shoot our arrival. Josh was a *very* good driver. His Cayenne Turbo was very fast, perhaps faster in a straight line than the M5. But I possessed one thing he did not, which I might never use again, at least not this way.

I had a purpose. I had a destination. And I couldn't be late.

INTERSTATE 10 WESTBOUND

9 MILES FROM SANTA MONICA PIER

1:24 A.M. (PST)

This was wrong. I was breaking every protocol in the book of Polizei. I was also breaking the law. We had to get there as quickly as possible. It was the only way to ensure the safety of the other drivers on the I-10. We were going to make it, perhaps by as little as one minute. Maybe. Unless SWAT teams were already en route, no one could stop us. Except for the red Ferrari 360 Modena up ahead going 80 mph, his date's long blond hair flying up from the open roof on the passenger side, of course. I could tell he was precisely the type of cowardly, Modena-leasing, valet-parking, Hollywood playboy/film guy/mattress tester who would take personal offense at being passed by a dirty, dented, blue BMW at 119 mph, and who, staking that night's manhood on his car's superiority to mine, might illegally cut into the HOV lane to stop us. The safety of my passengers—and *his* date—depended on maximum geographic separation between us, which is why I accelerated to 125 in order to both pass and minimize the duration of our proximity. Somewhere behind us, I was pretty sure I heard a howl, and I was sure it hadn't been manufactured in Italy.

INTERSTATE 10 WESTBOUND

PASSING UNDER FREEWAY 405

4 MILES FROM SANTA MONICA PIER

"Can't take my eyes off the road! Maher! What time is it?"

"Just drive!"

"Do you know where to turn?" shouted Cory.

"Fourth Street?! Here? Got it!"

I downshifted to fifth, then fourth, dropping from 109 to 67 mph just in time to bear right and follow the ramp to the traffic light at Colorado. I was ready to run this and the next three. Santa Monica Police Headquarters was a block away. Then the light turned green. It was one block to Colorado. Red light. A police car passed perpendicular, eastbound. Green light. I turned left. Red light. Green light.

One block from the pier.

Red light.

Green light.

I was almost finished.

We crossed Ocean Avenue and drove down the pier's concrete entrance ramp.

At the bottom of the ramp lay the pier itself, a wood structure that creaked as our front tires, then our rear, rolled over its wide planks. The finish line lay 50 feet and one left turn away, in the parking lot. The PolizeiAir crew would be there, Lelaine, Cory's parents, friends, and family, and all the official witnesses—David Johnson, Charles Graeber, Gary Jarlson, and all the others I couldn't remember because I'd been busy driving cross-country for slightly less than a day and a third.

My journey was coming to an end. First I had to punch our time card, then smile for our legitimacy pictures, then move the car off the pier before any SWAT teams showed up, then hide it at one of three nearby hotels where Cory had booked rooms under various names, then arrange the car's undercover shipping back to NYC, then rent a car, drive to Nevada, and fly home. I made a mental note to get the front right headlight fixed, since that was a ticketable offense in New York State, and I could tell from our headlight pattern that it had gone out once again. I wondered what the penalty was in California.

I didn't know the time—I'd lost track—but I knew we'd covered 2,800 miles *very* quickly, maybe even quickly enough. I knew our friends awaited us less than 60 seconds away, *just* around the corner of *that* building, and I knew, even in my hallucinatory, exhausted, criminally guilty-yet-already-remorseful elation and virtual blindness, that the white car oncoming was a late-model Ford Crown Victoria, that it was a Santa Monica police K-9 unit with a low-profile light bar, and that at our current closing speeds we would meet in approximately 10 seconds. I prayed he might tell me the time, and had a good, but not necessarily expensive, watch. Casios were very reliable.

Police officers waited their whole careers for traffic stops like this.

He saw us.

And kept going. I caught a surreal glimpse of his friendly, preoccupied face, hoped his commander never found out, then made the final left turn into the parking lot.

Maher pulled out the time card. We lowered our windows as Lelaine ran toward us, time clock in hand. I'd seen it before, an epochal lifetime ago. I stopped the car. The time clock *thunked* once, then twice more in quick succession.

The target was 31:07. Or better. Or else.

That meant 1:33 A.M. (PST), or 4:33 A.M., according to the time clock, still—for validation purposes—on EST.

Maher got out before I could ask. Cory took the card from him. I joined them in the light of Robin's camera. Wexler's Cayenne roared in and stopped behind the M5. He, Graeber, The Weis, Nine, the Captain, Johnson, and

Jarlson gathered around us. Cory peered at the time card. I leaned closer. She flipped it over, then flipped it again. Maher had punched it three times, at least 10 seconds apart.

Cory frowned, then looked up, right at me. And smiled.

I took the card. *OCT 7 P.M. 9:26*

I turned it over for L.A.

OCT 9 A.M. 4:31
OCT 9 A.M. 4:31
OCT 9 A.M. 4:30

Four-thirty A.M. Eastern meant 1:30 A.M. Pacific.

I knew we made it, but I was too shocked, elated, confused, tired, and stupefied to speak the four precious numbers.

"I can't believe it," said Maher. "So close, man."

"Me neither," said Cory.

We'd done it—31:04—by three minutes.

"Alex?" said Robin, pointing a camcorder at me. "Your thoughts?"

I grinned. "I'm never driving again."

CHAPTER 37

The Bravest Driver I Ever Met

"I could have been a painter," said my father, "or a musician."

"I know," I said, hoping to bring our conversation back to the prior day's topic.

"Or a photographer," he continued, "I'll never understand why you were so lazy about the piano. Why you never picked up photography. When you were a boy. You had no interest. Too many distractions."

"That was a long time ago."

He didn't seem to have heard me. "Did you know I could have been a painter?"

"Why weren't you?"

He looked at me sternly. He'd heard. "Because I had to make a life for you and your brother. A life better than mine. Here in America. So you would never go through what I did. Jack, my poor brother. And Jojo. I wanted you to have everything. You should be grateful."

I pulled the vibrating phone from my pocket.

"It's okay," he said, "go. I need to sleep. I'm tired."

"It's not important."

"I don't want to live anymore."

"What?!?" *This* was not my father. "What are you talking about?"

"I don't want to go through this any longer. I can't give you any more."

"But that's not true! I don't know anything . . . I need you! What am I going to do?"

"Enough. You know enough. Go, Alexander, just go."

I couldn't leave.

"Please go," he said, "and let me sleep."

"Wait . . . are you sure? I'll come back tomorrow. If you feel better we can talk then."

He closed his eyes. "Yes . . . yes."

I reluctantly stood up, leaned over, and kissed his forehead. "I'll see you tomorrow?"

He opened his eyes and nodded.

MONDAY, OCTOBER 9, 2006
CRESCENT BEVERLY HILLS HOTEL
LATE EVENING

I stirred awake and stared at the ceiling, as I had so many times before.

He *had* given me everything, yet until he died all I thought he ever wanted was to see himself reincarnated. Until we spoke of Sascha, and driving, and I set off on an odyssey whose end brought no clarity to its origin. He never told me any more about secret races or Cannonball or The Driver. What I learned, or thought I'd learned, disappeared in the haze of what I genuinely heard, or inferred, or wanted to believe—and what was true.

I *had* been lazy. I feared I could never live up to him. I long knew I hadn't earned what I was given. I wanted to believe he'd been wronged. I wanted to believe there was something he didn't—and couldn't—attain. I wanted to believe in the need to avenge him. I wanted what he couldn't have. I never wanted to be him, yet had to follow in his steps in order to transcend him.

And now, for the first time, I had woken up my own man.

I *had* found The Driver. Over and over. He was my father, then Rawlings, then every other enemy I'd found, or invented, or fought, until I'd set out against the very person to whom my father had told that strange tale under heavy sedation.

I could be The Driver. Lift the phone. Organize a race.

If I chose to be. If I willed it.

I'd always had everything anyone could ever want, yet I'd been ungrateful. Now that I was done, all I could remember was a white cross dancing against the afternoon sky, from which The Weis and Nine and the Captain watched over me, and my ever-supportive mother, and Skylar, and Maggie . . . all fearfully watched me leave. All waiting for me to come home.

I got home the same day the M5 arrived at AI. Matt called. There were cracks in both axles and the rear suspension. He said we were lucky to be alive.

Over the next few weeks I saw The Weis and Nine a handful of times, the Captain only once. We barely spoke of the run. Their story seemed hard to believe, as they said of the saga on the ground. The Weis said if he hadn't seen it with his own eyes, he'd have been sure I'd made the whole thing up.

Maher had no such outlet. Other than his girlfriend, he knew no one he could talk to about it but me, and so he dropped by with increasing frequency, bringing a welcome respite from preliminary research on my hilariously premature memoir. We agreed 30 hours was possible, but disagreed on the motivation required.

He was ready to go if and when someone broke our record. I was not.

We agreed it had been the best and worst experience of our lives. When the time came, I would humbly tell Digonis and Stander. Cory would tell Docherty and Diem.

We had no idea how they'd respond.

In researching this book, I contacted virtually every Gumball and Bullrun driver I thought qualified to compete in a cross-country run as we'd attempted. Almost all said yes. None were interested in money—or even thought 32:07 could be broken—except for Rawlings and Collins. Interestingly, three of the very best equivocated. Frankl thought it reckless, but I knew he'd go if asked. Spencer was interested, but not compelled; nor was Kenworthy.

Oliver Morley, whom I reached by satellite phone on what I believed to be his private island in the Caribbean, had quite an earful for me. He forgave remarks I'd made in Polizei guise, and said all he ever objected to was allowing fans to believe I was a better driver than I was. He suggested I forget racing cross-country and accept his offer of driving lessons the next time I was in England. I accepted. He made one more remark, one of the two greatest compliments ever paid to me. He said that on the 2005 Gumball, he and Spencer had coordinated with friends to monitor the ALK website. They'd tracked me as closely as I had them. The Battle of Rome had been far closer than I'd ever known. Only after Spencer told him of my unexpectedly fierce pursuit did Morley consider me more than a prankster. "Perhaps you're not such a bad driver, after all," he said over the hazy connection. "Spencer couldn't believe you kept that M5 on his Turbo. Impressive, I'll grant you that. You're very brave, Roy. Given your deficiencies as a driver, maybe the bravest driver I ever met."

Maher paid me the other on the Santa Monica Pier. Our twenty-strong group had gathered to recap our final moments over champagne. Josh was flabbergasted at my speed across the I-10. A rough calculation suggested an average of 99 mph over 58 miles, what may be the highest ever recorded (literally, on video). I asked Cory if and when she would destroy the tapes. She laughed.

"Alex," said Maher, "you *do* realize how close it was."

"I know. There were so many times it could have gone wrong. Dave, I'm considering never driving again, or becoming a driving instructor. For old people. Nothing fast."

"Seriously, Alex, what you did at the end . . . I didn't know you could do that."

"Neither did I. I thought you were lying, when you said we might not make it."

"We *had* to break 31:07. I *had* to push you, and you did it. Legitimately."

"*We* did it."

"Alex, I might have done the end cleaner, but I couldn't have done it faster."

"My God, Maher, when this gets out, I hope some copycat doesn't go out and kill someone."

"Just don't tell anyone exactly how."

"I won't, but you know, Dave, what *you* did . . . you *are* crazy."

"It takes two."

By November I was hermetically locked in the house once again, attempting to distill what could have filled three books into but one. However safe my desk overlooking Astor Place, an absurd sense of mortality drove me to write what I feared might be my first and last statement on the lessons learned. I spent weeks without venturing outside. I could see the headline—*Illegal Race Driver Killed by Taxi.* I had to complete the definitive history, for the full story seemed far greater than my own. If anything befell me, my unborn children might yet pursue archaeology, or music, and wouldn't take foolish risks to fill holes in their hearts, or egos.

Once the book was done, I owed Nicholas, Rob, Dennis, Jerry, Spencer, Malmstrom, and Oliver an apology and thanks. I owed each more than they were likely to understand.

As for Rawlings, we had a lot more to talk about. He'd earned it.

To Maggie—with whom I hadn't spoken in six months, who thought she hadn't mattered, whom I couldn't face until I was finished, *if* she would see me at all—I would hand the first galley. I hoped she would understand the *why*. I hoped she would forgive me.

Anything was possible. Once the book was done.

"Waaaasssssuuuupppp, Mr. Pol ccz cyc?"

"Richard," I said, "you don't know how good it is to hear your voice. I hear Bullrun's Montreal to Miami, you going?"

"Right on, brother. You Gumballin' again? London to Istanbul? Sheee-it!"

"My last one, just for fun. There's no one left to fight!"

"There's some tough new guys Bullrunning, but I hear ya. Done with that book yet?"

"Two weeks. I think you'll like it. I say some pretty nice things about you."

"I know you're lyin', Alex, but I'll give y'all the benefit of the doubt."

"You're a sweet man, *Herr Rowww-lings*, no matter what they say."

Richard took a deep breath. "I've been thinkin' about you, me and Dennis, mano-a-mano, cross country."

This was inevtiable. He had the will. *But would he go alone?*

"Dennis just put an extra tank in the 550. That thing'll do 700 miles without a refuel, and I just got this Cannonball book by that Yates guy, and he's talking about the record being 32:51. So I'm wondering, where'd you get 32:07? When we gonna see this movie?"

"Funny you should ask. Around the same time as my book. October, or right after."

"Hmm, sure is a long time. So whaddya think? A real race cross-country. Me and Dennis are busy this summer with Bullrun, so what about, say, October or November?"

"That's *exactly* what I was thinking."

"Alex, I'm real curious, though, 32:07 . . . man, you seen proof?"

"Richard, that's a long story."

Epilogue

The richest man in the world is one who stops counting.

Thirty-two hours. A mere day-and-a-third. Six years I spent trying to defeat it.

I never knew greater joy than when, six months after the final run, the first draft of this book was completed. I could stop counting. I yearned to give those I loved the hoard I'd so far spent only on myself.

Time.

But I had miscalculated.

Virtually everyone warned me. The 2007 Gumball was meant to be my last. I didn't need to go. I wanted to. So did Nine, who so regretted giving up his seat in October, but even he feared the worst. A questionable route through the Balkans. New and old competitors, eyes fixed on the myth that was Team Polizei.

I saw Maggie. She had waited. She said she understood. *When I get back,* I said, because I *was* scared, and I didn't want her to see that, or worry, or suffer through it yet again. I left for London a few days later.

On the afternoon of May 2, on a small, tree-lined road southwest of Struga, Macedonia, just a few kilometers from the Albanian border where UN escorts were waiting to accompany us to Tirana for dinner with the prime minister, a red VW Golf emerged from a side road—just as the lead Gumballers approached. And then it finally happened. The accident of my worst nightmares.

The Golf's passengers, Vladimir and Martina Cepuljoski, died of their injuries.

Nick Morley—Oliver's younger, level-headed brother—was the other driver.

He survived unscathed, was arrested, charged in their deaths, convicted, and later released on a suspended sentence.

Ross and I were on a parallel route hundreds of miles away, but I knew the truth. I'd seen my early videos. I knew how often I'd tempted fate. However much I sought to mitigate the risks, I could easily have been the one to strike that red Golf.

I was shattered, but not surprised. Ross and I withdrew and returned to London. The rest of Gumball '07 was cancelled.

Due to the extraordinary events surrounding the cancellation of Gumball, I'd been away one week longer than expected, breaking an earlier promise I'd made to myself. One day, I had gone to see my dad after visiting hours at the hospital had ended. He died the next morning. I vowed I'd never be late again.

On Friday, May 11, Nine called, and said something so shocking, so inconceivable, that I—uncertain I'd grasped the irrevocable truth—served him platitudes borne of our twenty-year friendship. Maggie hadn't waited. Not only had Gumball—the cauldron into which I'd once leapt—evaporated, so had the world I'd left behind. I went home. And stayed there. In silence.

On Monday, May 14, I received a text message from Dennis Collins. He and Rawlings had just arrived in L.A. From New York. In 31 hours and 59 minutes. *A New World Record!* he wrote. Strangely, I was happy for them, even proud. I knew what it took. I said nothing of my run. They deserved their summer of glory.

I began to understand why—against all wisdom—I'd ventured out one last time. Why Rawlings and Collins went without alone. Why conversation with old friends now seemed so stilted. Why Nine and Maggie were now together.

They, I, all of us—had changed, however unwittingly. We dream of stopping time, relish in its rare capture, lie to ourselves about its inexorable advance, but time has no mercy. Nor, in committing utterly to that for which our hearts yearn, should we. The costs of my journey were far higher and carried by many more than I could have known. But I would do it again, if I didn't now know better.

Someone, perhaps Rawlings, will inevitably make another run. Safely, I hope. And the Roy/Maher time will be broken. Someday. But if anyone suggests *I* venture back out in response, they have much to learn about the underrated pleasure of a full night's sleep, or a good book on a rainy Sunday, or ice cream on the beach.

If you see an old Targa by the dunes, you'll know where to find me.

Acknowledgments

So many people helped me write this book, I can't fit them all here. Omissions and obfuscation are my fault, of course.

Thanks to:

Andy McNicol, my agent at William Morris, who first suggested I write this, and Doug Grad, my editor at HarperCollins, a man of limitless patience, as well as everyone at Harper in sales, marketing, publicity, and production.

My mom, my brother Max, and my cousin Jack Lipton.

Michael Hogan and Punch Hutton at *Vanity Fair*.

Old friends Noah Shactman, Josh Shenk, and Deborah Schoeneman, who gave me essential guidance in the manuscript's early days, and Lelaine Lau, Tyler Neely, Sydney Lauren, Maggie Kaiser, Denise Mangen, Aaron Kenadi, and David Goldweitz, who saw me through to the end.

Team Polizei—my copilots: David Maher, Amanda Kinsley, Nicholas Frankl, Michele Shapiro, Alli Joseph, Michael Ross, and Jonathan "Nine" Goodrich, and my European support crew: Henry Fyshe, Gary Luckett, Nick and Josh Plotnick, Kathryn Hencken, Ester and Steve "Schtaven" Jennions, and Captain Jacob Wallace.

Team 3207, without whose bravery and loyalty the story would have had a very different ending: Cory Welles, Paul Weismann, Keith Baskett, Robin Acutt, James Petersmeyer, George Kruntschev, J.F. Musial, and Josh Wexler.

The journalists who bore witness to my most implausible exploits: Gary Jarlson, *Wired* magazine's Charles Graeber, *Jalopnik*'s Mike Spinelli and Davey Johnson, *Automobile*'s Ezra Dyer (who didn't even know it), *Vanity Fair*'s George Gurley, *Gizmodo*'s Noah Robischon and Joel Johnson, and photographers Jeff Forney, Gina LeVay, Kenny Morrison, and Jonathan Bushell.

My attorney, Seth Friedland.

The incredible AI Design team: Matt Figliola, Chris Van Steen, Jason Zhang, Henry Daza, Danny Torez, Billie Edwards, Jairo Ortiz, Kenny Kara-sinski and Marc Palines, and the man of the hour at BMW North America, Alexander Schmuck, and the staff of BMW Battersea, London.

The legends of the U.S. Express: Richard Docherty, Steve Stander, Mike Digonis, David Diem, Doug Turner, David Morse, Steve Clausman, George Egloff (my nominee for the bravest man in the world), and all those I've yet to meet.

Gumball 3000's Maximillion Cooper, Julie Brangstrup, Nick Wylyss, Antony Adel, Stockholm Lina, Duncan Schoales, and anyone else I may have forgotten.

Bullrun's "Handsome Dave" David Green, Andy Duncan, Steve Green, Ross Cottingham, and anyone else I may have forgotten.